SECOND LAN...
TEACHING &
LEARNING

David Nunan
University of Hong Kong

HEINLE & HEINLE PUBLISHERS
I(T)P *An International Thomson Publishing Company*
Boston, Massachusetts 02116 U.S.A.

New York • London • Bonn • Boston • Detroit • Madrid • Melbourne • Mexico City • Paris •
Singapore • Tokyo • Toronto • Washington • Albany, NY • Belmont, CA • Cincinnati, OH

The publication of *Second Language Teaching & Learning* was directed by the members of the Newbury House ESL/EFL Publishing Team at Heinle & Heinle:

Erik Gundersen, Editorial Director
Charlotte Sturdy, Market Development Director
Mike Burggren, Production Services Coordinator
Stanley J. Galek, Vice President and Publisher/ESL

Also participating in the publication of this program were:

Assistant Editor: Jill Kinkade
Manufacturing Coordinator: Mary Beth Hennebury
Cover Designer: Linda Dana Willis

Heinle & Heinle Publishers
An International Thomson Publishing Company
Boston, Massachusetts 02116 U.S.A.

Manufactured in Canada

ISBN: 0-8384-0838-9

10   9

TABLE OF CONTENTS

DEDICATION

In the late 1970s, I read a book that profoundly changed the way I thought and felt about language teaching and about myself as a teacher. The book was by Earl Stevick, and it was called *Memory, Meaning and Method*. In subsequent years, I had the honor of meeting Earl, and of becoming his friend. In the early 1990s, I had the pleasure of sharing an apartment with him, and teaching with him at the TESOL Institute in Barcelona. During that time, I was privileged to discover the truly remarkable human being behind the inspiring teacher. Some years later, Earl did me the great honor of inviting me to provide input to him as he prepared the second edition of *Memory, Meaning and Method*. Thank you Earl. It is to honor your work, and your influence on my own, that I respectfully dedicate *Second Language Teaching & Learning* to you.

INTRODUCTION and OVERVIEW

Over the last twenty-five years, there have been major changes in the theory and practice of second language teaching and learning. These changes have been driven by changes in educational theory, changes in the way we think about language and learning, and the development of an active research agenda that has provided important insights and ideas for classroom practitioners. The purpose of this volume is to provide a portrait of second language teaching and learning as we approach the millennium, to identify major trends and issues, to show where they have come from, and to illustrate, in practical ways, how teachers can incorporate these emerging ideas in their own teaching practice.

This is a personal account. It traces the development of my own thinking, reflects my own struggles with theoretical and conceptual issues, and illustrates the practical solutions that I have sought to the challenges posed by my learners. However, by linking my own ideas, struggles, disappointments and joys to the work of others, I hope that the account will not be seen as idiosyncratic, and will enable teachers, teacher educators, researchers, and teachers in preparation to make connections with their own work.

The main audience for this book is practicing teachers and teachers in preparation who want a practical introduction to the current state of second language teaching and learning, but who also want to know the theoretical and empirical background to this state.

PART I

The Context of Second Language Teaching and Learning

Introduction

The three chapters in Part 1 are intended as a 'concept map' for the rest of the book. Here, I present my own perspective on second-language teaching and learning (which, for convenience, I shall refer to as SLTL). The content is therefore selective and idiosyncratic, reflecting as it does a professional journey that has taken me down a number of different educational highways and byways as well as into the occasional blind alley.

Chapter 1 traces some of the trends and issues emerging from the general educational field that have had an important influence on the current state of SLTL. The chapter serves to remind us that the philosophy and principles of second language education are rooted firmly in the field of general education. As language teachers, we are a branch on a much larger tree, and our professional lives will be immeasurably enriched if we are knowledgeable about the rest of the tree.

Chapter 2 turns to some of the research that has influenced the current state of SLTL. Again, this is a selective review. To do full justice to the wealth of research in the diverse fields that feed into pedagogy would take several volumes, and a great deal of research is covered in other chapters of the book as well. My principal purpose in this chapter is to put two questions of critical importance to language teachers under the microscope, namely:

◊ What is the relationship between formal instruction and language acquisition?
◊ What tasks and patterns of classroom organization best facilitate second language acquisition?

The chapter therefore looks at research in second language acquisition, classroom interaction, task-based language teaching, and learning styles and strategies.

Chapter 3 is intended to highlight the main issues and themes that emerged from the two main chapters in the section. I do this by drawing a contrast between what, for want of better terms, I have called "traditional" and "contemporary" approaches to SLTL. I realize that in drawing this distinction I run the risk of placing in conceptual opposition what are, in fact, points on a continuum. What I shall be at pains to point out in the chapter is that contemporary practice represents an evolution, and that the best practice incorporates the best of "traditional" practice rather than rejecting it. To use a manufacturing or commercial metaphor, we should constantly strive to "add value" to what we do. In this chapter, I suggest that we can see that value has been added in the areas of syllabus design, the approach to teaching, roles of learners, the approach to language, use of classroom texts, facilities for learning, the approach to learning, classroom organization, assessment, and learning outside the classroom.

CHAPTER 1

The Conceptual Basis of Second Language Teaching and Learning

In order to understand the direction in which second-language teaching is moving as a profession, it is useful to know its origins. While it is unlikely that we will progress very far by driving in the rear view mirror, an understanding of the conceptual and empirical bases of SLTL will provide a solid foundation for looking forward. In this chapter, I shall explore the educational and philosophical bases for second language teaching and learning, and in the next I shall turn to the empirical foundations. The chapter covers the following issues and concepts:

The humanistic tradition and experiential learning
◇   competing concepts of education
◇   humanism and experiential learning
◇   inductive and deductive learning

Communicative language teaching
◇   reconceptualizing language
◇   tailoring courses to learners

Learner-centered education
◇   defining *learner-centeredness*
◇   learner involvement in the learning process
◇   learner-centeredness, another dimension
◇   principles of adult learning

Negotiated curricula
◇   learner contributions ot the learning process
◇   moving learners along the negotiation continuum

Task-based language teaching
◇   defining *task*
◇   *task* versus *exercise*
◇   the authenticity principle
◇   the form–function principle
◇   the task-dependency principle

HUMANISTIC EDUCATION AND EXPERIENTIAL LEARNING

◆ *COMPETING CONCEPTS OF EDUCATION*

For many people, education is about knowledge: What it is, and how it is to be acquired by succeeding generations of learners, and thus by succeeding generations of humanity. Politically, education has been a perennial hot topic, because those who control knowledge have potential access to privilege and wealth. However, this idea that knowledge is some kind of commodity to be traded in intellectual marketplaces known as schools and universities is only one of many characterizations. Attempting to define what it is to know has preoccupied philosophers just as much as attempting to answer the question of what it is to be. For much of this century, there has been a passionate debate, in Western educational contexts at least, between those who believe that the function of an educational system is the transmission of a received body of facts, values, and procedures for conceptualizing and adding to that body of knowledge, and those who believe that the function of an educational system is to create the conditions whereby learners might generate their own skills and knowledge. It is a debate between those who believe that education is a matter of making meaning for the learner on the one hand, and those who believe that the function of education is to facilitate the process whereby learners make their own meaning, on the other. Those subscribing to the second view, and I would count myself among them, would agree with Oscar Wilde, that "Education is an admirable thing, but it is well to remember from time to time that nothing that is worth knowing can be taught."

This ongoing debate within the wider world of general education has had a profound effect on language education, as we shall see. It is also complicated by the fact that for teachers who are native speakers of the language they teach, and who are working as foreign rather than second language teachers, a great deal of their work takes place in cultures that have very different concepts of education from the cultures in which those teachers grew up and within which they came to form their own educational values. This can lead to misunderstandings on the part of both the teacher and the students, which, in turn, can have a negative influence on the learning process.

All cultures have their own concepts of teaching, learning, and education. The native aborigines in the culture where I grew up do not educate their children by giving them lectures. Life skills are taught inductively: Children learn by observing their elders. Cultural customs and norms, and an understanding of who they are as a people, are passed on through myths and legends. Aboriginal children can find it profoundly difficult to adjust to the (often implicit) rules and norms of European schools, as Malcolm (1991) and others have pointed out. (I will return to the concepts of 'inductive' and 'deductive' learning at the end of this section.)

In English language teaching, there has long been a debate about the appropriateness of many of the methods used by expatriate teachers and those trained in expatriate methods, some commentators claiming that Western concepts of education are being applied, inappropriately, in non-Western contexts. Increasingly, it is being recognized that pedagogical action needs to be sensitive to the cultural and environmental contexts in which teaching takes place. Not one of my undergraduate students in the university where I currently teach has a parent who attended a university. Some of them have parents who never went to school.

The explosion in education in many developing countries has also brought about intergenerational misunderstandings, which sometimes leads to conflict between the participants in the educational process. These parents have very different concepts of education from those of their children. In negotiating how and what I should attempt to achieve with my students, I need to be sensitive to the cultural and educational backgrounds from which they come. I also need to be alive to the potentially alienating effect a university education might have on their lives outside the classroom.

The general debate over how education is to be conceptualized in general, and the question of whether learning is a matter of mastering a body of content "received" from former generations, or the development of skills and attitudes in particular, is reflected in a great deal of contemporary thinking in second language teaching and learning. As we shall see in the rest of this chapter, communicative language teaching, learner-centered instruction, and task-based language teaching are three concepts that have had a particularly important influence on our field over the last twenty years. These three ideas, which are all interrelated, are part of an interpretative view of education, a view that argues against the notion that learning is a matter of having skills and knowledge transmitted from the teacher to the learner. The interpretative tradition, which is strongly rooted in humanistic psychology, argues that, in order for learning to take place, learners must reconstruct the skills and knowledge for themselves; they cannot simply "receive" these from external sources. The cliché, "If students are to learn, then, ultimately they have to do the learning for themselves" is an apt summation of the belief.

◆ HUMANISM AND EXPERIENTIAL PSYCHOLOGY

Out of the notion that learners are at the center of the learning process, and that learning is a process of self-discovery, grew experiential learning. In experiential learning, the learner's immediate personal experiences are taken as the point of departure for deciding how to organize the learning process. According to Kohonen (1992), experiential learning has diverse origins, being derived from John Dewey's progressive philosophy of education, Lewin's social psychology, Piaget's model of developmental psychology, Kelley's cognitive theory of education, and the work of Abraham Maslow and Carl Rogers in the field of humanistic psychology. What draws these diverse philosophical and academic positions together is the construct of humanism.

Humanistic psychology attempts to make sense of experience at the point where sociology and psychology intersect. It captures the fact that

as humans we are simultaneously looking inwards and operating out-
wards, and that any attempt to understand what motivates behavior must
necessarily capture the individual in relation to the group. Attempts to
quarantine human action and motivation either to the individual or the
group aspect will result in a partial perspective. Kohonen (1992) captures
this dualistic perspective on experience:

> [T]he individual's self-concept is a social product that is shaped
> gradually through interaction with the environment. It is an organized,
> integrated pattern of self-related perceptions, which become increasingly
> differentiated and complex. The development of a healthy self-concept
> is promoted by a positive self-regard and an unconditional acceptance
> by the 'significant others'.
>
> *p. 15*

He argues for experiential learning on the grounds that it facilitates personal growth, that it helps learners adapt to social change, that it takes
into account differences in learning ability, and that it is responsive both
to learner needs and practical pedagogical considerations. As already
indicated, experiential learning builds a bridge from the known to the
new by taking the learner's perceptions and experiences as the point of
departure for the learning process.

The most comprehensively formulated model of experiential learning
is that of Kolb (1984). Kolb suggests that, through experiential learning,
the learner moves from the known to the new through a process of
making sense of some immediate experience, and then going beyond the
immediate experience through a process of transformation. In the field
of language education, the relevance of humanism and experiential learning has been highlighted by Legutke and Thomas, who link humanism
and experiential learning:

> The proponents of humanistic education have broadened our con-
> cept of learning by emphasising that meaningful learning has to be self-
> initiated. Even if the stimulus comes from outside, the sense of discovery,
> however, and the motivation which that brings has to come from inside
> driven by the basic human desire for self-realization, well-being and
> growth. . . . [I]n terms of personal and inter-personal competence the
> process-oriented classroom revolves around issues of risk and security,
> co-operation and competition, self-directedness and other-directedness;
> and meaningful and meaningless activities. We have also tried to make
> clear that 'teachers who claim it is not their job to take these phenomena
> into account may miss out on some of the most essential ingredients in
> the management of successful learning'.
>
> *Underhill 1989, 252 as cited in Legutke and Thomas 1991: 269*

To my mind, the most articulate examination of humanism and experiential learning in relation to language education is provided by Kohonen

(1992), who argues that the experiential model offers, "potential for a learning atmosphere of shared partnership, a common purpose, and a joint management of learning" (p. 31). He goes on to suggest that in classrooms infused with the vision promised by experiential learning, behavior is a joint responsibility of the whole class, and that the teacher is only one member within that class. He provides contrasts between traditional and experiential models of education in ten key dimensions. (See Table 1.1).

Table 1.1   Traditional and experiential educational models compared

Dimension	Traditional Model: Behaviorism	Experiential Model: Constructivism
1. View of learning	Transmission of knowledge	Transformation of knowledge
2. Power relation	Emphasis on teacher's authority	Teacher as "learner among learners"
3. Teacher's role	Providing mainly frontal instruction; professionalism as individual autonomy	Facilitating learning (largely in small groups); collaborative professionalism
4. Learner's role	Relatively passive recipient of information; mainly individual work	Active participation, largely in collaborative small groups
5. View of knowledge	Presented as "certain"; application problem-solving	Construction of personal knowledge; identification of problems
6. View of curriculum	Static; hierarchical grading of subject matter, predefined content and product	Dynamic; looser organization of subject matter, including open parts and integration
7. Learning experiences	Knowledge of facts, concepts and skills; focus on content and product	Emphasis on process; learning skills, self-inquiry, social and communication skills
8. Control of process	Mainly teacher-structured learning	Emphasis on learner; self-directed learning
9. Motivation	Mainly extrinsic	Mainly intrinsic
10. Evaluation	Product-oriented: achievement testing; criterion-referencing (and norm-referencing)	Process-oriented: reflection on process, self-assessment; criterion-referencing

◆ INDUCTIVE AND DEDUCTIVE LEARNING

Another important pair of concepts, which we shall return to constantly throughout this book, is inductive and deductive learning. Simply put, deductive learning is a process of adding to our knowledge by working from principles to examples. This has been an important intellectual tool within Western philosophical and scientific thinking since the time of Aristotle. According to Cohen and Manion (1980), deductive reasoning went unchallenged from the time of Aristotle to the Middle Ages, when the philosopher Francis Bacon turned the process of working from principles to examples on its head. Bacon argued for induction as a way of adding to our knowledge of the words. In induction, one works from examples to principles, rules, and generalizations.

It is all too easy to equate humanism and experiential learning with an inductive, discovery-oriented approach to education, but this is probably an oversimplification. In fact, even in the scientific area, the opposition between induction and deduction has been questioned. Mouly (1978), for example, has proposed a synthesis between the two, arguing that inquiry consists of:

> a back-and-forth movement in which the investigator first operates inductively from observations to hypotheses, and then deductively from these hypotheses to their implications, in order to check their validity from the standpoint of compatibility with accepted knowledge. After revision, where necessary, these hypotheses are submitted to further test through the collection of data specifically designed to test their validity at the empirical level.
>
> *Mouly 1978*

Although Mouly's comments were made within the context of research, it is not difficult to see their application to the field of learning in general, and of language learning in particular. The back and forth movement between language data and linguistic principles or "rules" that characterize an organic approach to language acquisition is taken up and elaborated in Chapter 4. It also seems consistent with the ways in which humans function cognitively.

> It seems to me that people respond to their environment by setting up a constant stream of hypotheses. The cumbersome cycle of inductive inquiry—first we do this and then that—comes nowhere close to reflecting the quicksilver oscillation between induction and deduction that I am inclined to believe reflects how people process language (amongst everything else), or how they respond to the learning tasks that we give them.
>
> *Nigel Bruce, personal communication*

In the rest of this chapter, we shall see how humanism and experiential learning have informed some of the most important and influential ideas to have emerged in language teaching over the last twenty years. These include communicative language teaching, learner-centered instruction, negotiated curricula, and task-based language teaching.

COMMUNICATIVE LANGUAGE TEACHING

Without doubt, the most pervasive changes to teaching practice over the last twenty years are those that can be described as *communicative language teaching* (CLT). In this section, I shall discuss some of the conceptual aspects of this development. In the section on the empirical background to SLTL, I review some of the research that has informed CLT.

◆ RECONCEPTUALIZING LANGUAGE

An important stimulus for changing the way we teach language came during the 1970s when linguists and language educators began a reappraisal of language itself. Up to, and including the 1960s, language was generally seen as a system of rules, and the task for language learners was to internalize these rules by whatever means were at their disposal (or, more usually, in formal contexts, at the disposal of the teacher or teaching institution). Language was seen as a unified system, and the ultimate aim of the learner was to approach the target language norms of the "native speaker." The priority for learners was to master the structures of the language, and, in this process, considerations of meaning were seen almost as peripheral. In fact, some language specialists argued that instruction should focus almost exclusively on teaching basic syntactic patterns, ignoring, or at least minimizing, the development of vocabulary and semantic systems. (There were exceptions to this. See, for example, Newmark and Reibel, 1968).

However, during the 1970s, a much richer conceptualization of language began to emerge. Language was seen as a system for the expression of meaning, and linguists began to analyze language as a system for the expression of meanings, rather than as a system of abstract syntactic rules. (For a view of how these changing concepts began to change the way methodologists approached the teaching of language, see Brumfit 1984.)

The realization that language could be analyzed, described, and taught as a system for expressing meanings had a profound effect on language teaching. At least it had a profound effect at the levels of syllabus design and textbook writing. Whether the effect was quite so pervasive or profound in language classrooms themselves is open to question. If language is a system for expressing meanings, and if different learners have different communicative ends in view, then surely these different communicative ends should be reflected in the things that learners are taught. In other words, there ought to be different syllabuses for different learners. It was this insight that led to the development of needs-based courses and the emergence of tools and techniques for analyzing and describing learner needs (Munby, 1978; Brindley, 1984). We shall look at some of these techniques in Chapter 6.

♦ TAILORING COURSES TO LEARNERS

The notion that it was not necessary for learners to master a particular grammatical structure or lexical item simply because it happened to be part of the system, coupled with the insight that what was learned should reflect the different needs of different learner groups, was in harmony with the interpretative view of knowledge being fashioned within humanistic psychology and experiential learning, as we saw in the preceding section. These traditions legitimized the idea that it was not necessary to attempt to learn everything, that a language was not an external body of knowledge into which the learner had to be "initiated", that, in fact, there may not actually be external bodies of knowledge.

In terms of methodology, this new view of language also had an important effect. If the aim of language teaching is to help learners develop skills for expressing different communicative meanings, then surely these ought to be reflected in classroom tasks and activities. Later in the chapter, we see how this insight led to the emergence of task-based approaches to language teaching.

The notion that different learners have different communicative requirements, and that these ought to be reflected, both in the content of the curriculum (what is taught) and learning processes (how it is taught), was also reinforced by an ideological shift in focus away from the teacher and the textbook and toward the learner. Learner-centered education, which grew partly out of the humanistic tradition that I have already discussed, was also reinforced by developments in SLTL.

LEARNER-CENTERED EDUCATION

♦ DEFINING LEARNER-CENTEREDNESS

The concept of learner-centered education has been controversial, mainly because it is susceptible to multiple interpretations. Some teachers react negatively to the concept, because they feel that, implicit in the notion, is a devaluing of their own professional roles. Others believe that it involves handing over to the learner duties and responsibilities that rightly belong to the teacher. I believe that both of these criticisms are misguided, and I spell out my reasons for this later in the section. First, however, I would like to describe how I became interested in the subject in the first place. It began years ago, when I began to notice a major gap between what I was focusing on as a teacher, and what my learners were taking away from the pedagogical opportunities I was providing. I quickly became obsessed with the question that was so admirably framed by Dick All-wright: "Why don't learners learn what teachers teach?" (Allwright, 1984). When I began collecting samples of learner language and analyzing these, I discovered that there was a gap between the sorts of things I was trying to get my students to learn and the things that they actually appeared to learn as evidenced by the things they said and wrote. In order to under-stand the complex processes underlying my students' attempts at learning, I realized that I had necessarily to see things from their point of view. I had to find out what they felt they wanted to learn, and how they went about the task of learning. I came to the belief that while teachers working in classrooms guided by a learner-centered philosophy would have to make similar decisions as those working in any other kind of classroom; a key difference would be that in a learner-centered classroom, key decisions about what will be taught, how it will be taught, when it will be taught, and how it will be assessed will be made with reference to the learner. Information about learners, and, where feasible, from learners, will be used to answer the key questions of what, how, when, and how well.

However, I found that it is often a mistake to assume that learners come into the language classroom with a sophisticated knowledge of pedagogy, or with a natural ability to make informed choices about their own learning processes. (This is what I characterize in the next section as the strong interpretation of learner-centeredness.) In fact, there are relatively few learners who are naturally endowed with the ability to make informed choices about what to learn, how to learn it, and when to learn from the moment that they first enter a learning arrangement. They have to go through a process, and often a lengthy process of learning how to learn, and they can usually only do this with the assistance and guidance of the teacher. The role of the teacher is therefore enhanced in a learner-centered system, and the skills demanded of the teacher are also greater. It is for this reason that I reject the notion that teachers are some-how devalued in a learner-centered system.

◆ LEARNER INVOLVEMENT IN THE LEARNING PROCESS

At this point, it is necessary to turn from the concept of learner-cen-teredness to the closely related concept of learning-centeredness. A learn-ing-centered classroom is designed to enable the learner to make critical pedagogical decisions by systematically training them in the skills they need to make such decisions. Such a classroom is constituted with complementary aims. While one set of aims is focused on language content, the other is focused on the learning process. Learners are therefore systematically educated in the skills and knowledge they will need in order to make informed choices about what they want to learn and how they want to learn. Rather than assuming that the learner comes to the learning arrangement possessing critical learning skills, the sensitive teacher accepts that many learners will only begin to develop such skills in the course of instruction.

Learner-centeredness is therefore not an all-or-nothing concept. It is a relative matter. It is also not the case that a learner-centered classroom is one in which the teacher hands over power, responsibility, and control to the students from day one. I have found that it is usually well into a course before learners are in a position to make informed choices about what they want to learn and how they want to learn, and it is not uncommon that this happens only at the end of the course. That said, I would advocate the development of curricula and materials that encourage learners to move toward the fully autonomous end of the pedagogical continuum.

From the above discussion, it can be seen that learner-centered instruction is not a matter of handing over rights and powers to learners in a unilateral way. Nor does it involve devaluing the teacher. Rather, it is a matter of educating learners so that they can gradually assume greater responsibility for their own learning. I shall discuss how this might be done in the next section, when I discuss negotiated curricula. In fact, learner-centered curricula are not radical alternatives to more traditional approaches to the design and delivery of language programs:

> [A learner-centered] curriculum will contain elements similar to those contained in traditional curriculum development, that is, planning (including needs analysis, goal and objective setting), implementation (including methodology and materials development), and evaluation (see, for example, Hunkins 1980). However, the key difference between learner-centered and traditional curriculum development is that, in the former, the curriculum is a collaborative effort between teachers and learners, since learners are closely involved in the decision making process regarding the content of the curriculum and how it is taught. This change in orientation has major practical implications for the entire curriculum process, since a negotiated curriculum cannot be introduced and managed in the same way as one which is prescribed by the teacher or teaching institutions. In particular, it places the burden for all aspects of curriculum development on the teacher.
>
> *Nunan 1988: 2*

A criticism that is sometimes made of this approach is that learners simply do not know what they want. While it is true to say that learners do not always have the necessary skills and insights to make informed choices (thus the reason for incorporating a learning-how-to-learn dimension into the classroom), I have yet to meet a learner who has absolutely no idea of what he or she wants. They may not be able to formulate and articulate their needs in any precise fashion, but the notion that they do not have ideas on the subject is belied by a substantial amount of research. Some years ago, I carried out a comparative study into the learning preferences of teachers and learners in the Australian Adult Migrant Education Program (Nunan 1988). When I compared the preferences of learners and teachers in relation to selected learning tasks and activities, I found some stark contrasts and dramatic mismatches. The results of this study are summarized in Table 1.2, where it can be seen that there are mismatches between teachers and learners on all but one of the items (students and teachers agreed that conversation practice was a very high priority). In all other cases, teachers and learners disagreed. For example, learners gave pair work a low rating, while teachers gave this item a very high rating. The same was the case with student self-discovery of errors. Now I am not suggesting that student views should be acceded to in all cases. However, I would argue that, at the very least, teachers should find out what their students think and feel about what they want to learn and how they want to learn and take this into consideration when planning their courses.

Unfortunately, when confronted with a mismatch between their own views and those of their students, teachers often feel that there are only two ways to resolve the dilemma, either to give in to the students (assuming that the students themselves are in agreement over what they want), or to adopt an "I'm the doctor and I know best for you" attitude. However, there are many positions in-between. Negotiation, as we saw above, is a two-way process. The key thing is to recognize that differences exist, and to create a win–win situation so that everyone gets something. (I shall look at the practicalities of doing this in the next section.)

Table 1.2   A comparison of student and teacher ratings of selected learning activities

Activity	Student	Teacher
Pronunciation practice	very high	medium
Teacher explanations	very high	high
Conversation practice	very high	very high
Error correction	very high	low
Vocabulary development	very high	high
Listening to/using cassettes	low	medium high
Student self-discovery of errors	low	very high
Using pictures/films/video	low	low medium
Pair work	low	very high
Language games	very low	low

As I write this chapter, I am confronting a situation with one of my classes in which there is conflict between the desires of the students and my own pedagogical agenda. Although it is ostensibly an academic writing class, the aim of which is to prepare students to write academic essays in English, the students want a "fun"-based course with lots of videos and small group work. I am in the process of trying to restructure the course to give them some of the things they want while at the same time achieving the original aims of the course. (I look at what these students had to say about the course in Chapter 5, when the issue of learner roles and contributions is examined.)

◆ LEARNER-CENTEREDNESS: ANOTHER DIMENSION

There is one other sense in which the term *learner-centered* is often used. This is when it refers to classrooms, not in which learners are involved in making choices about what and how to learn, but in which learners are actively involved in the learning process, classrooms in which the focus is on the learner in the sense in which they do all the work. As we shall see, this kind of classroom is, in fact, consistent with a particular line of second language acquisition research that suggests acquisition is facilitated when opportunities for learners to interact are maximized. In the next chapter, I review some of the research work that supports this view.

The potential benefits of engineering classroom interactions so that the focus is firmly on the learners rather than the teacher is nicely illustrated in a classroom sequence described in Barnes's (1976) classic book *From Communication to Curriculum*. While the episode took place in a content classroom, the outcomes could apply to any classroom. The input data for the task was a poem entitled "The Bully Asleep," in which a teacher fails to intervene when a group of children harass a sleeping bully. Barnes arranged the students into small groups, and simply told them to "Talk about the poem in any way you like and let me know when you've finished" (p. 25). He then recorded and analyzed the resulting small group discussions. From his analysis, Barnes concluded that the task worked because

> [T]he absence of a teacher has placed control of learning strategies in the pupils' hands. In this case, since no task was set, the children control the questions they choose to ask: the issue of whether the teacher acted wisely is theirs, not the poet's. But the teacher's absence removes from their work the usual source of authority. They cannot turn to him to solve dilemmas. Thus in this discussion . . . the children not only formulate hypotheses, but are compelled to evaluate them for themselves. This they can do in only two ways: by testing them against their existing view of 'how things go in the world', and by going back to the 'evidence'.

In this case the evidence is a poem, but it might equally have been a map, a facsimile of an historical document, a table of numerical data, or a piece of scientific apparatus.

Barnes, 1976: 29

◆ PRINCIPLES OF ADULT LEARNING

The characterization I have given above, in which learners are systematically sensitized into processes underlying their own learning, and are gradually encouraged to take greater and greater responsibility for their own learning, is what might be called a weak interpretation of learner-centeredness. A strong interpretation would argue (as, for example, Brundage and Macheracher (1980) have done), that, from the very first lesson, learners have a right to be involved in the decision making processes about what they should learn, how they should learn, and how they might be evaluated. This strong tradition emerged from studies into adult learning or *androgogy* (see, for example, Knowles 1983).

The following set of principles underpins the practice of adult learning. They were formulated by Brundage and Macheracher (1980), who have carried out extensive research into adult learning.

◊   Adults who value their own experience as a resource for further learning or whose experience is valued by others are better learners.

◊   Adults learn best when they are involved in developing learning objectives for themselves that are congruent with their current and idealized self-concept.

◊   Adults have already developed organized ways of focusing on, taking in, and processing information. These are referred to as *cognitive style.*

◊   The learner reacts to all experience as he/she perceives it, not as the teacher presents it.

◊   Adults enter into learning activities with an organized set of descriptions and feelings about themselves that influences the learning process.

◊   Adults are more concerned with whether they are changing in the direction of their own idealized self-concept than whether they are meeting standards and objectives set for them by others.

◊   Adults do not learn when overstimulated or when experiencing extreme stress or anxiety.

◊   Those adults who can process information through multiple channels and have learnt how to learn are the most productive learners.

◊   Adults learn best when the content is personally relevant to past experience or present concerns and the learning process is relevant to life experiences.

◊   Adults learn best when novel information is presented through a variety of sensory modes and experiences with sufficient repetitions and variations on themes to allow distinctions in patterns to emerge.

You can see that this list strongly reflects the humanistic and experiential traditions that emphasize the constructive role of the learner within the learning process. In fact, when I first came across these principles, it occurred to me that many of them may reflect the way *all* learners, and not just adults, approach learning.

Most of the work already cited has been carried out within general education. However, in 1984 Brindley did a detailed study of adult learning with immigrants in Australia and their teachers. From his research, he found that

> one of the fundamental principles underlying the notion of permanent education is that education should develop in individuals the capacity to control their own destiny and that, therefore, the learner should be seen as being at the centre of the educational process. For the teaching institution and the teacher, this means that instructional programmes should be centred around learners' needs and that learners themselves should exercise their own responsibility in the choice of learning objectives, content and methods as well as in determining the means used to assess their performance.
>
> *Brindley 1984: 4–5*

In Chapter 5, we shall look at some of the practical implications of placing learners at the center of the learning process.

NEGOTIATED CURRICULA

The philosophy of learner-centeredness has been given practical effect in the form of negotiated curricula in which the views of the learners as well as the pedagogical agenda of the teacher are satisfied through a process of give-and-take. In a classroom where the content and process are negotiated, neither learners nor teacher have it all their own way. As the label suggests, what gets taught, and how it is learned, are arrived at through discussion and compromise.

◆ *LEARNER CONTRIBUTIONS TO THE LEARNING PROCESS*

On a number of occasions, I have worked in contexts in which it has been feasible to negotiate with learners at all stages of the learning process. In most situations, however, it is at the stage of curriculum implementation that negotiation is a reality. For those who question the feasibility of negotiating with learners in certain contexts, I would argue that there is an element of negotiation in every classroom encounter. It is not possible to maintain an exclusively non-negotiable classroom for any length of time. In other words, negotiation is a variable commodity within the pedagogical transactions of the classroom. It is simply not the case, at the level of curriculum implementation, that learning is either negotiated or mandated. Negotiations can involve not only big ticket items relating to the overall content and procedure of a lesson, but many more modest items such as whether to do a particular task in groups or in pairs.

Is there any evidence that justifies the notion that learners should be given a say in their own pedagogical destiny? I believe there is. In 1992, Slimani decided to find out what learners actually learn from classroom interaction, and posed the following questions:

◇   What is it that individual learners claim to have learned from interactive classroom events (this claimed learning she terms *uptake*)?

◇   What is it that happens in the lesson that can account for this uptake?

Her learners were a group of Algerian learners of English as a foreign language who were preparing to undertake engineering studies in English. Slimani found that topics initiated in the classroom by the learners were much more likely to be nominated as having been learned than those nominated by the teacher. In other words, when learners had an opportunity to contribute to the content of the lesson, that was the content that learners would claim to have learned. She reports that:

> about 77.45 per cent of the topicalisation was effected by the teacher. This is not particularly surprising in view of the fact that the discourse was unidirectionally controlled by the teacher . . . What appears to be strikingly interesting though is that a further analysis of the effect of the teacher's versus the learners' scarce opportunities . . . for topicalisation showed that the latter offered much higher chances for items to be up-taken. Learners benefited much more from their peers' rare instance of topicalisation than from the teacher's. . . . *topics initiated by learners attracted more claims from the learners than the ones initiated by the teacher.* [italics added—D. N.]
>
> Slimani 1992: 211

♦   MOVING LEARNERS ALONG THE NEGOTIATION CONTINUUM

As I have already indicated, negotiation is not an all-or-nothing process. There are levels and degrees of negotiation. In fact, it is a continuum. In my own classrooms, I work hard at moving learners along the continuum. This can be done by incorporating a series of steps into the educational process. Although I have set the following steps out sequentially, some of the steps overlap, and can be introduced simultaneously. This is particularly true of Steps 4–9, which focus on learning processes, and can be introduced alongside Steps 1–3, which are more content oriented.

◇   **Step 1:** *Make instruction goals clear to learners*
A first step in giving learners a voice is to make instructional goals clear to them. If the evidence that I have gathered in many classrooms over many years

Unit Goals

In this unit you will:

Make comparisons

"Which do you prefer, the bus or the subway?"

"I guess I like the subway better."

Make plans

"I'm going to fly to Spain for my vacation."

Figure 1-1 *ATLAS* - Book 3, © Heinle & Heinle Publishers

is anything to go by, this is relatively rare. In a study I carried out some years ago into aspects of classroom management, there was only a single teacher who spelled out the pedagogical agenda for her learners. An extract from the start of one of her lessons illustrates her method. She is using a mandated textbook in which the goals and objectives are implicit, and yet she is able to make the goals of the lesson explicit to the learners. She does so by actively involving them in the process, rather than simply informing them.

T: *Today we're going to practice talking about likes and dislikes, and we're going to talk about music and movies and stuff. OK? OK Kenji? Now, I want you to open your books at page 22, that's where the unit starts, and [inaudible comment from student] . . . What's that? . . . Yeah, that's right. Now, I want you to look quickly through the unit and find one example, one example of someone saying they like something, and one example of someone saying they don't like something? OK? One example of each. And I'm going to put them here on the board.*

If you are producing your own materials, or adapting those written by others, it is relatively easy to make the goals explicit. Once again, learners can be actively involved, as the following example shows:

The unit initiated by the goals in Figure 1-1 could be completed by asking the learners to carry out a self-checking exercise such as that in Figure 1.2. While this has been extracted from a commercial source, it is the sort of exercise that teachers can readily create.

As I indicated above, I believe that the idea of making the pedagogical agenda explicit to the learners is relatively uncontroversial, and something

Review the language skills you practiced in this unit.
Check [√] your answers.

CAN YOU:

Make comparisons?   ☐ yes   ☐ a little   ☐ not yet

Find or give an example: ....

Make plans?   ☐ yes   ☐ a little   ☐ not yet

Find or give an example: ....

Figure 1-2   *ATLAS* - Book 3, © Heinle & Heinle Publishers

that can be done with all but the youngest of learners. This provides a basis for learners to be involved in selecting their own goals and content. Dam and Gabrielsen (1988) found that even relatively young learners were capable of making decisions about the content and processes of their own learning. Learners, regardless of their aptitude or ability, were capable of a positive and productive involvement in selecting their own content and learning procedures. Furthermore, learners were also positive in accepting responsibility for their own learning.

◊   ***Step 2:*** *Allow learners to create their own goals*

The next step in giving learners a voice would be to allow learners to create their own goals and content. An interesting and practical way of involving learners at this level is reported in Parkinson and O'Sullivan (1990). They report on the notion of the action meeting as a way of involving learners in modifying course content.

> A mechanism was needed for course management: as the guiding and motivating force behind the course, it would have to be able to deal with individual concerns and negotiate potential conflicts of interest, need, and temperament. It would also have to satisfy the individual while not threatening the group's raison d'être. As foreshadowed in the orientation phase, the group would now experiment with a mechanism suggested by the teachers, namely a series of Action Meetings. . . . [These] would provide an opportunity for individuals to participate (interpersonally and interculturally) in an English-medium meeting, negotiating meaning and authentic content. They would also be a means of facilitating group cohesion and motivation and would be a primary mechanism for ongoing program evaluation by the participants.
>
> *Parkinson and O'Sullivan 1990: 119–120*

◇   *Step 3: Encourage learners to use their second language outside the classroom*

A logical extension of this idea is to get learners activating their language outside the classroom itself. The following classroom extract illustrates the way in which one teacher encouraged students to think about activating their language outside of the classroom.

[The students are sitting in small groups of two to four as the teacher addresses them.]

T: *Well students, as you know, this morning we're going to be looking at ways that we can help learners improve their English—without a teacher, without, um, a class to come to. What've we got all around us that can help us? Well the first thing that we're going to be looking at are these things. [She bends down and picks up a plastic shopping bag.] Now in the bag—I've got a bag full of mystery objects in here—different things, but they all have one thing in common. We can use them to help improve our language. Now this is going to be lucky dip type activity. Have you ever done a lucky dip?*

Ss: *Yes, yes.*

T: *Yes. Where you put your hand in and you take one thing out. I'll do it the first time. Put my hand in and I'll just bring . . . something out.*

[She pulls out a mirror.]

   Oh, a mirror. Now how can this help us improve our language—you got any ideas? Irene?

S: *We can help, er, our voc . . . vocabulary.*

T: *Vocabulary's one thing, yes. How?*

S: *We can look, er, how we pronounce the words. (Mmm) We can look in the mirror and see how our mouth moves.*

T: *Good. Yes, we can see how our mouth moves—by looking at our reflection in the mirror. For example, the sound th. Can you all say th?"*

Ss: *No. [Laughter]*

[The teacher distributes the rest of the objects in the bag and the students, working in groups, spend ten minutes discussing the ways in which the different objects they have chosen can be used for practicing English outside the class. The teacher then calls the activity to a halt.]

   Nunan 1991: 182

◇   *Step 4: Raise awareness of learning processes*

So far, I have talked about giving learners a voice in deciding *what* to learn. However, it's also important to give them a voice in *how* they learn. I have found that the best place to begin in this is to raise their awareness of the strategies underlying classroom tasks. This is something that all teachers can do, regardless of whether they are working with a mandated curriculum and materials, or are relatively free to decide what to teach and how to teach it. This is illustrated in the following classroom extract.

T: *One of the things, er, we practice in this course . . . is . . . or some of the things we practice are learning strategies. And one of the learning strategies that will help you learn new words is the learning strategy of "classifying". Do you know what* classifying *means?*

Ss: *No no*

T: *Have you heard this word before?*

Ss: *No*

T: *Classifying means putting things that are similar together in groups. OK? So if I said, er, I want all of the girls to go down to that corner of the room, and all the boys to go into this corner of the room, I would be classifying the class according to their sex or their gender. What I'd like you to do now in Task 5 is to classify some of the words from the list in Task 4. OK? [In the preceding task, students had read a postcard and circled the words that describe people. They were then given a three-column table with the headings: "color", "age", and "size".]*

◊   *Step 5: Help learners identify their own preferred styles and strategies*

The next step in the development of a learner-centered classroom is to train learners to identify their own preferred learning styles and strategies. Detailed guidance on how this might be achieved are taken up later in the book when I focus on the learning process.

Once I have helped my learners to identify their own preferred styles and strategies, I begin to give them choices from a range of options. The notion that learners are capable of making choices has been questioned by some commentators. It has also been suggested that the notion of choice is a Western one, which doesn't work in Eastern educational contexts. All I can say is that it works in Hong Kong. I was also able to make it work in Thailand. There is evidence from other sources as well. Widdows and Voller (1991), for example, investigated the ability of Japanese university students to make choices. As a result of their study they found that students were able to make choices, and that their preferences were often markedly at odds with the content and methodology that they were exposed to in class. They report that,

> Students do not like classes in which they sit passively, reading or translating. They do not like classes where the teacher controls everything. They do not like reading English literature much, even when they are literature majors. Thus it is clear that the great majority of university English classes are failing to satisfy learner needs in any way. Radical changes in the content of courses, and especially in the types of courses that are offered, and the systematic retraining of EFL teachers in learner-centered classroom procedures are steps that must be taken, if teachers and administrators are seriously interested in addressing their students' needs.
>
> *Widdows and Voller 1991*

◇ **Step 6:** *Encourage learner choice*

In some foreign language contexts, the notion of student choice may be a relatively unfamiliar, or even alien, one. In such a case it is preferable to engage the learners in a relatively modest level of decision making. For example, if the data for a lesson include a reading passage and a listening text, learners might be asked to decide which they would rather do first, the reading or the listening. If teachers are uncomfortable with the idea of students doing different things at the same time, then it can be put to a class vote. They could then gradually be involved in making choices such as the following, in which the activity type and task is similar. The point is not that learners in different groups will be doing things that are radically different, but that they are being sensitized to the notion of making choices.

> You choose: Do A or B.
>
> *A Group Work.* Think about the last time you went grocery shopping. Make a list of all the things you bought. Compare this list with the lists of three or four other students. Whose list is the healthiest?
>
> *B Group Work.* Think about all the healthy things you did last week. Make a list. Compare this list with the lists of three or four other students. Who had the healthiest week?

Once learners are used to the idea, they can be invited to make more elaborate choices, as in the following example, in which learners are asked to preview three tasks that they will be doing in a lesson, to identify the major skills focus, and to decide the order in which they will do the tasks.

You Choose

a. Look quickly at the next three tasks and decide whether these are listening, speaking, reading, or writing tasks.
b. Now decide the order in which you wish to do them. Circle your choices.

	I'll do this task . . .		
Task 1: A _____ task	1st	2nd	3rd
Task 2: A _____ task	1st	2nd	3rd
Task 3: A _____ task	1st	2nd	3rd

These examples illustrate the point that even within the various points on the learner-centered continuum, it is possible to identify subcontinua.

◇ **Step 7:** *Allow learners to generate their own tasks*

Having encouraged learners to make choices, the next step is to provide them with opportunities to modify and adapt classroom tasks. This could be a preliminary step to teaching them to create their own tasks. This need not involve highly technical materials design skills, which would clearly be unrealistic. I have started learners on the path towards developing their own materials by giving them the text but not the questions in a reading comprehension task and asking them, in small groups, to write their own questions. These are then exchanged with another group to be answered and discussed.

◇ **Step 8:** *Encourage learners to become teachers*

At a more challenging level, learners would become teachers. There is nothing like the imminent prospect of having to teach something for stimulating learning. Lest this should be thought utopian, I can point to precedents in the literature. Assinder, for example, gave her students the opportunity of developing video-based materials that they subsequently used for teaching other students in the class. The innovation was a success, the critical factor of which, according to Assinder, was the opportunity for the learner to become the teacher:

> I believe that the goal of 'teaching each other' was a factor of paramount importance. Being asked to present something to another group gave a clear reason for the work, called for greater responsibility to one's own group, and led to increased motivation and greatly improved accuracy. The success of each group's presentation was measured by the response and feedback of the other group; thus there was a measure of in-built evaluation and a test of how much had been learned. Being an 'expert' on a topic noticeably increased self-esteem, and getting more confident week by week gave [the learners] a feeling of genuine progress.
>
> *Assinder 1991: 228*

◇ **Step 9:** *Encourage learners to become researchers*

Finally, it is possible to educate learners to become language researchers. Once again, for those who think this notion fanciful or utopian, there is a precedent in the literature. Heath (1992), working with educationally disadvantaged children in the United States, asked her collaborators to document the language they encountered in the community beyond the classroom.

> Students were asked . . . to work together as a community of ethnographers, collecting, interpreting, and building a data bank of information about language in their worlds. They had access to knowledge I wanted, and the only way I could get that knowledge was for them to write to me. They collected field notes, wrote interpretations of patterns they discovered as they discussed their field notes, and they answered the questions I raised about their data collection and their interpretations.
>
> *Heath 1992: 42*

Despite the struggle involved, students learned through the process of becoming ethnographic researchers that communication is negotiation, and they got to reflect on the important relationships between socialization, language, and thought. In substantive terms, all students moved out of the Basic English into regular English classes, and two moved into honors English. As Heath reports, "Accomplishments were real and meaningful for these students."

In this section, I have provided some practical illustrations of how philosophical concepts of humanism and experiential learning can lead, through learner-centered attitudes and negotiated curricula, to practical classroom action. In the next, and final section in the chapter, I review an approach to language pedagogy known as task-based language teaching (TBLT), which draws on all of these ideas and practices. It forms a useful bridge to Chapter 2, which focuses on the research basis for SLTL. As we shall see, in addition to drawing on the conceptual developments outlined in the first part of this chapter, task-based language teaching has sought to develop a research agenda so that ideas put forward by advocates of TBLT can be tested against empirical data from teaching and learning.

TASK-BASED LANGUAGE TEACHING

Task-based language teaching is an approach to the design of language courses in which the point of departure is not an ordered list of linguistic items, but a collection of tasks. It draws on and reflects the experiential and humanistic traditions described above, as well as reflecting the changing conceptions of language itself. As we shall see in the next section, it also draws on a growing body of empirical research.

◆ DEFINING TASK

Within the literature, tasks have been defined in a variety of ways. Long, for instance, suggests that a task

> is a piece of work undertaken for oneself or for others, freely or for some reward. Thus, examples of tasks include painting a fence, dressing a child, filling out a form, buying a pair of shoes, making an airline reservation, borrowing a library book, taking a driving test, typing a letter, weighing a patient, sorting letters, taking a hotel reservation, writing a cheque, finding a street destination, and helping someone across a road. In other words, by *task* is meant the hundred and one things people do in everyday life, at work, at play, and in-between.
>
> *Long 1985: 89*

In my 1989 book on task-based language teaching, I drew a distinction between pedagogical tasks and real-world or target tasks. The tasks Long sets out above are target tasks. They are the sorts of things that individuals typically do outside the classroom. The ultimate rationale for language instruction is to enable learners to do these things using language, and it is to be expected that classroom time will be taken up with the rehearsal of making reservations, writing letters, finding street destinations in a directory, and so on. However, learners will also do many things in class that are not rehearsals for performance outside of the classroom. Listening to a tape and repeating, doing a jigsaw reading task, solving a problem in small groups, these tasks are undertaken, not because learners will do them outside of the classroom, but because it is assumed that they facilitate the development of a learner's general language proficiency. They have a pedagogical or psycholinguistic rationale.

Richards, Platt and Weber have such a rationale when they suggest that a task is

> an activity or action which is carried out as the result of processing or understanding language (i.e., as a response). For example, drawing a map while listening to a tape, listening to an instruction and performing a command, may be referred to as tasks. Tasks may or may not involve the production of language. A task usually requires the teacher to specify what will be regarded as successful completion of the task. The use of a variety of different kinds of tasks in language teaching is said to make language teaching more communicative.
>
> *1986: 289*

Pedagogical Tasks Defined

. . . a piece of classroom work that involves learners in comprehending, manipulating, producing, or interacting in the target language while their attention is focused on mobilizing their grammatical knowledge in order to express meaning, and in which the intention is to convey meaning rather than to manipulate form. The task should also have a sense of completeness, being able to stand alone as a communicative act in its own right with a beginning, a middle and an end.

Nunan 1989: 10

Examples of classroom tasks include:
◇ listening to a weather forecast and deciding what to wear;
◇ responding to a party invitation;
◇ completing a banking application form;
◇ describing a photograph of one's family.

◆   *TASK* VERSUS *EXERCISE*

At the risk of oversimplification, the essential difference between a task and an exercise is that a task has a nonlinguistic outcome, while an exercise has a linguistic outcome. Thus, in the first example given in the box above, the outcome will be the selection of appropriate clothing, given (and assuming the accuracy of) a weather forecast. This is a nonlinguistic outcome, and success will be measured in nonlinguistic terms (whether the person is too hot, too cold, or comfortable). In contrast, the following is an exercise (and, a creative one at that!), because the outcome will be a set of structures. Success will be decided in linguistic terms.

Imagine you are a travel buff and write sentences describing your standard equipment. Use a nonrestrictive relative clause with a subject relative pronoun for each item.

Example: laptop

I always bring a laptop, which is a portable computer.

1.	luggage cart	5.	travel calculator
2.	money belt	6.	detergent
3.	travel iron	7.	a Swiss army knife
4.	adapter	8.	book light

Frodesen and Eyring 1993: 159

Elsewhere, I have suggested that tasks have some sort of input data (I use this term rather than *text* because the data may not contain language. It may be a set of pictures, diagrams, or other nonverbal material). It will also contain a set of procedures that specify what learners are to do in relation to the data. Implicit in any task will be a pedagogical goal, as well as particular roles for teachers and learners. One final dimension worth considering is the setting in which the task will be performed. Will this be within the classroom or outside? Will the learners work in teacher-fronted, small group, or individual mode?

In describing, analyzing and creating tasks, it is useful to think of the four essential dimensions of *task*. These are the dimensions of language, procedure, learner, and learning process. In each of these dimensions there are several key considerations that I shall summarize here, and take up in greater detail later in the book. In the rest of this chapter, I look at three important principles of task design.

1. the authenticity principle;
2. the form/function principle;
3. the task dependency principle.

◆ THE AUTHENTICITY PRINCIPLE

In terms of language, key considerations concern the extent to which linguistic data that learners work with are authentic, and to what extent the relationships between linguistic form and communicative function are clear to the learner. As a rough rule of thumb, we can say that authentic data are samples of spoken and written language that have not been specifically written for the purposes of teaching language. Much has been made of the fact that authenticity is a relative matter, and that as soon as one extracts a piece of language from the communicative context in which it occurred and takes it into the classroom, one is "de-authenticating" it to a degree. I would not disagree with this. Nor would I argue that nonauthentic data should be banned from the classroom. However, I would argue that learners should be fed as rich a diet of authentic data as possible, because, ultimately, if they only encounter contrived dialogues and listening texts, their task will be made more difficult.

The advantage of using authentic data is that learners encounter target language items (in the case of the example below, comparative adjectives and adverbs) in the kinds of contexts where they naturally occur, rather than in contexts that have been concocted by a textbook writer. Ultimately, this will assist learners because they will experience the language item in interaction with other closely related grammatical and discourse elements. The disparity between contrived and authentic data can be seen in the following extracts that, themselves, have been turned into a classroom task.

Task

Study the following extracts. One is a piece of genuine conversation, the other is taken from a language teaching textbook. What differences can you see between the two extracts? What language do you think the nonauthentic conversation is trying to teach? What grammar would you need in order to take part in the authentic conversation?

Text 1

A: *Excuse me, please. Do you know where the nearest bank is?*

B: *Well, the City Bank isn't far from here. Do you know where the main post office is?*

A: *No, not really. I'm just passing through.*

B: *Well, first go down this street to the traffic light.*

A: *OK.*

B: *Well, first go down this street to the traffic light.*

Text 2

A: *How do I get to Kensington Road?*

B: *Well you go down Fullarton Road . . .*

A: *. . . what, down Old Belair, and around . . .?*

B: *Yeah. And then you go straight . . .*

A: *. . . past the hospital?*

B: *Yeah, keep going straight, past the racecourse to the roundabout. You know the big roundabout?*

Text 1
A: *OK.*
B: *Then turn left and go west on Sunset Boulevard for about two blocks. The bank is on your right, just past the post office.*
A: *All right. Thanks!*
B: *You're welcome.*
[I have not acknowledged the source of this extract, because I do not wish to appear to be criticizing the text from which it was extracted. It is cited here for contrastive purposes only.]

Text 2
A: *Yeah.*
B: *And Kensington Road's off to the right.*
A: *What, off the roundabout?*
B: *Yeah.*
A: *Right.*

[Source: D. Nunan 1993.]

◆ THE FORM–FUNCTION PRINCIPLE

When designing tasks, the second key consideration concerns teaching language in ways that make form and function relationships transparent. I suspect that one of the reasons for the mismatches between teaching and learning is that learners often find it difficult to see the functional purpose for having different linguistic forms. For example, exercises in which learners are required to carry out various kinds of linguistic transformations (such as changing active voice sentences into passives and back again), may be fine for teaching new linguistic forms, but not for showing students how to use the forms for making meanings. In the case of the active/passive voice example, the implicit message for the learner is that these two forms carry the same meaning, that they are alternative ways of saying the same thing.

The challenge, in activating this principle, is to design tasks that require learners to use inductive and deductive reasoning to develop their own understanding of the relationship between form and function. This is a developmental process, and it often takes learners many years to develop an accurate understanding of a particular relationship.

The following task sequence, adapted from Hall and Shepheard (1991), illustrates how such an approach might be used to help students make sense of time relationships.

Example

◇ Working with another student, match the uses of the present perfect with the following sentences by writing a letter in the column.

A. indefinite future period   B. indefinite past   C. definite future period
D. recent action   E. past–present period: unfinished

1. The rains have just brought hope to   PAST   NOW   FUTURE
    the starving of Africa.   _____ X__|_____

2. Giant swarms of locusts have been
    reported in Cape Verde.

3. Experts who have been in the FAO in
    Mali for years were amazed by the size
    of one swarm.

4. Other countries are waiting until
    international meetings have been held
    in two months' time.

5. Government cannot wait until locust
    swarms have eaten their crops.

◇   Now draw timelines for sentences 2–5 similar to that for sentence 1.

◇   Answer the following questions.

  1. a. The rains have just brought hope to the starving of Africa.
      b. The rains just brought hope to the starving but no solution

      Which adverbs can replace *just* in (a) and (b)?

  2. a. Great swarms of locusts have been reported in Cape Verde.
      b. Great swarms of locusts were reported in Cape Verde.

      To which sentence can the words *two days ago* be added?

  3. a. Experts who have been with the FAO for years were amazed.
      b. Experts who were with the FAO for years were amazed.

  4. a. Other countries are waiting until international meetings have been
         held in two months' time.
      b. Other countries are waiting until international meetings are held in
         two months' time.

      Are these countries waiting until the meetings are over or until they
      begin in (a), in (b)?

  5. a. Other countries are waiting until international meetings have finished.
      b. Other countries are waiting until international meetings finish.

      True/False: There is no objective difference betwen the two events.
      Which sentence emphasises the completion of the event?

[Adapted from N. Hall & J. Shepheard, 1191
The Anti-Grammar Grammar Book. London. Longman.

◆ THE TASK DEPENDENCY PRINCIPLE

In relation to pedagogical procedures, that is, what learners actually do
in relation to the data they are working with, the key question is: What

principles can the teacher, materials developer, or course designer draw on in order to arrive at an instructional sequence in which tasks flow logically from one to the next? In my own work, I have sought to do this by invoking the "task dependency" principle, in which each succeeding task in the instructional sequence flows out of, and is dependent on, the one that precedes it. In this way, a series of tasks in a lesson or unit of work forms a kind of pedagogical ladder, each task representing a rung on the ladder, enabling the learner to reach higher and higher levels of communicative performance. As a general principle (and *not* as an unvarying rule), I also sequence tasks from reception to production. In other words, listening and reading tasks generally come before writing and speaking tasks. The earlier tasks can therefore act as models for the learner, providing them with language and content to draw on when they come to produce their own language. A final principle that facilitates coherence is to arrange an instructional sequence so that what I call "reproductive tasks" precede "creative" tasks. A reproductive task is one in which the student reproduces language provided by the teacher, the textbook, or the tape.

In contrast to reproductive tasks, creative tasks are those that require learners to come up with language for which they have not been specifically cued. In other words, they are asked to put together familiar elements in new or novel combinations. The final task in the sequence presented in Figure 1-3a, 1-3b, is an example of a creative task, in that learners are recombining, in novel ways, familiar elements from earlier tasks.

In designing sequences of tasks, it is important to consider the salience for learners of the pedagogical goals of the task, the extent to which learning strategies are made explicit, the extent to which the task incorporates an experiential philosophy of learning by doing, and the opportunities provided to learners for inductive learning. We also need to consider the extent to which learners are given space to contribute their own ideas, feelings and attitudes, the extent to which they are given active (rather than reactive) roles, and the opportunities they have to make choices. These and the other aspects of *task* touched on in this chapter are taken up in greater detail in later chapters.

In placing *task* at the center of the curriculum development process, I have blurred the distinction between syllabus design (which is concerned with selecting and sequencing linguistic and experiential content) and methodology (which is concerned with the selection and sequencing of pedagogical procedures). The danger in designing courses based on a collection of tasks is that we have no principles for selecting, sequencing, and integrating our material, and the curriculum ends up as little more than a collection of classroom "tricks." There are two ways to get around this problem. The first is to reference the selection of tasks against a clearly specified set of curricular goals. The second is to invoke the task

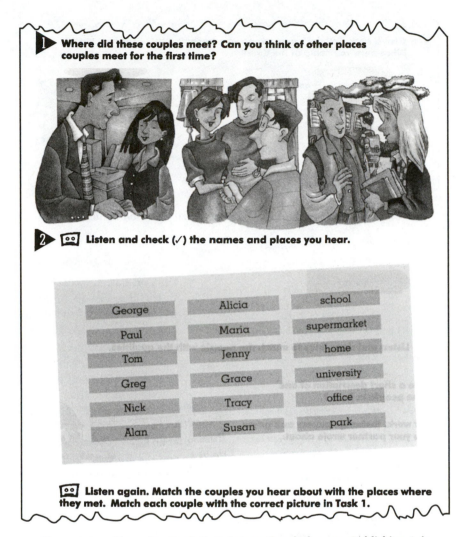

1▶ Where did these couples meet? Can you think of other places couples meet for the first time?

2▶ 🔊 Listen and check (✓) the names and places you hear.

George	Alicia	school
Paul	Maria	supermarket
Tom	Jenny	home
Greg	Grace	university
Nick	Tracy	office
Alan	Susan	park

🔊 **Listen again. Match the couples you hear about with the places where they met. Match each couple with the correct picture in Task 1.**

Figure 1-3a   *Listen In* - Book 2, © International Thomson Publishing Asia

dependency principle, sequencing and integrating tasks into sequences of task ladders, in which succeeding tasks evolve out of the ones that go before.

The following table of contents for LISTEN IN Level 1, a three-level oral skills series, illustrates the first principle. The general aim of this course is to help learners develop skills for taking part in a wide variety of transactional and interpersonal encounters.

The task dependency principle is illustrated in the following sequence.

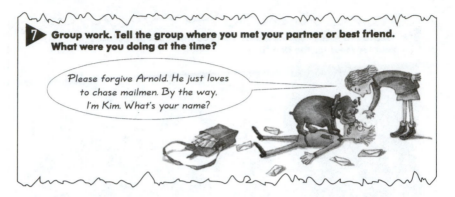

Figure 1-3b ***Listen In*** **- Book 2, © International Thomson Publishing Asia**

CONTENTS

Unit 1	-	How do you do?	1
Unit 2	-	This is my family.	5
Unit 3	-	That's her over there.	9
Unit 4	-	What languages are you studying?	13
Unit 5	-	Where are you from?	17
Units 1-5	-	Review	21
Unit 6	-	This is where I live.	23
Unit 7	-	Where can I find the sporting goods?	27
Unit 8	-	What do you do?	31
Unit 9	-	We're meeting in the conference room.	35
Unit 10	-	Do you have a computer?	39
Units 6-10	-	Review	43
Unit 11	-	I usually get up at six.	45
Unit 12	-	I'd like a table for five.	49
Unit 13	-	Tennis is a great game.	53
Unit 14	-	What movies are playing?	57
Unit 15	-	Where do you get your news?	61
Units 11-15	-	Review	65
Unit 16	-	I didn't know how to meet anyone.	67
Unit 17	-	Why don't we buy a new car?	71
Unit 18	-	My new boss is really nice.	75
Unti 19	-	How do you like to learn?	79
Unit 20	-	How often do you see your friends?	83
Units 16-20	-	Review	87

Figure 1-4 ***Listen In*** **- Book 1, © International Thomson Publishing Asia**

As you can see, each task in the chain evolves out of the one that comes before. Prior tasks provide learners with the language models and experiential content that they will need to carry out the tasks that follow. Note also that although each task builds on the one that goes before, it is also self-contained, being able to stand alone in its own right.

Task 1

1. You are about to watch a video in which eight exchange students talk about their experiences. Make notes on what they have to say, for example, where they went, what advice they would give to others, what they did that was culturally inappropriate, what they thought was strange about the host culture.

	Where?	*Advice*	*Positive*	*Negative/Odd*
S1:				
S2:				
S3:				
S4:				
S5:				
S6:				
S7:				
S8:				

2. Compare responses with two or three other students.

Task 2

1. Imagine that you are going as an exchange student to another country. Complete the following survey (check the appropriate space under the 'YOU' column.)

	YOU			YOUR PARTNER		
This would bother us	a lot	a little	not at all	a lot	a little	not at all
a. the weather	___	___	___	___	___	___
b. the food	___	___	___	___	___	___
c. getting around	___	___	___	___	___	___
d. tipping	___	___	___	___	___	___
e. language	___	___	___	___	___	___
f. social customs	___	___	___	___	___	___
g. being away from home	___	___	___	___	___	___

	YOU			YOUR PARTNER		
This would bother us	a lot	a little	not at all	a lot	a little	not at all
h. meeting people	____	____	____	____	____	____
i. money matters	____	____	____	____	____	____
j. shopping	____	____	____	____	____	____

2. Pair Work. Now survey another student, and tick off the responses under the 'YOUR PARTNER' column.
3. Work with another pair, and tell them about your partner.

Task 3

1. Pair Work. Imagine that you are about to move to another country to do work experience. You know very little about this country. Brainstorm ideas for meeting people and finding out about your new country.
2. Work with another pair and write down ten ideas. Rank the ideas from most to least interesting (1 = most interesting) and from most to least practical (1 = most practical).
3. Compare your list with another pair. Which pair has the most interesting ideas overall?

Task 4

What would you want to know about a country that you were going to visit for the first time either for study or work? How would you try and find out? Imagine that you met a person from this country in Hong Kong. Make a list of the questions you would ask.

Interview someone from another country who is living in Hong Kong. Make a summary of that person's comments and be prepared to discuss these in the next class.

[SOURCE: *Adapted from D. Nunan. 1995.* ATLAS: Learning-Centered Communication. *Level 3. Student's book and video. Boston: Heinle & Heinle/ITP*]

◆ CONCLUSION

In this chapter, I placed second language teaching and learning firmly within an educational context, and showed that many of the issues confronting language teachers are also preoccupying content teachers. I framed the chapter within the long-running controversy over the nature of knowledge and learning, and made clear my own bias toward a constructivist view of knowledge. Such a view is in harmony with ruling concepts on the field, including communicative language, task-based language teaching, learner-centeredness, and negotiated curricula.

While the primary purpose of the chapter is to provide a conceptual framework for understanding current directions in the field, I also tried to put practical flesh on these conceptual bones by illustrating the points with extracts from classrooms and teaching materials. In the next chapter, I shall look at some of the research that has informed our understanding of pedagogy and language acquisition.

◆ CONCEPT MAP OF CHAPTER 1

The following concept map shows the main ideas introduced in the chapter and the relationships between them.

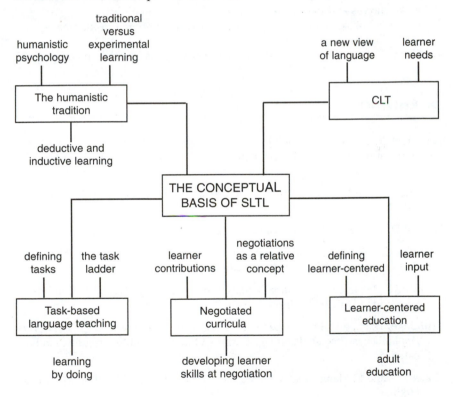

◆ QUESTIONS AND TASKS

1. What two competing views of education are presented in the first section of the chapter?
2. In your view, what are the three most important points about experiential learning made in the chapter?
3. What is the difference between inductive learning and deductive learning?

4. What is communicative language teaching, and what factors led to its emergence in ELT?
5. Identify two different senses in which the term *learner-centered* can be used.
6. Would a learner-centered approach work in your situation? Why or why not?
7. Which of the principles of adult learning articulated by Brundage and MacKeracher do you agree with? Which do you disagree with? How do the principles relate to a humanistic, experiential view of education?
8. Do you agree with the assertion that there is a degree of negotiation in every classroom? Think of a class that you taught, observed, or took part in as a learner in which negotiation occurred and give three to five examples of negotiation.
9. Identify three differences between a "traditional" and a "task-based" language classroom.
10. Study a unit of work from a textbook that you are familiar with. Identify ways in which the unit can be modified to give learners an opportunity to make choices and decisions, and contribute their own ideas.
11. Design a link sequence of tasks using the ideas presented in the final section of the chapter.
12. Carry out a survey of your students and colleagues like the one on page 33.

◆ REFERENCES

Allwright, R. L. 1984. Why don't learners learn what teachers teach?—The interaction hypothesis. In D. M. Singleton and D. G. Little (eds.), 1984. *Language Learning in Formal and Informal Contexts*. (pp. 3–18) IRAAL: Dublin.

Assinder, W. 1991. Peer teaching, peer learning; one model. *ELT Journal*, 45, 3, 218–229.

Barnes, D. 1976. *From Communication to Curriculum*. London: Penguin.

Brindley, G. 1984. *Needs Analysis and Objective Setting in the Adult Migrant Education Service*. Sydney: NSW Adult Migrant Education Service.

Brumfit, C. 1984. *Communicative Methodology in Language Teaching*. Cambridge: Cambridge University Press.

Brundage, D. H., and D. MacKeracher 1980. *Adult Learning Principles and Their Application in Program Planning*. Toronto: Ontario Institute for Studies in Education.

Cohen, L., and L. Manion. *Research Methods in Education*. 2nd Ed. London: Croom Helm.

Dam, L., and G. Gabrielsen. 1988. Developing learner autonomy in a school context. A six-year experiment beginning in the learners' first year of English. In H. Holec (ed.), *Autonomy and Self-Directed Learning: Present Fields of Application*. Strasbourg: Council of Europe.

Frodesen, J., and J. Eyring. 1993. *Grammar Dimensions Four*. Boston: Heinle & Heinle.

Hall, N., and J. Shepheard. 1991. *The Anti-Grammar Grammar Book*. London: Longman.

Heath, S. B. 1992. Literacy skills or literate skills? Considerations for ESL/EFL learners. In D. Nunan (ed.), *Collaborative Language Learning and Teaching*. Cambridge: Cambridge University Press.

Knowles, M. 1983. *The Adult Learner: A Neglected Species*. Houston: Gulf Publishing Company.

Kohonen, V. 1992. Experiential language learning: Second language learning as cooperative learner education. In D. Nunan (ed.), *Collaborative Language Learning and Teaching*. Cambridge: Cambridge University Press.

Kolb, D. 1984. *Experiential Learning: Experience as the Source of Learning and Development*. Englewood Cliffs, N.J.: Prentice-Hall.

Legutke, M., and H. Thomas. 1991. *Process and Experience in the Language Classroom*. London: Longman.

Long, M. H. 1985. A role for instruction in second language acquisition. In K. Hyltenstam and M. Pienemann (eds.) *Modelling and Assessing Second Language Acquisition*. Clevedon Avon: Multilingual Matters.

Malcolm, I. 1991. "All right then, if you don't want to do that . . ." Strategy and counterstrategy in classroom discourse management. *Guidelines*, 13, 2, 1–17.

Mouly, G. J. 1978. *Educational Research: The Art and Science of Investigation*. Boston: Allyn and Bacon.

Munby, J. 1978. *Communicative Syllabus Design*. Cambridge: Cambridge University Press.

Newmark, L., and D. Reibel. 1968. Necessity and sufficiency in language learning. *International Review of Applied Linguistics*, 6, 145–164.

Nunan, D. 1991. *Language Teaching Methodology*. London: Prentice-Hall.

Nunan, D. 1988. *The Learner-Centred Curriculum*. Cambridge: Cambridge University Press.

Nunan, D. 1993. *Introducing Discourse Analysis*. London: Penguin

Nunan, D. 1995. *ATLAS: Learning-Centered Communication*. Boston: Heinle & Heinle/ITP.

Nunan, D. 1998. *Listen In*. Singapore: International Thomson ELT.

Parkinson, L., and K. O'Sullivan. 1990. Negotiating the learner-centred curriculum. In G. Brindley (ed.), *The Second Language Curriculum in Action*. Sydney: National Centre for English Language Teaching and Research.

Richards, J. C., J. Platt, and H. Weber. 1986. *A Dictionary of Applied Linguistics*. London: Longman.

Slimani, A. 1992. Evaluation of classroom interaction. In J. C. Alderson and A. Beretta. (eds.), *Evaluating Second Language Education* (pp.197–211). Cambridge: Cambridge University Press.

Widdows, S., and P. Voller. 1991. PANSI: A survey of ELT needs of Japanese university students. *Cross Currents*, XVIII, 2,

CHAPTER 2

The Empirical Basis of Second Language Teaching and Learning

A major shift in perspective over the last twenty years has been the development of a much more empirical approach to SLTL. Until relatively recently, proposals for classroom action were derived less from empirical data than speculation. In recent years, however, there has been a veritable explosion in the number of data-based studies in the field. This is not to say that change is, or even should, always be empirically driven. New ways of approaching SLTL can also emerge from reconceptualizations of the nature of language, learners, and the learning process. It can also emerge from the struggle to find new ways of addressing problems, challenges, or puzzles that emerge in the course of teaching. However, many people, and I would include myself here, have argued that at some stage new ideas should be tested in some shape or form through research. By the amount of activity in the field, there is evidence that this is beginning to happen. In this chapter, I review some of the research that has influenced the way that I think about language teaching and learning. In keeping with the rest of the book, this is a personal selection. Even if I had wished to offer comprehensive coverage, it would have been well beyond the scope of this chapter. I should also point out that many other studies are referred to in other sections of the book. The purpose of this chapter is to focus on research into a number of hypothesized relationships between environmental–instructional factors and acquisition. The following issues are dealt with in the chapter.

First versus second language acquisition
◇ psycholinguistic mechanisms
◇ the acquisition of syntax
◇ discourse acquisition

Chronological age and second language acquisition
◇ age-related differences in acquisition
◇ the "critical" period hypothesis

The effect of instruction on acquisition
◇ the "morpheme order studies,"
◇ conscious learning versus subconscious acquisition
◇ comprehensible input
◇ comprehensible output
◇ developmental stages in the acquisition process
◇ interaction and acquisition

The relationship between task types/modes of classroom organization and acquisition
◇   modified interaction and the negotiation of meaning
◇   small group work
◇   task types and discourse
The relationship between learning strategies and acquisition
◇   defining learning strategies
◇   strategy preferences and biographical variables
◇   learner "types"
◇   the "good" language learner
◇   strategy training and task performance

IS LEARNING A SECOND LANGUAGE LIKE LEARNING A FIRST?

♦ *PSYCHOLINGUISTIC MECHANISMS*

In the early 1970s, one of the first issues to preoccupy researchers working in the fledgling discipline of second language acquisition related to the relationship between first and second language acquisition. The question addressed by researchers had to do with whether or not psycholinguistic mechanisms in second language acquisition were basically the same as or different from those in first language acquisition (See, for example, Ervin–Tripp, 1974). In relation to the acquisition of grammatical morphemes, Dulay and Burt (1974a; 1974b) began with the premise that first and second language acquisition in children were the same process, and that the kinds of errors made by a second language learner would be the same as those made by a first language learner of the same language. However, as a result of their research, they concluded:

> we can no longer hypothesize similarities between L2 and L1 acquisition as we did at the outset of our investigations. Although both the L2 and L1 learner reconstruct the language they are learning, it is intuitive to expect that the manner in which they do so will differ. Children learning a second language are usually older than L1 learners; they are further along in their cognitive development, and they have experienced a language once before. These factors should combine to make the specific strategies of the creative construction process in L2 acquisition somewhat different for those of the creative construction process in L1 acquisition.
>
> *Dulay and Burt 1974b: 225*

♦ *THE ACQUISITION OF SYNTAX*

Recent experiments into first language acquisition based on the work of Chomsky strongly suggest that a first language is "hard wired" into the brain, in other words, that our first language is an innate endowment bequeathed to us by virtue of our membership of the human race. Arguments for the Innateness Hypothesis have recently been popularized by Stephen Pinker (1994) in his book *The Language Instinct*. While Pinker tends to gloss over the interactional aspects of language acquisition (for an account of these, see Foster 1990), the evidence of for an innate ability is strong. All children with normal hearing and articulatory mechanisms acquire their first language. This is not the case with second or third languages. Comparatively few individuals who begin the study of a second language after they have mastered their first ever develop the equivalent of native mastery. While some would argue that the jury is still out over whether learning a second language is like learning a first, I believe there is sufficient evidence to suggest that the two skills are fundamentally different, certainly insofar as syntax and phonology are concerned.

Innateness Hypothesis
The innateness hypothesis suggests that the ability to acquire language is a facility unique to the human species. We inherit this ability genetically in the same way as other species inherit such things as the ability to migrate to certain parts of the world to mate and breed.

◆ DISCOURSE ACQUISITION

Turning from syntax to discourse, in my own dissertation work I investigated the discourse processing operations of first and second language learners (Nunan 1984). I looked in particular at the perception of semantic and discourse relationships in written texts, and found a high level of agreement between first and second language readers. While the second language readers had greater overall difficulty with the texts than the first language readers, in relative terms, those relationships that first language readers found difficult were also found to be problematic for second language readers, and those that the first language readers found easy were also found to be easy by the second language readers.

Similarities and differences between first and second language acquisition have most often been inferred from comparative studies into language processing and production by first and second language users. Such studies are generally experimental or quasi-experimental in nature, and also usually employ some sort of elicitation device. For example, the study referred to in the preceding paragraph elicited data from first and second language readers through a modified cloze procedure. The problem with elicitation devices, and particularly with forced production tasks, is that one can never be entirely certain that the results obtained have not been determined, at least in part, by the elicitation devices and instruments themselves (for a discussion, see Nunan, 1992).

WHAT IS THE ROLE OF CHRONOLOGICAL AGE ON THE ACQUISITION OF A SECOND LANGUAGE?

♦ AGE-RELATED DIFFERENCES

The effect of age on acquisition has been extensively documented, the issue being whether younger learners acquire a second language more efficiently and effectively than older learners. Research to date has not conclusively settled the issue of age one way or another (Scovel 1988), largely because, from a research perspective, the issue is more complex than it might seem at first. As Ellis (1985), points out, it is necessary to distinguish between the effect of age on the route of acquisition (whether the same target language items are acquired in the same order for different learners), the rate (how rapidly the learners acquire the language), and ultimate attainment (how proficient they end up being). Ellis concludes from his review of the available literature that, while age does not alter the route of acquisition, it does have a marked effect on the rate and ultimate success. However, the results are by no means straightforward. For example, in terms of rate, adults appear to do better than children (6 to 10 years), while teenagers (12 to 15 years) appear to outperform both adults and children. Ellis concludes that:

1. Starting age does not affect the route of SLA. Although there may be differences in the acquisitional order, these are not the result of age.
2. Starting age affects the rate of learning. When grammar and vocabulary are concerned, adolescent learners do better than either children or adults, when the length of exposure is held constant. When pronunciation is concerned, there is no appreciable difference.
3. Both number of years of exposure and starting age affect the level of success. The number of years' exposure contributes greatly to the overall communicative fluency of the learners, but starting age determines the levels of accuracy achieved, particularly in pronunciation.

Ellis 1985: 106

♦ THE CRITICAL PERIOD HYPOTHESIS

These age-related differences have been explained in terms of a biological mechanism known as the "critical period." This construct refers to a

The Critical Period Hypothesis
According to proponents of the critical period hypotheses, biological changes in the brain around puberty result in the two hemispheres of the brain functioning independently. After this neurological change takes place, acquiring native-like competence in a second language becomes difficult, if not impossible. This hypothesis has been controversial, and, with the development of recent technology allowing scientists to map mental activity, has been called into question.

limited period of time in the development of an organism during which a particular behavior can be acquired. Psycholinguists have looked for evidence of the critical period in both first- and second-language acquisition. It has been argued (see, for example, Penfield and Roberts 1959) that the optimum age for acquiring another language is in the first ten years of life because it is then that the brain retains its maximum "plasticity" or flexibility (the plasticity metaphor, suggesting as it does that the brain is like a lump of plasticine that gradually hardens with age, seems a favored one among investigations of the critical period). It is suggested that, at around puberty, the brain loses its plasticity, the two hemispheres of the brain become much more independent of one another, and the language function is largely established in the left hemisphere. The critical period hypothesis argues that, after these neurological changes have taken place, acquiring another language becomes increasingly difficult.

The hypothesis, however, is not without its critics. As Ellis (1985) points out, it is only partially correct to suggest that acquisition is easier for younger children. In fact, pronunciation is the only area where the younger the start the better, and the hypothesis is at a loss to explain *why* the loss of plasticity only affects pronunciation.

Evidence relating to brain plasticity and the differential functions of the two hemispheres of the brain have come, not from research into language acquisition, but from clinic work on both children and adults who have suffered physical injury, or who have brain or speech disorders of one sort or another. Investigations into the effect of age on acquisition have come from experiments and quasi-experiments. Such experiments typically take subjects from two contrasting age groups, such as children versus adolescents, or children versus adults, teach some aspect of the target language such as a grammatical form or phonological feature, and then test the subjects to determine whether one group has learned more effectively than the other. For example, Asher and Price (1967) compared the efforts of a group of pre-adolescents to learn Russian with a group of college students, and found that the adults outperformed the children. One of the major shortcomings of these experiments, however, is that they are generally extremely selective, looking at a small subset of the features of one aspect of the target language. They also tend to be carried out over relatively short periods of time. For instance, the study carried out by Asher and Price was based on a mere 25 minutes of instruction.

WHAT IS THE EFFECT OF INSTRUCTION ON ACQUISITION?

While researchers are by no means in agreement about the most effective way of teaching a second language, they are now beginning to agree on the most appropriate kinds of questions to ask. The two most important questions for language educators are: What is the relationship between instruction and acquisition? (In other words, how does what the teacher teaches relate to what the learner learns?) What task types and modes of classroom organization and intervention facilitate acquisition? In this section, I shall review studies that have investigated the first question, and then, in the section that follows, I shall turn to the issue of task types/modes of pedagogical organization and acquisition.

◆ THE MORPHEME ORDER STUDIES

One of the most influential scholars to have written on the relationship between instruction and acquisition is Krashen (1981, 1982). Krashen developed his hypotheses out of a series of investigations carried out during the 1970s. Known as the "morpheme order studies," these investigations set out to determine whether there is a "natural sequence" in the acquisition of second language grammar. The researchers found that, in fact, learners from very different first language backgrounds (for example, Spanish and Chinese), appeared to acquire a set of grammatical items (or morphemes) in English in virtually the same order (Dulay and Burt 1973, 1974). The first studies were carried out with children. Later investigations involving adults came up with very similar acquisition orders (Bailey *et al.* 1974). From these investigations, researchers concluded that it was the nature of the language being learned, and not, as had previously been thought, a contrast between the first and second languages, that determined the order of acquisition. The next step was to see whether these orders could be "overturned" by instruction. The results were disappointing (at least for those who wanted to make strong claims about the relationship between instruction and acquisition). Not one study showed that the so-called natural order could be changed through instruction. It was also found that knowledge of grammatical rules was no guarantee of being able to use those rules for communication. Learners who were able to identify instances of rule violation, and who could even state the rule, frequently violated the rules when using language for communication.

◆ CONSCIOUS LEARNING VERSUS SUBCONSCIOUS ACQUISITION

It was against this empirical background that Krashen formulated a controversial hypothesis. He argued that there are two mental processes operating in second-language acquisition: conscious learning and subconscious acquisition. Conscious learning focuses on grammatical rules, enabling the learner to memorize rules and to identify instances of rule violation. Subconscious acquisition is a very different process, and facilitates the acquisition of rules at a subconscious level. According to Krashen, when using the language to communicate meaning, the learner must draw on subconscious knowledge. There was nothing particularly new or radical in the suggestion that there were conscious and subconscious processes functioning in language development. What was new and radical was Krashen's assertion that these processes were totally separate; in other words, that learning could not become acquisition.

> A very important point that also needs to be stated is that learning does not 'turn into' acquisition. The idea that we first learn a new rule, and eventually, through practice, acquire it, is widespread and may seem to some people intuitively obvious. This model of the acquisition process was first presented to me when I was a student of TESL, and seemed very sensible at the time. It was, I thought, exactly the way I learned languages myself.
>
> *Krashen, 1982: 83*

◆ COMPREHENSIBLE INPUT

According to Krashen, language acquisition takes place through comprehension. In other words, when the student understands a message in the language containing a structure that is one step in advance of that learner's current level of competence, then that structure will be acquired. The hypothesis was an explicit rejection of the notion that "skill getting" was a necessary prerequisite for "skill using" (Rivers and Temperley 1978).

Many teachers found Krashen's disjunction between learning and acquisition to be intuitively appealing, as it was consistent with the observable fact that there is often little tangible evidence of any direct relationship between teaching and learning. It was also reassuring for those teachers who were demoralized by the fact that their learners did not learn what they had taught. On the other hand, the notion that learners could develop the ability to speak simply by understanding messages in the language seemed counterintuitive.

In the wake of Krashen's work, numerous researchers sought to contest the notions (a) that structures are impervious to acquisition, and (b) that comprehensible input is all that is required for acquisition. In 1984, Rod Ellis published a study reporting his investigations into the effect of formal instruction on the acquisition of question forms. (Ironically, this study was published in the same issue of *Applied Linguistics* as a detailed attack on Krashen's work by Kevin Gregg, 1984). Ellis set out to investigate the effects of approximately three hours of teaching on the ability of 13 children between the ages of 11 and 13 to ask *Wh*-questions. While three hours is very little, it was felt that, as the children were beginning to use *Wh*-question forms spontaneously, they were developmentally ready to learn, and some degree of impact should be discernible. At the beginning, and again at the end of the three-hour instructional period, the children were given cue cards for *who*, *what*, *where*, and *when*, and asked to make up questions based on a picture of a classroom scene. Ellis found that there was no significant increase for the 13 children as a whole in their ability to use *Wh*-questions, although individual children did show a marked improvement. In addition, he found that those children who interacted least in class appeared to improve the most. In order to account for this finding, Ellis was required to go back to the lesson transcripts. Here, he found that it appeared to be the quality rather than the quantity of the interactions that mattered. When the teaching sequences contained communicatively rich exchanges, in which the learner was required to take part in relatively spontaneous interactions, rather then straight drills, he or she showed some development. Ellis concluded that:

> it would seem that 'exposure' . . . is far more important than 'instruction'. In other words, it is not focusing on the form of 'when' questions that helped some of the children to develop, but the opportunity to negotiate a communicative task.
>
> *p. 149*

◆ COMPREHENSIBLE OUTPUT

In 1985, Krashen's comprehensible input hypothesis came under challenge from Swain (1985), who investigated immersion programs in Canada. In these programs, children receive their content instruction in another language. If the children are native speakers of English, they receive instruction in math, science, and so forth in French. If their first language is French, they receive instruction in English. These children therefore receive massive amounts of comprehensible input. Despite this, their second language development is not as advanced as it should be according to the comprehensible input hypothesis. When Swain looked at what actually went on in the classroom, she found that the basic instructional pattern was one in which the teachers talked a great deal, but the students got to say very little. Based on her observations, Swain formulated an alternative hypothesis, which she called the "comprehensible output" hypothesis, suggesting that opportunities to produce language were important for acquisition.

At about this time Montgomery and Eisenstein (1985) carried out a study that also supported the idea that opportunities to practice the language in communicative situations was important for language acquisition. They carried out an experiment in which a control group received grammar instruction only. An experimental group received instruction, plus opportunities to use their language communicatively outside the classroom. At the end of the experiment, they tested both groups. Not surprisingly, the experimental group outperformed the control group on tests of communicative interaction. What was surprising was the fact that this group also outperformed the control group on tests of grammar, even though they had received comparatively less grammatical instruction. Montgomery and Eisenstein concluded that both instruction and interaction were necessary for acquisition.

The same conclusion was reached by Schmidt, who carried out a case study of his own experiences learning Portuguese in Brazil. He found that formal instruction plus opportunities to communicate out of class were both necessary for acquisition. He also challenged the idea of subconscious acquisition, arguing that he only acquired items when they were consciously noticed. Out of his study he formulated what he called the "notice the gap" principle. This was based on the insight that his own language only improved when he noticed the gap between his own production and that of the native speakers with whom he was interacting (Schmidt and Frota, 1986).

◆ DEVELOPMENTAL STAGES

During the 1980s a number of researchers studying the acquisition of German and English came up with an interesting explanation for the disparity between instruction and acquisition based on speech processing constraints (Pienemann, 1989). They argued that grammatical items can be sequenced into a series of stages, each more complex than the last. However, this complexity is determined by the demands made on short-term memory, rather than by the conceptual complexity of the items in question. For example, as Krashen had already pointed out, in English third person -s is a late acquired item. These researchers were able to give an explanation for why this was so. According to pedagogical grammars, the item is relatively straightforward. If the subject of a sentence is singular, add -s to the main verb. However, in speech processing terms, it can be quite complex, because the speaker has to hold the information as to whether the noun phrase is singular or plural in working memory. Because many speech processing operations are very complex, and also because the time available for speaking or comprehending is limited, it is only possible to focus on a limited part of the whole speech processing operation at one time.

Another perspective on the processing complexity of third person -s is described in the popular book on language, *The Language Instinct*:

The Teachability Hypothesis
According to the teachability hypothesis, grammatical structures can be classified according to the demands they make on the learner's working memory. The greater the demands the more difficult the structure is to learn. An item will only be acquired, and therefore should only be taught, when the learner is developmentally ready to acquire it.

Any speaker committed to using it (i.e., third person -*s*) has to keep track of four details in any sentence uttered:

Whether the subject is in the third person or not: *He walks* versus *I walk.*

Whether the subject is singular or plural: *He walks* versus *They walk.*

Whether the action is present tense or not: *He walks* versus *He walked.*

Whether the action is habitual or going on at the moment of speaking (its "aspect"): *He walks to school* versus *He is walking to school.*

Pinker: 1994: 43–44

Out of the work on speech processing, the researchers formulated their "teachability/learnability hypothesis," arguing that an item is only learnable, and therefore should only be taught, when learners are at the developmental stage immediately preceding that of the item to be learned. (For a more detailed explanation of this hypothesis, see Hyltenstam and Pienemann 1985. For a critique of the hypothesis, see Nunan 1991.)

♦ INTERACTION AND ACQUISITION

Much recent work has taken up Swain's comprehensible output hypothesis, investigating in greater detail the importance to acquisition of opportunities to interact in the target language.

In a 1990 paper, Spada reviewed much of the research carried out by herself and others in Canada, looking in particular at the question of what type of curricular organization seems to result in the most successful second language acquisition. Spada summarizes studies that have investigated three types of curricular organization: traditional curricula (here she was looking basically at grammar translation); immersion courses of the type already described, in which content instruction is delivered in the target language, but in which there is no formal instruction in grammar, and "communicative" classes, in which there was a focus on form, but in which learners were also provided with an opportunity to deploy their language in communication. Spada concluded that classrooms that were basically "communicative" in orientation, but that contained opportunities for explicit grammatical instruction, were superior to both traditional classrooms that focused heavily on grammar, and to immersion programs that eschewed explicit grammatical instruction.

One of the problems with a great deal of SLA research, and, I suspect, one of the reasons for a great deal of the conflicting, and even contradictory outcomes, is that the terms *acquisition*, and *instruction* are relatively imprecise terms. *Acquisition* can refer to any number of grammatical items (it is interesting in itself that virtually all SLA research has focused on the acquisition of morphosyntax), while *instruction* can refer to the many different kinds of instructional opportunities that teachers arrange for their students. In a 1989 book on classroom observation and action research, I reproduced a checklist devised by Koziol and Call that identifies 27 different ways of introducing a new grammatical item, and this is probably not an exhaustive list!

Recognizing that different linguistic forms might be susceptible to different forms of pedagogical intervention has prompted recent researchers to specify both the types of grammatical items under investigation, and the nature of the instruction. For example, Doughty (1988), who was interested in the effect of instruction versus exposure (or implicit versus explicit instruction) limited the focus of her investigation to relativization. The results she obtained were consistent with those of Spada: Learners receiving instruction outperformed learners who received exposure only.

In a longitudinal study spanning a two-year period, Lim (1992) investigated the relationship between the extent to which learners used the target language and both qualitative and quantitative aspects of acquisition. She found that the frequency and quality of learner participation related significantly to qualitative aspects of learner participation, such as the range of speech acts and control of conversational management techniques. Furthermore, learner participation in class related significantly to improvements in language proficiency. In other words, those who use the language more progress more rapidly.

Fotos (1993), working with adult EFL students in Japan, found that small group, problem-solving tasks are as effective as formal teacher-fronted instruction for grammatical consciousness-raising. Her study places squarely on the agenda the issue of just what it is that we mean when we talk of instruction. I suggested above that there are many ways of conceptualizing and defining instruction, and the study by Fotos shows that it is not necessarily or even primarily a case of the teacher standing up and delivering the good linguistic news to his or her students.

In an adult EFL context in China, Wudong Wu (1994) found that declarative knowledge (that is, the ability to identify errors and state rule violations) did not automatically lead to procedural knowledge (the ability to put known forms to communicative effect). Subjects in his study were able to identify errors in written texts, and even state the rules that had been violated. However, when it came to producing texts themselves, that is, in Krashen's terms, when their attention was focused on meaning, not form, they made the same mistakes themselves. In contrast with Krashen, however, Wudong Wu found that, by having learners engage in communicative tasks in which the target structures were activated, it was possible for these structures to be acquired. He concluded that, in addition to formal instruction, opportunities to activate knowledge through output activities, was a significant factor in acquisition.

Zhou (1991), also working in China, although with children rather than adults, found that formal instruction resulted in acquisition of some structures (passives) but not others (tense and aspect). Zhou also claims on the basis of the research that explicit (declarative) knowledge can be converted to implicit (procedural) knowledge through practice, an outcome remarkably similar to the arrived at by Wudong Wu. This study also underlines the importance of identifying specific structures for investigation, rather than simply attempting to measure acquisition in general.

Finally, Möllering & Nunan (1994) investigated the acquisition of modal particles by adult learners of German as a Foreign Language in Australia. They found that instruction made a difference, but once again, only in certain areas.

> [Subjects'] use of modal particles in a given context deviated from native speaker expectations, especially with regard to the modal particle *doch*. Production data revealed an underrepresentation of *doch* although it had occurred in modal particle function more often than any other particle in the texts the students had read, as the concordance data showed. Thus, *doch* was chosen as the focus of instruction and was used with considerably more frequency after the instruction phase, though in what might be called 'semi-obligatory' contexts rather than optional ones. Less than half of the students were able to explain or translate *doch* in a way which showed that they fully understood its illocutionary force. Thus, an improved understanding cannot be posited for the group as a whole but should be seen as a tendency. Acquisition is a complex 'organic' rather than linear 'all-or-nothing' process.
>
> *Möllering and Nunan 1995: 59*

The studies reviewed in this section are summarized in Table 2.1.

From Table 2.1, it may seem that this research is confusing and confused. In some ways it is. I suggested above that the apparent contradictory results may well be a reflection of the relative imprecision with which the terms *instruction* and *acquisition* are used, although the effects are not uniform from one linguistic item to another. It is also clear that instruction can make a difference for grammatical acquisition. However, it also seems from the studies reviewed in this section that there is another important variable at play here: interaction in the target language. It seems that, in order to maximize the effects of instruction, learners need opportunities to use the structures they are learning in communicative interaction.

The conclusion that a balanced diet of form-focused instruction plus opportunities to use the language in meaningful interaction is supported by Lightbown and Spada (1993), in their review of second-language learning in instructional contexts:

> Classroom data from a number of studies offer support for the view that form-focused instruction and corrective feedback provided within the context of a communicative program are more effective in promoting second language learning than programs which are limited to an exclusive emphasis on accuracy on the one hand or an exclusive emphasis on fluency on the other.
>
> *Lightbown and Spada 1993: 105*

Table 2.1 What is the relationship between instruction and acquisition?

Study	*Outcomes*
Krashen (1982)	Instruction does not lead to acquisition. Comprehensible input is necessary and sufficient for acquisition.
Ellis (1984)	Formal instruction on question forms had little effect on the acqusition of question forms.
Swain (1985)	Comprehensible input does not lead to acquisition.
Montgomery & Eisenstein (1985)	Grammar + opportunities to communicate led to greater improvements in fluency and grammatical accuracy than grammar only.
Schmidt & Frota (1986)	Instruction and opportunities to communicate out of class were both necessary. Improvement occurred when subject consciously "noticed the gap."
Pienemann (1989)	Grammatical forms will only be acquired when instruction matches the learner's developmental stage.
Spada (1990)	"Communicative" classrooms with instruction plus opportunities for interaction were superior to "traditional" instruction and also to immersion programs.
Doughty (1988)	Learners receiving instruction (both meaning- and form-focused) outperformed those receiving only instruction.
Lim (1992)	Frequency/quality of learner participation related significantly to qualitative aspects of learner participation, e.g., range of speech acts and control of conversational management techniques. Learner participation in class related significantly to improvements in language proficiency.
Fotos (1993)	Small group tasks are as effective as formal teacher-fronted instruction for SLA.
Wudong (1994)	Declarative knowledge (ability to identify errors and state rule violations) does not lead to procedural knowledge (ability to use grammar to communicate) without opportunities to activate knowledge through output activities.
Zhou (1991)	Formal instruction resulted in acquisition of some structures (passives) but not others (tense and aspect). Explicit (declarative) knowledge can be converted to implicit (procedural) knowledge through practice.
Möllering & Nunan (1994)	Instruction made a difference in the acquisition of German modal particles, although acquisition is relativistic, complex, and organic.

The observation that interaction is an important variable takes us on to the second key empirical question that I posed at the beginning of this section: What task types and modes of classroom organization facilitate acquisition? It is to research that looks at this question that I now turn.

WHAT IS THE RELATIONSHIP BETWEEN TASK TYPES/MODES OF CLASSROOM ORGANIZATION AND ACQUISITION?

◆ MODIFIED INTERACTION AND THE NEGOTIATION OF MEANING

The second key question confronting second language pedagogy concerns the relationship between task types, modes of classroom organization, and second-language acquisition. Most of these studies have posited an indirect relationship between task types/modes of interaction and acquisition. By this I mean that they have not attempted to measure a direct relationship between, say, certain types of tasks and acquisition, but have assumed that a relationship exists. Let us assume for example, that quantity of learner talk will lead to acquisition (and we have some evidence to suggest that it does from the research of people such as Shirley Lim 1992). If we then find that problem-solving tasks result in significantly greater quantities of learner talk than brainstorming tasks, we can then conclude that problem-solving tasks are more likely to result in acquisition than brainstorming tasks. However, the relationship between the type of task and second-language acquisition is an indirect one. Long (1985) has used the indirect approach in his research into the relationship between conversational adjustments and language acquisition. He advances the following argument in favor of tasks that promote conversational adjustments or interactional modifications on the part of the learners taking part in the task:

Step 1:   Show that (a) linguistic/conversational adjustments promote (b) comprehensible input.

Step 2:   Show that (b) comprehensible input promotes (c) acquisition.

Step 3:   Deduce that (a) linguistic/conversational adjustments promote (c) acquisition. Satisfactory evidence of the a > b > c relationships would allow the linguistic environment to be posited as an indirect causal variable in SLA. (The relationship would be indirect because of the intervening "comprehension" variable.)

Long 1985: 378

The Interactional Hypothesis
According to this hypothesis, language is acquired as learners actively engage in attempting to communicate in the target language. The hypothesis is consistent with the experiential philosophy of "learning by doing." Acquisition will be maximized when learners engage in tasks that "push" them to the limits of their current competence.

♦ SMALL GROUP WORK

One of the first studies to be carried out as a result of developing views of language as communication was that by Long *et al.* (1976). Small group communicative tasks were (and still are) an important mode of organiza-tion in many communicative classrooms. Long and his colleagues sought to compare the language produced by students in group work tasks with that produced in teacher-fronted activities. Not surprisingly, they found that students produced a greater quantity of talk in group tasks. However, when they studied the language functions performed by students, they also found a much greater range. As students produced a greater quantity and variety of language in small group as opposed to teacher-fronted tasks, such small group tasks could be seen as facilitating acquisition. (Note that this is an example of a study positing an indirect causal relation-ship between the variable of mode of classroom organization and acquisi-tion, as no attempt was made to measure directly the effect of group work tasks on acquisition.)

Long followed up his work on organizational patterns in the classroom with an investigation of the characteristics of small group tasks most likely to facilitate acquisition. In a study reported in 1981, he found that two-way tasks (in which all students in a group discussion had unique information to contribute) stimulated significantly more modified interac-tions than one-way tasks (that is, in which one student possessed all the relevant information). Similarly, Doughty and Pica (1986) found that required information exchange tasks generated significantly more modi-fied interaction than tasks in which the exchange of information was optional. (The term *modified interaction* refers to those instances during an interaction when the speaker alters the form in which his or her language is encoded in order to make it more comprehensible. Such modification may be prompted by lack of comprehension on the part of the listener.)

These investigations of modified interaction were theoretically moti-vated by Krashen's hypothesis (1981; 1982) that comprehensible input was a necessary and sufficient condition for second language acquisition; in other words, that acquisition would occur when learners understood messages in the target language.

Porter (1983) extended the work on group tasks, looking at the effect on the quantity of output of proficiency level and language status of interlocutors. She found that learners produce a greater quantity of talk when working with other learners than with native speakers. She also found that learners do not learn each other's errors. This was an important finding, because one of the criticisms of group work tasks is that learners will pick up bad linguistic habits from one another. (Of course, convincing learners that this is not necessarily the case is another matter.)

Drawing on his own research, as well as synthesizing the research of others, Ellis (1988) argued that the following factors were likely to enhance second language acquisition in instructional contexts:

◇   Quantity of "intake."
◇   A need to communicate.
◇   A choice on the part of learners over what is said.
◇   The performance of a range of speech acts.
◇   An input rich in "extending" utterances: These are teacher utterances that pick up, elaborate, or in other ways extend the learner's contribution.
◇   Uninhibited practice.

◆ TASK TYPES AND DISCOURSE

Another line of research has focused on the question of the types of language and discourse patterns stimulated by different task types. Berwick (1993) investigated the different types of language stimulated by *transactional* and *interpersonal tasks*. (A *transactional task* is one in which communication occurs principally to bring about the exchange of goods and services, whereas an *interpersonal task* is one in which communication occurs largely for social purposes.) He found that the different functional purposes stimulated different morphosyntactic realizations.

In a similarly motivated study, I investigated the different interactional patterns stimulated by open and closed tasks. An *open task* is one in which there is no single correct answer, while a closed task is one in which there is a single correct answer or a restricted number of correct answers. I found that the different task types stimulated very different interactional patterns, and that this needed to be taken into consideration by curriculum developers and discourse analysts. (This study and its pedagogical implications are reported in Nunan 1991, 1993). In addition to the fact that the different task types stimulated different interactional patterns, the research also indicated that some task types might be more appropriate than others for learners at particular levels of proficiency. In particular, I found that with lower-intermediate to intermediate learners, relatively closed tasks stimulate more modified interaction than relatively more open tasks. This is not to say that such students should engage in closed tasks to the exclusion of open tasks. The important thing is that program planners and teachers should select a mix of tasks to reflect the pedagogic goals of the curriculum. This work also underlines the need for SLA researchers and curriculum specialists to work together if the fruits of researchers' labor are to find their way into the classroom.

In a recent study, Martyn (1996) investigated the influence of certain task characteristics on the negotiation of meaning in small group work. Martyn looked at the following variables:

Interaction relationship: Whether one person holds all of the information required to complete the task, whether each participant holds a portion of the information, or whether the information is shared.

Interaction requirement: Whether or not the information must be shared.

Goal orientation: Whether the task goal is convergent or divergent.

Outcome options: Whether there is only a single correct outcome, or whether more than one outcome is possible.

The results seem to indicate that, while the task variables do appear to have an effect on the amount of negotiation for meaning, there appears to be an interaction between task variables, personality factors, and interactional dynamics. This research, which is ongoing, underlines the complexity of the learning environment, and the difficulty of isolating psychological and linguistic factors from social and interpersonal ones.

The studies described in this section are summarized in Table 2.2.

Table 2.2 What task types and modes of classroom organization facilitate acquisition?

Study	Outcome
Long *et al.* (1976)	Students produce a greater quantity and variety of language in group work versus teacher-fronted activities.
Porter (1983)	In group work, learners produce more talk with other learners than with native speaking partners; learners do not learn each other's errors.
Pica *et al.* (1987)	Learners who have opportunities to negotiate meaning (make clarification requests and check comprehension) as they listened to a set of instructions comprehended much more than students who received a simplified set of instructions.
Spada (1987)	Instruction that focuses primarily on meaning (i.e., is communication based) but allows for a focus on grammar within meaningful contexts works better than grammar-only, or communication-only instruction.
Ellis (1988)	Factors enhancing acquisition: Quantity of "intake." A need to communicate. Learners have a choice over what is said. [The performance of a range of speech acts.] An input rich in "extending" utterances: These are teacher utterances that pick up, elaborate, or in other ways extend the learner's contribution. [Uninhibited practice.]
Nunan (1991)	Task type will determine the range of functions and types of discourse students use.
Martyn (1996)	Task variables have an effect on the amount of negotiation for meaning, but there appears to be an interaction between task variables, personality variables, and interactional dynamics.

WHAT IS THE RELATIONSHIP BETWEEN LEARNING STRATEGIES AND ACQUISITION?

Learning strategies are the mental and communicative procedures learners use in order to learn and use language. Learning styles are the general orientations to the learning process exhibited by learners. For many years now, researchers have been interested in the following questions related to learning styles and strategies:

◇   What is the relationship between learning strategy preferences and other learner characteristics such as educational level, ethnic background, first language?
◇   Do effective learners share certain strategy preferences?
◇   Can strategies be taught?
◇   Does strategy training make a difference to second-language acquisition?

◆ DEFINING LEARNING STRATEGIES

Despite the current interest in learning styles and strategies, investigations into the effect of learner strategy training are relatively uncommon, and results are rather mixed. Around fifteen years ago, Cohen and Aphek (1980) looked at the effect of strategy training on vocabulary acquisition. They found that certain techniques, such as the paired associates technique, did result in successful acquisition. At about the same time, Carroll (1981) looked at inductive learning. In this study, it was found that the ability to study samples of language and induct the rules governing that particular aspect of language was an aspect of language aptitude. O'Malley (1987) studied the effect of different types of strategy training (metacognitive, cognitive, and socioaffective) on different language skills, and found that the training had a significant effect on speaking, but not on listening.

Language Learning Strategies
The mental and communicative processes that learners deploy to learn a second language.

◆ STRATEGY PREFERENCES AND BIOGRAPHICAL VARIABLES

In a major study of learning styles among adult learners of English as a second language, Willing (1988) obtained data on the learning preferences of 517 students. Willing was looking for possible correlations between learning preferences and biographical variables. The principal means of data collection was a questionnaire that learners completed in the course of an interview. Low proficiency learners were interviewed in their first language. One of the major aims of the investigation was to explore possible learning style differences attributable to different learner bio-graphical variables. It is widely accepted by teachers that such things as ethnicity, age, and other factors will have an effect on preferred ways of learning. Willing investigated the following variables:

ethnic group

age group

level of previous education

length of residence in Australia

speaking proficiency level

type of learning program (e.g., whether in full-time or part-time courses).

The study came up with several surprising findings. In the first place, there were certain learning activities that were almost universally popular. In several instances, these were activities that did not enjoy similar popu-larity among teachers, as a follow-up investigation of teachers' preferences by Nunan showed (1988). For example, error correction by the teacher was highly valued by almost all learners, while student self-discovery of error was given a low rating. For teachers, the reverse was true.

Perhaps the most surprising finding was that none of the biographical variables correlated significantly with any of the learning preferences.

> none of the learning differences as related to personal variables were of a magnitude to permit a blanket generalization about the learning preference of a particular biographical sub-group. Thus, any statement to the effect that 'Chinese are X' or 'South Americans prefer Y', or 'Younger learners like Z' or 'High-school graduates prefer Q', is certain to be inaccurate. The most important single finding of the study was that for any given learning issue, the typical spectrum of opinions on that issue were represented, in virtually the same ratios, within any biographical sub-group.
>
> *Willing 1988:150–151*

This finding, which runs counter to the folk wisdom of the classroom and staffroom, suggests that personality factors are more significant than sociocultural variables and educational background for learning strategy preferences. Of course, the fact that the study was conducted in a second rather than foreign language environment may have had a significant effect on the outcomes, and it would be useful to replicate the study in foreign language contexts.

◆ LEARNER TYPES

One final finding of note was that learners could be categorized by type according to the pattern of their responses on the questionnaire. Learner "types" and their preferences are set out in Table 2.3.

◆ THE GOOD LANGUAGE LEARNER

In a rather different type of study, Jones, *et al.* (1987) set out to determine whether there were differences between effective and ineffective learners in terms of their awareness of different types of strategy. They found that effective learners are aware of the processes underlying their own learning and seek to use appropriate learning strategies to control their own learning. Nunan (1991) also found that one of the characteristics of the "good" language learner was an ability to reflect on and articulate the processes underlying their own learning. Similarly, in an overview of research into strategy training, O'Malley and Chamot (1990) found indications that more effective learners differed from less effective ones in their use of strategies. In particular, they found that students who were designated by their teachers as more effective learners use strategies more frequently, and use a greater variety of strategies, than students who were designated as less effective.

In their well-known study of the good language learners, Rubin and Thompson (1983) suggest that good or efficient learners tend to exhibit

Table 2.3   Learner types and learning preferences

Type 1 "Concrete" learners
These learners tend to like games, pictures, films, video, using cassettes, talking in pairs, and practicing English outside class.

Type 2 "Analytical" learners
These learners liked studying grammar, studying English books and reading newspapers, studying alone, finding their own mistakes, and working on problems set by the teacher.

Type 3 "Communicative" learners
These students like to learn by watching, listening to native speakers, talking to friends in English and watching television in English, using English out of class in stores, trains, and so on, learning new words by hearing them, and learning by conversations.

Type 4 "Authority-oriented" learners
These learners preferred the teacher to explain everything, liked to have their own textbook, to write everything in a notebook, to study grammar, learn by reading, and learn new words by seeing them.

specific characteristics, presented in Table 2.4, as they go about learning a second language.

A few years ago, I investigated 44 good language learners in order to find out whether there were any common patterns in their experiences. The learners had all learned English as a foreign language in a variety of Southeast Asian countries including Hong Kong, Thailand, Indonesia, the Philippines, Malaysia, and Singapore. They were all good learners in that they had all attained bilingual competence in the language, and all were teachers of English as a foreign language. There were two strands to this research, one that looked at the good language learner, and the other that explored the effect of teachers' learning strategy preferences on their own teaching style. I shall not be concerned with this second strand here.

There were two reasons for selecting language teachers as research subjects. In the first place, by selecting English language teachers, it was easier to locate subjects with high levels of proficiency. Secondly, it was felt that because teachers would have the metacognitive and metalinguistic wherewithal to conceptualize their experiences, they would be better able to reflect on and articulate their foreign language learning experiences.

Table 2.4   Characteristics of the good language learner

Good learners:

◇ find their own way

◇ organize information about language

◇ are creative and experiment with language

◇ make their own opportunities, and find strategies for getting practice in using the language inside and outside the classroom

◇ learn to live with uncertainty and develop strategies for making sense of the target language without wanting to understand every word

◇ use mnemonics (rhymes, word associations, and so forth) to recall what has been learned

◇ make errors work

◇ use linguistic knowledge, including knowledge of their first language in mastering a second language

◇ let the context (extralinguistic knowledge and knowledge of the world) help them in comprehension

◇ learn to make intelligent guesses

◇ learn chunks of language as wholes and formalized routines to help them perform 'beyond their competence'

◇ learn production techniques (e.g., techniques for keeping conversation going)

◇ learn different styles of speech and writing and learn to vary their language according to the formality of the situation

Data for the study were provided by a questionnaire and a follow-up interview. The questionnaire was an adaptation of the one used by Willing, and asked subjects to rate 30 statements about learning preferences such as "In English class, I like to learn by reading," "I like the teacher to explain everything to us," "I like the teacher to let me find my mistakes," "I like to study grammar." The subjects completed the questionnaire and then took part in a one-to-one discussion of their strategy preferences, how they learned, how they would go about learning another language, and how they went about finding practice opportunities out of class.

During the investigation, subjects were asked to record what they found most helpful, and what they found least helpful in learning English as a foreign language. Despite the different contexts and environments in which the learners learned, the responses were surprisingly homogeneous.

The most striking thing about this study was the fact that, despite the diverse contexts and environments in which the subjects learned English, practically all agreed that formal classroom instruction was insufficient. Motivation, a preparedness to take risks, and the determination to apply their developing language skills outside the classroom characterized most of the responses from these good language learners (see Beebe 1983 for an interesting study on risk-taking). The free-form responses reinforced the general pattern of responses provided by the questionnaire. Given these responses, I believe that it is premature to reject the notion that there is no correlation between certain learning strategy preferences and the good language learner.

In a follow-up study, a group of advanced second language learners were asked to nominate the things that helped them most and least in learning English. Similar results to those from the foreign language subjects were obtained. These are set out in Table 2.5, the items being rank-ordered from most to least frequently nominated.

Despite the range of responses, there was a large measure of agreement about what helped and what did not help these subjects master a second language. Conversation practice inside and outside the classroom and opportunities for activating English outside class were by far the most frequently nominated things that facilitated development. Least helpful were grammar drills, these being nominated over twice as often as the next item, lack of opportunity to activate language use outside class.

Data such as these need to be interpreted carefully. For example, they do not mean that we should abandon the teaching of grammar. However, we may need to think again about how we go about teaching grammar, we need to be more explicit in showing learners how grammar instruction relates to the achievement of communicative objectives.

Table 2.5

Things that helped most	*Things that helped least*
1. Conversation with English speakers/in groups	1. Learning grammar/drills
2. Finding opportunities to practice outside class	2. Lack of opportunity to use English outside class
3. Accessing media: radio, TV, newspapers	3. Poor teaching
4. Formal classes/learning with a teacher	4. Being criticized/punished
5. Motivation	5. Practicing with L2 speakers/poor L1 speakers
6. Reading	6. Classes too big/too many levels
7. Grammar rules/drills	7. Use L1 too much
8. Listening	8. Accessing media
9. Pronunciation	9. Fear of making mistakes
10. Vocabulary	10. Lack of motivation
	11. Childish materials, e.g., picture books
	12. Lack of audio-visual facilities
	13. Rigid timetables and programs
	14. Reading aloud in classroom
	15. Memorizing
	16. No time to study
	17. Writing

◆ STRATEGY TRAINING AND TASK PERFORMANCE

In the field of foreign languages, Barnett (1988) investigated the effect of strategy training on the reading of French as a foreign language. While the experimental group outperformed the control group, the differences were not statistically significant. However, this study is a little difficult to interpret, as the strategies themselves were not made explicit to the students.

A recent study by Green and Oxford (1995) looked at patterns of variation in strategy use by students at different levels of proficiency. They found a significant relationship between strategy use and language learning success. In particular, they found that active use of the target language, with a strong emphasis on practice in naturalistic situations, was the most important factor in the development of proficiency in a second language. They concluded from their study that active use strategies help students attain higher proficiency.

In an investigation into the effect of providing opportunities for reflection, self-reporting, and self-monitoring among university students in Hong Kong, Nunan (1997) found that opportunities to reflect on their learning led students to a greater sensitivity to the learning process over time. Students were also able to make greater connections between their English classes, and content courses conducted in English. Finally, opportunities to keep guided journals helped learners to develop skills for articulating what they wanted to learn and how they wanted to learn it.

In a North American context, Cohen *et al.* (1995) and Cohen (1996) studied the impact of strategy training on a group of 55 foreign language students at the University of Minnesota. The researchers sought to identify the effect of explicit instruction in strategies on speaking proficiency, and the relationship between reported frequency of use of strategies and ratings of task performance. They were also interested in how students characterized their rationale for strategy use while performing speaking tasks. In the study, three experimental groups received the same instruction as three comparison groups over a ten-week period. In addition, the experimental groups were given explicit instruction in the application of speaking strategies to the skill of speaking. On the question of whether strategy training made a difference on task performance, they found that the experimental group outperformed the comparison group on two of the three post-test tasks used in the experiment. While the researchers argue for the beneficial effect of strategy training, they point out that the results were complex and in some cases not easy to interpret. (For example, there seemed to be a language proficiency factor, with learners at certain levels of proficiency seeming to benefit more from proficiency training than those at other levels.)

Recently, I investigated the effect of strategy training on a group of undergraduates at the University of Hong Kong. This study was motivated by two factors. The first of these was the fact that, even though they pay lip service to the importance of English for their future careers, many students come into the English courses at the University of Hong Kong with low motivation to learn English. Most of them have learned English throughout their secondary schooling, and are demotivated by their perceptions of a lack of progress, by what many report as poor instructional methods, and by an increasing pressure, with the change of sovereignty, from Britain to China, to devote their language learning efforts to Putonghua. The second factor has to do with the limited amount of time that students are given to develop skills in Academic English (48 hours with an additional 12 hours of self-directed learning in the form of a contract.) It was felt that the incorporation of a learning strategy dimension into the curriculum could help to maintain or enhance motivation, and might also lead to greater appreciation on the part of learners of the processes underlying their own learning. (Previous research has shown that the effective learner is one who is aware of learning strategies, Jones *et al.* 1987.) It was also hoped that strategy training would help learners develop greater independence and control over their learning, and this, in turn, would encourage them to continue learning English on their own once their classes had stopped.

I decided to explore the effects of systematically incorporating a learning strategy dimension into the courses being developed by students in the Arts faculty at the University. The study was designed to investigate the following questions:

1. What is the effect of learner strategy training on student motivation?
2. What is the effect of learner strategy training on students' knowledge of learning strategies?
3. What is the effect of learner strategy training on the levels of strategy utilization by students (that is, do those who receive strategy training use them more)?
4. What is the effect of learner strategy training on students' attitude toward the use of strategies in language learning (in particular, do those who receive training think more highly of strategies as tools for learning)?

A group of 60 students were randomly assigned to four different classes. Two classes were designated as experimental classes, and two were designated as control classes. All students were given precourse questionnaires to measure their motivation, their knowledge of 15 key strategies, their use of these strategies, and their perception of the value of the strategies. All four classes then took part in a regular first semester (English for Arts Students) course, the only difference being that the experimental group was systematically introduced to some of the key learning and study skills strategies underpinning the course. The strategy training was incorporated into the regular language teaching program, rather than being taught as a separate component. At the end of the semester, the questionnaires were readministered, and the results statistically analyzed. These results showed that the experimental groups significantly outperformed the control groups on measures of motivation, knowledge of strategies, and appreciation of the value of strategies. There was no significant difference on their use of strategies. (All groups increased their use of strategies during the course of the semester.)

When I carried out an item-by-item analysis of individual strategies, some interesting differences between the strategies and the training emerged, and it was clear that training did not have a uniform effect on strategies. The item-by-item analysis is summarized in the appendix on page 317.

When the lesson plans and transcripts were reviewed, it transpired that, because of programming exigencies, the sessions in which the two strategies of classifying and personalizing were to be introduced to the experimental groups had been canceled and it had not been possible for them to be rescheduled. The experimental groups therefore never had an opportunity to focus explicitly on them, nor to practice applying them to their own learning. The data here, therefore, provide a kind of negative evidence on the effect of strategy knowledge, use, and utility.

This study provides evidence that strategy training does make a difference in several key areas. First, it had a significant effect on student motivation. This result is consistent with and confirms other recent research into strategy training and motivation. It also had a significant effect on students' knowledge of strategies, and their appreciation of the use of strategies in their language learning. The results of strategy training on use of the strategies is less clear. This may reflect the fact that students had relatively few opportunities to take control of their learning in the context in which the study took place.

It is also clear from the analysis of individual strategies presented in the preceding section that the effect of strategy training is not uniform across all strategies. In some cases the effect appeared to be quite dramatic. In other cases the effects were less apparent. Individual analyses, as well as an interpretative analysis of the qualitative interview data, showed that prior knowledge, and the subjects' evaluation of the utility of particular strategies for university level study, had an important effect on their reaction to and willingness to deploy particular strategies. Analysis of the classroom observation data and lesson notes and materials also revealed the fact that not all strategies received equal amounts of attention in the classroom, and that this differential attention had an effect on students' responses. In short, the greater the attention, the greater the effect. However, as amount of focus on individual strategies was not one of the variables focused on in the study, it is not possible to comment on it in greater detail here. On the other hand, it is important to note the value of collecting qualitative data, in the form of student interviews, as well as classroom observation data in studies of this kind. Without such data, some of the quantitative results would have been uninterpretable. In fact, some would simply not have made sense. (For a discussion on the importance of collecting both qualitative and qualitative data, see Spada, 1990.) In Chapter 6, we shall look at the practical application of these ideas to classroom instruction and the design of teaching materials.

◆ CONCLUSION

In this chapter, I have taken a selective look at some of the empirical research that has influenced my own approach to pedagogy. I have done this to show that in the last 20 years the field has gone a long way toward overcoming the pendulum effect in which teaching fashions have come and gone with monotonous regularity, and the profession has been held in thrall by numerous persuasive rhetoricians. The data presented in this chapter show that we have gone a long way toward rectifying this situation.

◆ **CONCEPT MAP OF CHAPTER 2**

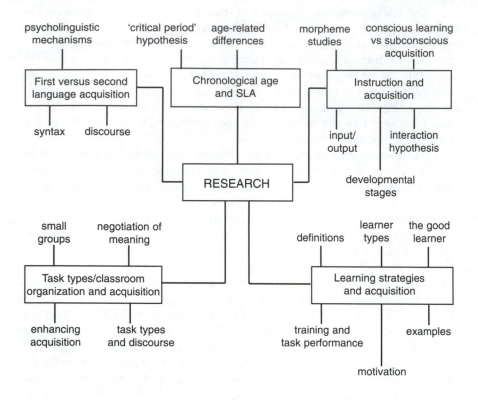

◆ **QUESTIONS AND TASKS**

1. Why is second language acquisition fundamentally different from first language acquisition?
2. Why is the issue of the effect of chronological age on acquisition more complex than it at first appears?
3. What is the "critical period," and what is it meant to explain?
4. What is the "comprehensible input hypothesis" and what is it meant to explain?
5. In what areas does instruction make a difference to acquisition? In what area does it not make a difference?
6. Why is small group work beneficial for language acquisition?
7. Make a summary of the research into the effect of learner strategy training on acquisition.
8. What do you think are the three most important characteristics of the good language learner? If possible, interview a number of good learners (learners who have developed high levels of communicative skill in a relatively short time). Are there any patterns? Do the results reflect in any way the results obtained by Rubin and Thompson?

9. Interview several language learners about what works for them and what doesn't work for them. Can you identify any patterns? What similarities and differences emerge?

◆ REFERENCES

Aiken, G., and M. Pearce. 1994. *Learning Outside the Classroom*. Sydney: National Centre for English Language Teaching and Research.

Asher, J., and B. Price. 1967. The learning strategy of total physical response: Some age differences. *Child Development*, 38.

Bacon–Shone, J., K. Bolton, and D. Nunan. 1997. Language use, policies and support at the tertiary level. Research Report to the Committee for Research and Conference Grants, University of Hong Kong.

Barnett, M. A. 1988. Teaching reading strategies: How methodology affects language course articulation. *Foreign Language Annals*, 21/2: 109–119.

Berwick, R. 1993. Towards an educational framework for teacher-led tasks. In G. Crookes and S. Gass (eds.), *Tasks in a Pedagogical Context*. Clevedon Avon: Multilingual Matters.

Block, D. 1994. A day in the life of an English class: Teacher and learner perceptions of task purpose in conflict. *System*, 22, 4.

Block, D. 1996. A window on the classroom: Classroom events viewed from different angles. In K. Bailey & D. Nunan (eds.), *Voices and Viewpoints: Qualitative Research in Second Language Education*. New York: Cambridge University Press.

Carroll, J. B. 1981. Twenty-five years of research on foreign language aptitude. In K. C. Diller (ed.), *Individual Differences and Universals in Language Learning Aptitude* (pp. 83–118). Rowley, Mass.: Newbury House.

Chamot, A. U. 1987. The learning strategies of ESL students. In A. Wenden and J. Rubin (eds.), (1987) *Learner Strategies in Language Learning*. Oxford: Pergamon Press.

Cohen, A. D. 1996. Language learning strategies instruction and research. AILA '96 Symposium on Learner Autonomy, Finland, August.

Cohen, A. D. and Aphek, E. 1980. Retention of second language vocabulary over time: Investigating the role on mnemonic associations. *System*, 8: 221–235.

Cohen, A. D., S. Weaver, and T. Y. Li. 1995. The impact of strategies-based instruction on speaking a foreign language. Research Report, National Language Resource Center, University of Minnesota.

Doughty, C. 1988. *The effect of instruction on the acquisition of relativization in ESL*. Unpublished Ph.D. dissertation, University of Pennsylvania.

Doughty, C., and T. Pica. 1986. 'Information gap' tasks: Do they facilitate second language acquisition? TESOL Quarterly, 20, 2.

Dulay, H., and M. Burt. 1973. Should we teach children syntax? *Language Learning*, 23.

Dulay, H., and M. Burt. 1974. Natural sequences in child second language acquisition. *Language Learning*, 24.

Ellis, R. 1984. Can syntax be taught? *Applied Linguistics*, 5, 2.

Ellis, R. 1985. *An Introduction to Second Language Acquisition*. Oxford: Oxford University Press.

Ellis, R. 1988. *Classroom Second Language Development*. London: Prentice-Hall.

Ellis, G. and B. Sinclair. 1989. *Learning to Learn English: A Course in Learner Training*. Cambridge: Cambridge University Press.

Ervin–Tripp, S. 1974. Is second language learning like the first? *TESOL Quarterly*, 8.

Foster, S. 1990. *The Communicative Competence of Young Children*. London: Longman.

Fotos, S. 1994. Integrating grammar instruction and communicative language use through grammar consciousness-raising tasks. *TESOL Quarterly*, 28, 2, 323–351.

Gardner, D., and L. Miller (eds.). 1994. *Directions in Self-Access Language Learning*. Hong Kong: Hong Kong University Press.

Gregg, K. 1984. Krashen's monitor and Occam's razor. *Applied Linguistics*, 5, 2, 79–100.

Green, J. M., and R. Oxford. 1995. A closer look at learning strategies, L2 proficiency, and gender. *TESOL Quarterly*, 29, 2: 261–297.

Heath, Shirley Brice. 1992. Literacy skills or literate skills? Considerations for ESL/EFL learners. In D. Nunan (ed.), *Collaborative Language Learning and Teaching*. Cambridge: Cambridge University Press.

Ho, B. 1997. Using reflection to raise consciousness of strategies in technical report-writing. Unpublished doctoral dissertation. Macquarie University, Sydney, Australia.

Holec, H. 1979. *Autonomy and Foreign Language Learning*. Oxford: Pergamon Press.

Hyltenstam, K., and M. Pienemann. (eds.) 1985. *Modelling and Assessing Second Language Acquisition*. Clevedon Avon: Multilingual Matters.

Jones, B., A. Palincsar, D. Ogle, and E. Carr. 1987. *Strategic Teaching and Learning: Cognitive Instruction in the Content Areas*. Alexandria, Va.: Association for Supervision and Curriculum Development.

Jones, V., and L. Jones. 1990. *Classroom Management: Managing and Motivating Students*. Needham Heights, Mass.: Allyn and Bacon.

Krashen, S. 1981. *Second Language Acquisition and Second Language Learning*. Oxford: Pergamon.

Krashen, S. 1982. *Principles and Practice in Second Language Acquisition*. Oxford: Pergamon.

Lightbown, P., and N. Spada. 1993. *How Languages are Learned*. Oxford: Oxford University Press.

Lim, S. 1992. *Investigating learner participation in teacher-led classroom discussions in junior colleges in Singapore from a second language acquisition perspective.* Unpublished doctoral dissertation.

Littlewood, W., and F. N. Liu. 1997. *The LEAP Project*. The English Centre, University of Hong Kong.

Long, M. L., 1985. Input and second language acquisition theory. In S. Gass and C. Madden (eds.), *Input in Second Language Acquisition*. Rowley, Mass.: Newbury House.

Long, M., L. Adams, and F. Castanos. 1976. Doing things with words: Verbal interaction in lockstep and small group classroom situations. In R. Crymes and J. Fanselow (eds.), *On TESOL '76*. Washington, D.C.: TESOL.

Martyn, E. 1996. The influence of task type on the negotiation of meaning in small group work. Paper presented at the Annual Pacific Second Language Research Forum, Auckland, New Zealand 1996.

Möllering, M., & D. Nunan. 1994. Pragmatics in interlanguage: German modal particles. *Applied Language Learning*, 6, 1 & 2.

Montgomery, C., and M. Eisenstein 1985. Real reality revisited: An experimental communicative course in ESL. *TESOL Quarterly*, 19, 317–334.

Nunan, D. 1984. *Discourse Processing by First Language, Second Phase, and Second Language Learners*. Unpublished doctoral dissertation. Flinders University of South Australia.

Nunan, D. 1988. *The Learner-Centred Classroom*. Cambridge: Cambridge University Press.

Nunan, D. 1989. *Understanding Language Classrooms*. London: Prentice-Hall.

Nunan, D. 1991. *Language Teaching Methodology*. London: Prentice-Hall.

Nunan, D. 1993. From learning-centeredness to learner-centeredness. *Applied Language Learning*, 4,

Nunan, D. 1995. *ATLAS. Learning-centered communication*. Boston: Heinle & Heinle.

Nunan, D. 1996. Hidden voices: Insiders' perspectives on classroom interaction. In K. Bailey and D. Nunan (eds.), *Voices and Viewpoints: Qualitative Research in Second Language Education*. New York: Cambridge University Press.

Nunan, D. 1997. Does learner strategy training make a difference? *RELC Journal*, December 1997.

O'Malley, J. M. 1987. The effects of training in the use of learning strategies. In A. Wenden and J. Rubin (eds.), *Learning Strategies in Language Learning*. Englewood Cliffs, N.J.: Prentice-Hall.

O'Malley, J. M., and A. U. Chamot. 1990. *Learning Strategies in Second Language Acquisition*. Cambridge: Cambridge University Press.

Parkinson, L., and K. O'Sullivan. 1990. Negotiating the learner-centred curriculum. In G. Brindley (ed.) *The Second Language Curriculum in Action*. Sydney: NCELTR.

Penfield, W., and L. Roberts. 1959. *Speech and Brain Mechanisms*. New York: Atheneum Press.

Pienemann, M. 1989. Is language teachable? *Applied Linguistics*, 10, 1,

Pinker, S. 1994. *The Language Instinct*. London: Penguin.

Porter, P. 1983. *Variations in the conversations of adult learners of English as a function of the proficiency level of the participants*. Unpublished Ph.D. dissertation, Stanford University.

Reilly, P. 1994. *Motivation in language learning*. Unpublished masters dissertation. University of Mexico.

Rivers, W., and M. Temperley. 1978. *A Practical Guide to the Teaching of English as a Second or Foreign Language*. New York: Oxford University Press.

Rubin, J. 1975. What the good language learner can teach us. *TESOL Quarterly*, 9, 41–51.

Rubin, J., and I. Thompson. 1983. *How to be a More Successful Language Learner*. Boston: Heinle & Heinle.

Schmidt, R., and S. Frota. 1986. Developing basic conversational ability in a second language: A case study of an adult learner of Portuguese. In R. Day (ed.), *Talking to Learn: Conversation in Second Language Acquisition*. Rowley, Mass.: Newbury House.

Scovel, T. 1988. *A Time To Speak: A Psycholinguistic Inquiry into the Critical Period for Human Speech*. Rowley, Mass.: Newbury House.

Spada, N. 1990. *Second Language Teacher Education*. Cambridge: Cambridge University Press.

Swain, M. 1985. Communicative competence: Some roles of comprehensible input and comprehensible output in its development. In S. Gass and C. Madden (eds.), *Input in Second Language Acquisition*. Rowley, Mass.: Newbury House.

Tsui, A. 1996. Reticence and anxiety in second language learning. In K. Bailey and D. Nunan (eds.), *Voices and Viewpoints: Qualitative Research in Second Language Education*. New York: Cambridge University Press.

Widdows, S., and P. Voller. 1991. PANSI: A survey of ELT needs of Japanese university students. *Cross Currents*, XVIII, 2,

Willing, K. 1988. *Learning Styles in Adult Migrant Education*. Adelaide, Australia: National Curriculum Resource Centre.

Wu, W. 1994. *English language development in China*. Unpublished doctoral dissertation. University of Tasmania, Australia.

Zhou, Yan–Ping. 1991. The effect of explicit instruction on the acquisition of English grammatical structures by Chinese learners. In C. James and P. Garrett (eds.), *Language Awareness in the Classroom*. London: Longman.

CHAPTER 3

From the Traditional to the Contemporary in Second Language Teaching and Learning

From what I said in Chapters 1 and 2, it is clear that there have been some dramatic developments in language teaching in recent years. We have reconceptualized the nature of language, reevaluated the role of the learner within the learning process, and generated new insights into instructed second language acquisition. Together, these developments have led to an increasingly sophisticated view of second language teaching and learning.

Our greatest challenge now is not to throw out well-established practices, as so often happened in the past, but to incorporate new ways of doing things into existing practice. In this sense, change will be evolutionary rather than revolutionary. One of the things holding us back as a profession has been the "pendulum" effect; teaching fashions have swung wildly from one extreme to another. By linking developments in language teaching firmly to the educational mainstream, and by testing new ideas critically, we should reach a phase in the evolution of the profession in which we are not ashamed to admit to merit in past practices, while, at the same time, being able to acknowledge that significant improvements are necessary.

Insights from theory and research have led to some fundamental changes in our beliefs about the nature of language and learning, and this has led inevitably to a change in the ways in which we go about the business of language teaching. However, as I have already indicated, I believe that current trends are basically evolutionary rather than revolutionary in nature, as methodologists and curriculum developers seek to add value to tried and tested practices rather than to subvert or reject them.

In this chapter, I will show how contemporary trends have added value to practice, or have prompted a reassessment and reevaluation of practice in the areas of syllabus design, approaches to teaching, the role of the learner, approaches to language, the role of texts, resources, and approaches to learning, classroom organization, and assessment. The chapter deals with the following issues and concepts:

Stimuli for change
◇ ineffectiveness of traditional approaches
◇ relevance of language learning to general education

Syllabus design
◇ difficulty of separating content and process in a communicative syllabus
◇ linguistic specification as second-order activity

Approach to teaching
◇ transmission versus interpretation models of learning
◇ high-structure versus low-structure pedagogical environments

Role of learners
◇ passive versus active roles
◇ reproductive language tasks
◇ encouraging creative language use

Approach to language
◇ shortcomings of grammar-translation and audiolingualism
◇ teaching grammar communicatively

Using language texts
◇ authenticity
◇ student-generated data

Facilities for learning
◇ textbooks and support resources
◇ information technology and the Internet

Approach to learning
◇ learning styles and strategies
◇ adding a "process" dimension

Classroom organization
◇ teacher-fronted versus small group classrooms
◇ communication patterns in the workplace

Assessment
◇ shortcomings of standardized tests
◇ student self-assessment

Language out of class
◇ strategies for activating language out of class

STIMULI FOR CHANGE

♦ *INEFFECTIVENESS OF TRADITIONAL APPROACHES*

A perennial stimulus for change in language education has been a dissatisfaction with the results obtained by traditional methods, often at great cost to schools and language systems, and the expenditure of tremendous effort by students and teachers. In grammar-translation classrooms, learners typically spent years learning English and yet many of them were still unable to use the language effectively. They often knew a good deal about the language but were unable to use this knowledge to communicate appropriately. In systems where grammar-translation gave way to audio-lingualism, students were able to parrot responses in predictable situations of use, but had difficulty communicating effectively in the relatively un-predictable world beyond the classroom.

Many concluded that it was a poor investment if all that work seemed to offer so little practical result. Students had a basic foundation of language knowledge but they did not know how to put that knowledge to active use. To help them to communicate and use that language knowledge, it was gradually recognized and accepted that a new approach to language learning and teaching was needed. Learners needed to understand that language is not just a list of grammatical patterns and a collection of words. Language as communication involves the active use of grammar and vocabulary to listen and read effectively and to speak with and write to other people. Language needs to be learned functionally so that learners are able to see that different forms communicate different meanings.

One response to the perception that language educators are relatively ineffective was to question the value of learning another language. I would challenge that perception. I believe that language learning should have a central place in any educational system. If we accept what Pinker (1994) and his colleagues have to say, then language is arguably the defining characteristic of the human species, and a knowledge of language in general, as well as an ability to use one's first, and at least one other language, should be one of the defining characteristics of the educated individual. As the bumper sticker says: "Monolingualism is curable!" In a world that is increasingly intermeshed economically, environmentally, and electronically, the ability to communicate effectively is crucial.

◆ RELEVANCE OF LANGUAGE TEACHING TO GENERAL EDUCATION

It is only through language that we can communicate with each other, share our ideas, tell people what we have experienced, express our wishes and desires, solve complex problems by drawing on information we read or hear, and, above all, communicate in the workplace and across cultures with people from other countries. To achieve these objectives, however, we need to learn language as communication, not just as a list of facts to be memorized or a set of symbols to be manipulated. This, as we saw earlier, has been an important force in the evolution of a new approach to language learning, one that begins from the active use of language and involves learners in cooperative learning tasks using language, helped by their teachers and specially designed learning materials. This is a central aim of contemporary approaches to language teaching.

The skills developed through the application of active, cooperative learning principles can extend to other subjects as well. Effective foreign language learning produces learners with the social and cognitive problem-solving skills that can be used in other subjects in the school curriculum. If only we could get language teachers and subject teachers communicating with each other, it might be possible to fashion a new type of school curriculum, one in which the familiar elements are not jettisoned, but recombined. Then, the relevance of the intellectual knowledge, learning skills, interpersonal development, and intercultural sensitivities fostered in the language classroom might be appreciated by others with a vested interest in education.

SYLLABUS DESIGN

Traditionally, the field of curriculum development has been divided into syllabus design, methodology, and evaluation (Tyler 1949). Syllabus design has to do with selecting and sequencing content, methodology with selecting and sequencing appropriate learning experiences, and evaluation with appraising learners and determining the effectiveness of the curriculum as a whole.

◆ DIFFICULTY OF SEPARATING CONTENT AND PROCESS IN A COMMUNICATIVE SYLLABUS

In general education, Stenhouse (1975) changed perspectives with a compelling rationale for the elevation of process (traditionally the domain of methodology) to the same status as content. His ideas found their way into language education through people such as Mike Breen (1984) and Leo van Lier (1988). (These developments are described in some detail in my 1989 book on syllabus design.) Breen used the metaphor of the journey to describe his approach to language teaching. Traditionally, he argued, content was seen as the destination ("We want learners to know how to contrast the simple past and perfect tenses"). Methodology was the route, the means whereby we reach the destination ("We'll get learners to do a set of substitution drills involving present perfect and simple past"). However, with the emergence of new views on the nature of language teaching, and a reconceptualization of what it was to know and use the language, this separation was difficult to sustain. With the emergence of a communicative, skills-based approach ("We want learners to be able to give an informal oral presentation on a subject of their choice"), a rigid

Syllabus
A syllabus consists of lists of content to be taught through a course of study. Key tasks for the syllabus designer are the selection of the items and their sequencing and integration.

In writings on second language teaching, it is possible to identify two views on the nature of syllabus design. The narrow view draws a clear distinction between the selection and sequencing of content (the domain of syllabus design) and the selection and sequencing of learning tasks and activity (the domain of methodology). With the emergence of CLT has come a group of curriculum specialists who take a broader view, and who question the sustainability of this strict separation.

separation became difficult to sustain because, if our method of achieving the target performance is to rehearse that performance in class, then the route *becomes* the destination. This reconceptualization changed the way that course designers and materials writers go about their jobs.

In traditional language teaching, syllabus design issues (*what* students learn) and methodology (*how* they learn), were decided with reference to the classroom rather than with reference to learners' real communicative needs in actual situations in the world outside. As a result, learners often had difficulty using what they learned beyond the classroom. With grammar-translation and audiolingual drills, it was often difficult for learners to make the conceptual leap from the classroom to genuine communication outside the classroom. This is not to say that drills of various kinds, and even translation tasks, have no place in the language classrooms, but that, in and of themselves, they are insufficient.

◆ LINGUISTIC SPECIFICATION AS A SECOND-ORDER ACTIVITY

In classrooms based on the principles set out in Chapter 1, and the research described in Chapter 2, syllabus designers begin by choosing language content and learning experiences that match the needs of learners as users of language beyond the classroom. In designing courses they are guided by specified communicative tasks that learners can perform at the end of their period of learning. In consequence, it is easier for learners to apply what they have learned in class to the challenge of communicating in the real world, and for employers to know what learners can do. In practical terms, syllabus designers no longer begin with a structurally graded list of linguistic items, and then cast around for ways of teaching those items. Instead, they begin with an inventory of target skills and ask what learners need to know and be able to do in order to perform those skills. Listing, sequencing, and integrating target items becomes a second-order activity rather than the first thing that they do.

APPROACH TO TEACHING

◆ *TRANSMISSION VERSUS INTERPRETATION MODELS OF LEARNING*

In traditional language classrooms, learners are taught chiefly about language and its rules. They learn facts about language rather than how to use it communicatively to express ideas, to talk and write to other people, to read and listen to real language, and to learn how to cooperate with others. As we saw in Chapter 1, in educational systems functioning under a transmission model, the primary role of the learner is as a relatively passive recipient of knowledge. The teacher's role is to provide that knowledge by transmitting it to the learner, largely through lockstep, teacher-fronted modes of learning.

◆ *HIGH-STRUCTURE VERSUS LOW-STRUCTURE TEACHING*

In a book on the management of the teaching process that I co-authored some years ago, a distinction was drawn between high-structure and low-structure teaching. Generally speaking, classrooms informed by current communicative views on language pedagogy will involve a change in teaching approach away from a high-structure orientation towards a more low-structure orientation. The impact of changing views about the nature of language on the teaching process was described in the following way:

> The insight that communication was an integrated process rather than a set of discrete learning outcomes created a dilemma for language education. It meant that the destination (functioning in another language) and the route (attempting to learn the target language) move much closer together, and, in some instances (for example, in role plays and simulations), become indistinguishable. . . . In educational terms, a useful way of viewing this emerging dilemma in language education is in terms of high- and low-structure teaching. High-structure tasks are those in which teachers have all the power and control. Low-structure tasks are those in which power and control are devolved to the students. . . . [we believe that] an association exists between low-structure and CLT, and that the incorporation of communicative tasks with low-structure implications into the classroom increases the complexity of the decision-making process for the teacher.
>
> *Nunan and Lamb 1996: 16–17*

In contemporary classrooms, while direct instruction and high-structure tasks are not eschewed, much more time will be devoted to low-structure tasks. In addition, direct instruction, when it occurs, will be integrated into instructional sequences in which learners are actively involved in using the language, guided and helped by their teachers. The teacher's

High-structure versus low-structure teaching
High-structure teaching situations are those in which the teacher is very much in control of the instructional process. In these situations, learners have relatively little power or control over either the content or process of learning. Low-structure situations, on the other hand, provide learners with numerous options and a great deal of autonomy. According to Biggs and Telfer (1987: 362) all instructional decision making can be located on a continuum, which has 'high-structure' decisions at one extreme and 'low-structure' decisions at the other.

primary role is the provision of pedagogical opportunities through which learners might structure and restructure their own understanding. The ultimate goal is to enable the learner to communicate with others in the world beyond the classroom where they will not have a teacher on hand. In helping learners achieve this goal, however, teachers need to redefine their approach to teaching.

ROLE OF LEARNERS

♦ *PASSIVE VERSUS ACTIVE LANGUAGE ROLES*

As indicated in the preceding section, learners in classrooms characterized by a transmission model of learning are cast in a relative passive role. They are passengers, being carried forward in the learning experience by the teacher. In language classrooms operating within such a transmission mode, learners practice patterns provided by teachers, textbooks, and tapes. They are thus cast into passive, reproductive roles. Rather than learning how to use language creatively themselves, they spend most learning time copying and reproducing language written down by others. They learn how to communicate in model and predictable situations, but they don't learn how to respond appropriately in novel and authentic communicative situations. Such a drill-based pedagogical culture is most commonly associated with audiolingualism, and, although audiolingualism is supposedly dead and buried, the drill-based culture is very much alive and well, as is evident in most so-called communicative curricula.

♦ *REPRODUCTIVE LANGUAGE TASKS*

The following task, adapted from a recent textbook, is an example of a task that is purportedly a communicative exercise, but is, in reality, a reproductive exercise practicing comparative adjectives.

Instructions: Working with a partner, take turns asking and answering these questions. If you agree on the answer, circle the word. If you disagree, put your initials next to the answer that you think is correct.

Example: Q: *Which is taller, the Sears Building, or the Empire State Building?*
A: *The Sears Building is taller.*

1.   Which has more sides, a pentagon or a rectangle?
2.   Which country has more cars per person, Taiwan or Japan?
3.   Which is closer to the equator, Singapore or Malaysia?
4.   Which is bigger, the Earth or the Moon?
5.   Which country has the larger population, Pakistan or the U.S.A.?
6.   Which country has more television sets per person, Australia or Singapore?
7.   Which planet is closer to the Earth, Venus or Mars?
8.   Which is an older capital city, Madrid or Rome?

As I have indicated several times already, there is nothing wrong with drills, and there is certainly nothing wrong with exercises such as the one above. They are an essential ingredient in the learning process for most learners, and provide the enabling skills for later communicative performance. However, by themselves, they do not go far enough in equipping learners to communicate. In addition to reproducing language models provided by others, even in disguised forms such as the task above, learners need opportunities for creative language use. By creativity, I do not mean that we should have learners writing poetry in class (although the use of imaginative literature could be used much more extensively than it is). Rather, by creativity, I mean the recombination of familiar elements into new, and previously unrehearsed, forms.

◆ ENCOURAGING CREATIVE LANGUAGE USE

In classrooms and textbooks in which the creativity principle is activated, learners are given structured opportunities to use the language that they have been practicing in new and unexpected ways. They are provided with the language that they will need to take part in genuine communicative tasks, and they are given opportunities to respond appropriately in new situations outside the classroom. Tasks allow learners to practice identifying the key grammar and vocabulary in real-world texts and to develop the skills of reading, writing, speaking, and listening in an integrated way, just as in authentic communicative situations. Tasks also give learners practice in cooperating with other learners and with their teachers, making creative use of the language they have learned. In this way, classrooms themselves act as a bridge to the outside world rather than as a linguistic quarantine station where learners are protected from the risks involved in having to engage in genuine communication.

Creative language use
Creative language use involves the recombination of familiar elements (words, structures, and prefabricated patterns) in new ways to produce utterances that have never been produced before by that particular individual (for that individual, they are therefore unique.) In role plays, simulations, and problem solving tasks, learners are given opportunities for creative language use.

Understanding learner roles is crucial to an understanding of problems and potential solutions in contemporary language classrooms (see, for example, Wright, 1987). In Chapter 5, we shall look in greater depth at the relationship between roles and tasks, and will explore ways in which learners themselves can be encouraged to redefine their roles.

APPROACH TO LANGUAGE

◆ *SHORTCOMINGS OF GRAMMAR-TRANSLATION AND AUDIOLINGUALISM*

Grammar-translation and audiolingualism adopted very different approaches to the treatment of grammar. In fact, audiolingualism developed partly in reaction to grammar-translation's excessively deductive approach to the teaching of grammar. Audiolingual methodology was based on an inductive approach in which rules were "caught" rather than "taught." (Richards and Rodgers, 1986). "Get students to learn by analogy, not analysis," "Language is a set of habits," and "Teach the language, not about the language," were pedagogical catchcries when audiolingualism was most popular as a teaching method (Moulton, 1963).

Audiolingualism
Of all modern methods of teaching languages, audiolingualism has undoubtedly had the greatest impact. In fact, it is probably still the most influential method used today. Numerous principles underpinned audiolingualism, although the two key contributions are probably the following:

1. Language learning is a process of habit formation.
2. Teachers should teach the language, they should not teach about the language.

Despite their marked differences, grammar-translation and audiolingualism did share one thing in common. They both separated the teaching of grammatical form from communicative meaning. In grammar-translation classrooms, grammar was taught as a set of rules to be memorized and repeated. In audiolingual classrooms, learners were expected to come to an inductive understanding of the rule through processes of analogy. In both approaches, it was difficult for learners to make connections between different parts of the grammatical system. It was also difficult to see how to apply the grammar they had learned in communication. Words were usually learned as individual items in lists so that learners did not develop an understanding of how they are grouped by their meanings into semantic sets.

The other thing that both grammar-translation and audiolingualism shared was an assumption that acquiring a second language was a linear process, that learners learn one item at a time, mastering the simple items first, and then moving on, in a step-by-step fashion to more complex items. However, as we saw in Chapter 2, this is an oversimplification (and, in some ways, a misrepresentation) of the way that second language grammar is actually acquired. Learners do not acquire information, perfectly, one thing at a time. They learn numerous things imperfectly at the same time. They structure and restructure their understanding of the language in complex nonlinear ways that we shall explore in greater detail in Chapter 4.

◆ TEACHING GRAMMAR COMMUNICATIVELY

In a teaching methodology that reflects what we currently know about second language acquisition, grammar and vocabulary are taught communicatively. Grammatical patterns are matched to particular communicative meanings so that learners can see the connection between form and function. Learners learn how to choose the right pattern to express the ideas and feelings that they want to express. They learn how to use grammar to express different communicative meanings. Words are grouped meaningfully and are taught through tasks involving semantic networking, concept mapping, and classifying. Such a methodology enables learners to recombine the familiar in unique ways and thus achieve the creativity in language use that I described in the preceding section.

USING LANGUAGE TEXTS

In traditional classrooms, learners listen to and read specially written classroom texts. These texts are usually produced by textbook writers and teachers to exemplify particular grammatical points, or to teach core vocabulary items. For example, the following text is designed to teach prepositions of place (*next to, across from, between*) existential *there*, and core vocabulary associated with neighborhoods, and it is difficult to imagine a context other than a language teaching textbook in which the text could conceivably appear.

> Jane's apartment building is in the center of town. Jane is very happy because the building is in a very convenient place.
> Across from the building, there's a laundromat, a bank, and a post office. Next to the building, there's a drug store and a restaurant. Around the corner from the building, there are two gas stations.
> There's a lot of noise near Jane's apartment building. There are a lot of cars on the street, and there are a lot of people walking on the sidewalk all day and night.
> Jane isn't very upset about the noise, though. Her building is in the center of town. It's a very busy place, but for Jane, it's a very convenient place to live.
>
> *Molinsky and Bliss 1989: 58*

As I pointed out in Chapter 1, there is nothing wrong in introducing texts such as these into the classroom. They demonstrate target language items within controlled contexts. However, I do have a problem with the notion that students should be fed an exclusive diet of such texts, because they do not give learners first-hand experience of how language is used in genuine communicative situations beyond the classrooms. Learners who only encounter texts such as this frequently have difficulty understanding the language and the texts that are used by speakers and writers authentically in the real world. The reasons for this were pointed out in Chapter 1 (see the section on task-based language teaching), and I shall not rehearse them here.

◆ AUTHENTICITY

In my own teaching, learners study spoken and written texts brought into the classroom from authentic contexts outside the classroom. In fact, learners are strongly encouraged to bring in their own samples of authentic language data. They practice listening to and reading genuine language

---

Authenticity
Authentic texts are those that have been produced in the course of genuine communication, not specially written for purposes of language teaching. They provide learners with opportunities to experience language as it is used beyond the classroom. Of course, there is a great deal of language generated within the classroom itself that is authentic, and this can very often be used for pedagogical purposes.

drawn from a wide variety of contexts, including TV and radio broadcasts, conversations, discussions and meetings of all kinds, talks, and announcements. They read magazines, stories, printed material and instructions, hotel brochures and airport notices, bank instructions, and a wide range of written messages. This practice helps them cope successfully with genuine communication outside the classroom.

While the learners that I teach are at upper-intermediate levels of proficiency, exercises and tasks help even the learners at the lower levels to make sense of these real texts, and to develop effective learning strategies for reading and listening, speaking and writing. Some years ago, when writing a series aimed at beginning and post-beginning learners, I was able to draw on a wide variety of authentic texts, including the materials listed in Table 3.1.

◆ STUDENT-GENERATED DATA

With appropriate guidance and support, even low level learners can benefit from opportunities to work with everyday spoken and written texts such as these. Older learners can be given a greater sense of ownership and control over their own learning by being encouraged to bring their own authentic data into the classroom. Bringing authentic data into the classroom can assist learners to see how grammatical forms operate in context and enable speakers and writers to make communicative meanings. Another advantage of using authentic data is that learners encounter target language items in the kinds of contexts that they naturally occur, rather than in contexts that have been concocted by a textbook writer. Ultimately, this assists the learner because he/she will experience the

Table 3.1

Spoken Data	Written Data
casual conversations	invitations
telephone conversations	airline tickets
answering machine messages	postcards
office conversations	enrollment forms
public announcements	business cards
stories and anecdotes	family trees
oral histories	classified advertisements
descriptions	airline boarding passes
directions	licenses
store announcements	handwritten notes
advertisements	movie reviews
interviews	maps
	business letters
	menus

language item in interaction with other closely related grammatical and discourse elements. By distorting the contexts of use in which grammatical items occur, nonauthentic language, in some respects, actually makes the task for the language learner more difficult.

FACILITIES FOR LEARNING

In traditional classrooms, learners usually have to rely only on the textbook as an aid to language learning. Often these textbooks are not especially provided with interesting visuals and supporting material, and rapidly become boring and uninteresting to the learner.

◆ TEXTBOOKS AND SUPPORT RESOURCES

In contemporary approaches to language teaching, the design of textbooks has become much more sophisticated. The incorporation of realia and authentic data brings the content to life, and helps learners make connections between the classroom world and the world beyond it. In addition to classroom texts, published textbook series these days typically contain self-study workbooks, cassette tapes, and videotaped materials that bring the real world into the classroom. For example, the highly innovative *Grammar Dimensions* (Larsen–Freeman, 1995), which introduces a new approach to the teaching of grammar, contains the following components in addition to the Student Text:

> instructor's manual
> audio tape
> student workbooks
> tests
> World Wide Web site for interactive grammar and writing

◆ INFORMATION TECHNOLOGY AND THE INTERNET

Increasingly, access to the Internet also brings the world into the classroom. Students can access and even download a wide range of informative, educational, and entertaining information. They can also establish contact with other first and second speakers of English around the world through chat lines and pen pal links. In addition to increasing their intercultural awareness and sensitivies, this also provides them with opportunities for genuine communication beyond the classroom. Such opportunities are not always easy to find in foreign language settings, and so the explosion in Internet usage has been particularly valuable to EFL students. My own learners, once they discover and begin to tap the potential of the Internet and the World Wide Web, find it both liberating and empowering. These same students also submit their assignments and class journals to me on e-mail. In the case of the assignments, I can embed comments on their work, and return the assignments to them, without the red ink scribbles that necessitate lengthy, time-consuming, and often wasteful retyping. Having them submit their journals electronically saves class time (in the past, the last ten minutes of each class was devoted to journals), and increases the amount of time that they devote to working on their English out of class.

In his practical introduction to the use of e-mail for English Teaching, Mark Warschauer (1995) gives the following examples of how the e-mail revolution has facilitated teaching and learning:

◇ In Hungary, students correspond daily on international discussion lists with students from Norway, the United States, Canada, Korea, Japan, Australia, and Indonesia. They later decide to jointly publish an international student news magazine called *Wings*.

◇ ESL students in Eugene, Oregon, submit their dialogue journals by e-mail rather than on paper. The students communicate much more naturally and frequently this way, and the teacher can respond much more quickly and easily.

◇ A teacher in New York learns she's teaching a class in English pronunciation for Spanish speakers, but she has no experience in this area. She posts a question via e-mail on an English teachers' list, and within 24 hours half a dozen colleagues around the world have e-mailed her concrete suggestions.

◇ ESL pupils and a Washington, D.C. elementary school find keypals (keyboard penpals) in several other states and countries. Their attitude towards writing changes dramatically in two months.

◇ A teacher in Japan would like to teach the story "Rip Van Winkle" but doesn't have the text. She finds it from home in ten minutes by using her personal computer and a modem connection to the Internet.

◇ EFL and ESL university students in Finland, Hong Kong, and the United States engage in an international competition to find a solution to a real-world environmental problem. They work in international teams to write technical reports, three-year plans, and abstracts for an international environmental conference, and then vote on the winning entry and post it electronically for others around the world to see (Warschauer 1995: 2–3).

These examples illustrate how new technologies can help us to activate the experiential, student-centered philosophies described in Chapter 1.

APPROACH TO LEARNING

◆ *LEARNING STYLES AND STRATEGIES*

In traditional classrooms, learners typically did not learn how to become better language learners on their own once they left a school or college.

While they learned how to memorize individual words and grammatical patterns, and to practice them in contrived contexts, the underlying strategies behind the classroom tasks were rarely made explicit. As a result, students rarely learned how to make use of this stored knowledge in an organized and creative way. Ways of learning language better and more effectively was not on the pedagogical agenda, and practice was therefore often unfocused and not directed at those skills they needed to improve.

◆ ADDING A PROCESS DIMENSION

As we saw in Chapter 2, a substantial amount of research has now been carried out on learning styles and strategies, and, in classrooms where teachers have been able to draw on this research, their students are able to develop a range of effective language learning strategies. They learn how to read and listen effectively, how to work out what texts mean, how to gather important information, how to work well in cooperation with others, how to use what they know in new and unpredictable situations, how to speak and write appropriately, and so on. They also learn metacognitive strategies for monitoring and reflecting on their learning (Oxford, 1990). These strategies are explicitly taught as part of the curriculum, and learners are shown how to apply these strategies to their own learning outside the classroom. In this way, they learn how to become better language learners outside of formal language learning contexts. In Chapter 6, I look at some of the practical techniques that teachers can use to add a learning strategy dimension to their teaching.

CLASSROOM ORGANIZATION

◆ TEACHER-FRONTED VERSUS SMALL GROUP CLASSROOMS

As we have seen, the traditional mode of classroom organization was a teacher-fronted one, with learners sitting in rows facing the teacher. They spent most of their time repeating and manipulating models provided by the teacher, the textbook and the tape, and developed skills in choral speaking and repeating. The physical set-up of classrooms was (and, in many schools, still is) predicated on this mode of organization, with desks set out in rows, and even, in many cases, screwed to the floor, thus making any other mode of organization almost impossible. Students in such classrooms do not learn how to express their own ideas and to share these ideas by communicating in small groups.

In Chapter 1, we saw that experiential learning was based on a constructivist approach to education. Such a philosophy is realized at a classroom level by cooperative, task-based learning, with learners working in small groups and pairs. Students become skilled at cooperating with others, and express their own opinions, ideas, and feelings, guided by the teacher. They learn how to solve language problems in a systematic way and to decide what language to use in the different situations that their teachers present in the classroom. Role plays and simulations help to make the task-based classroom a lively and rich language environment for learners of all abilities. As we saw in Chapter 2, tasks such as these stimulate the production of a much richer array of language functions than teacher-fronted modes of classroom organization. They also result in the negotiation of meaning, something that is largely absent in teacher-fronted tasks.

♦ COMMUNICATION IN THE WORKPLACE

Interestingly, these skills of communicating and cooperating in groups are also increasingly required in the workplace. Over the last few years, the old, hierarchical models of production in which communication is a one-way, downward process from line managers to workers on the shop floor, are giving way to small, integrated production teams in which communication occurs horizontally between members of the team.

> **Group Work**
> Group work is essential to any classroom that is based on principles of experiential learning. Through group work, learners develop their ability to communicate through tasks that require them, within the classroom, to approximate the kinds of things they will need to be able to do to communicate in the world beyond the classroom.

However, many educational institutions have not kept pace with changes in the workplace and in society at large. Educational institutions are inherently conservative, and it is probably fair to say that most are still predicated on a transmission mode of education, a mode that is even reflected in the physical setting of the classroom. Within such institutions there is often an ideological tussle between the dominant, transmission ideology of the institution itself, and the interpretative, constructivist approach advocated by the language teacher.

ASSESSMENT

♦ SHORTCOMINGS OF STANDARDIZED TESTS

In traditional learning environments, assessment practices are characterized by standardized tests designed, administered, and graded by outside authorities. Teachers have little control of what is assessed, or how it is assessed, and the examination system has a disproportionate influence over the curriculum. In such environments, learners do not develop their own ability to assess how much they have learned and how much they need to learn. As a result they often do not know exactly what they have learned and how much they still have to learn. The assessment is typically through quizzes and tests that do not reflect actual language use.

Assessment and evaluation

In many textbooks on curriculum development, the terms *assessment* and *evaluation* are used synonymously. However, I have always drawn a clear distinction between the two concepts. *Evaluation* is the collection and interpretation of information about aspects of the curriculum (including learners, teachers, materials, learning arrangements, etc.) for decision making purposes.

Assessment is a subcomponent of evaluation. *Assessment* refers to the tools, techniques, and procedures for collecting and interpreting information about what learners can and cannot do. In evaluating one's teaching, it is obviously important to include assessment data. This tells us what learners can and cannot do as a result of the instructional process. However, in order to make sense of this information, and to decide what worked and what did not work, it is important to collect other information that will tell us whether it was the teaching materials, instructional procedures, or some other aspect of the instructional process that needs to be changed.

♦ STUDENT SELF-ASSESSMENT

In contemporary language teaching, learners are trained systematically in ways of assessing their own learning progress. Learners can identify their own strengths better, and where they need more help from the teacher. When they leave the program we can indicate their proficiency level in the language they have been studying, and also provide a profile of their strengths and weaknesses in many other factors that influence effective communication. In this way, learners, parents, and employers can see precisely what progress has been made and what communicative tasks learners can successfully carry out. Increasingly, portfolios of work, providing concrete instances of learner achievement, are being accepted by employers and educational institutions. The following example, from *Writing Workout* (Huizenga & Thomas–Ruzic), shows how student-centered records of work can be built up over time.

These records have a number of purposes. In the first place, they serve to remind learners of the content covered in the unit. Secondly, over time, they provide a record of achievement, as well as reminding learners of work still to be done. Finally, and most importantly, they develop skills in self-assessment and self-evaluation, skills, as we saw in Chapter 1, that are important ingredients in a learner-oriented instructional system. (For a detailed description and inventory of learner-oriented tasks, see Brindley, 1989. See also the special issue of the *TESOL Journal* on learner assessment).

COOLING DOWN: A unit review

1. Write five to ten new words or phrases from this unit. Can you spell and pronounce each one?

   _____

   _____

   _____

   _____

2. Complete the cluster with things that you learned about some American cities.

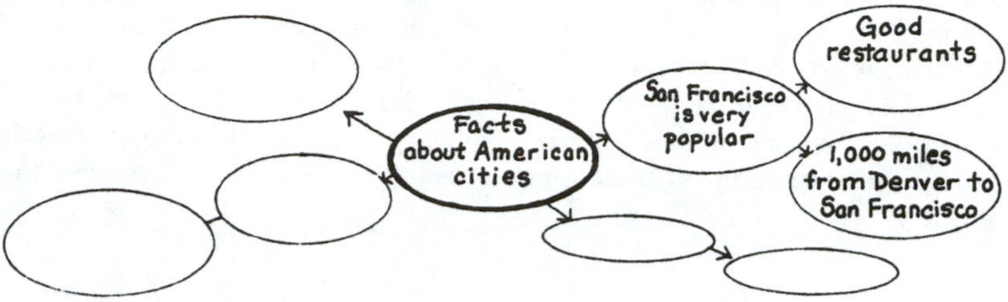

3. Write sentences about the future. Use *will* or *be + going to* in these sentences.

   Example: Later this afternoon *I will go to the library*.

   a. Tonight _____.

   b. _____ tomorrow.

   c. Next week _____.

   d. _____ next summer.

4. Write the names of three to five specific places or locations in the state or city where you are living. Include, for example, the name of a park, lake, building, mountain peak, river, school, or street. Watch capital letters!

   _____

   _____

Figure 3-1   *Writing Workshop,* © **Heinle & Heinle Publishers**

LANGUAGE OUT OF CLASS

In traditional classrooms, learners are rarely encouraged to make use of their language skills in the real world. The only practice they have is in class. This, of course, is not surprising in foreign language contexts in which opportunities to use the language are limited. However, as we saw in the preceding chapter, one of the things that characterizes good language learners is their ability to find opportunities to activate their language outside of the classroom.

♦ STRATEGIES FOR ACTIVATING LANGUAGE OUT OF CLASS

In contemporary approaches to language teaching, learners are involved in role plays and practice simulations, and through these develop an ability to carry out creative and imaginative learning projects outside of the language classroom. These projects are carefully connected to the kinds of language tasks that they will have to perform when they complete their studies. In this way they develop independence, they learn how to function as communicators themselves, and they learn to use language as a working tool to achieve their objectives outside of the classroom. In my own teaching, I try to structure out-of-class learning opportunities for students on a ratio of three to one. In other words, for every hour they spend with me, I try to find ways in which they will spend three hours outside the classroom systematically working on their language. In addition to increasing the overall quantity of language use, this sends the message to the learners that they have power and control over their own learning. It also shows them that, even in foreign language situations, there are many opportunities for them to practice their language. Out-of-class tasks include:

◊   engaging in peer review sessions, in which they collaborate with a fellow student to review projects and assignments;

◊   conducting dialogue journals with me via the Internet;

◊   taking part in conversation exchanges with foreigners who want to practice their Chinese (students are paired with foreigners, and arrange, at their own convenience, to spend forty minutes a week in conversation, twenty minutes in English and twenty minutes in Chinese);

◊   projects and surveys, (in which they collect information in English, and bring it back to a subsequent class);

◊   doing language improvement projects in the independent learning center (in these projects they identify an aspect of their English they want to improve, they formulate a learning objective, and write up a learning contract, which they carry out independently).

(Other ideas for fostering independent learning outside the formal language classroom can be found in Pemberton *et al.* (1996) and Gardner and Miller (1996).

♦ CONCLUSION

In this chapter, I have drawn together the major ideological and empirical themes that emerged in the first two chapters. I have illustrated the changes that have been brought about to pedagogical practice as a result of changing views on the nature of language and learning, and also through the incorporation into classroom teaching of insights from research. We can summarize the changes to theory and practice as follows:

◊ learners practice skills they will need outside of the classroom
◊ learners are actively involved in using the language they are learning, and in learning through doing
◊ learners communicate authentically and learn to use language appropriately
◊ learners learn how to use grammar and vocabulary to express different communicative meanings
◊ learners listen to and read authentic texts of different kinds
◊ learners develop strategies to become better language learners
◊ learners work together in small cooperative groups
◊ learners develop skills in self-assessment and self-evaluation
◊ learners learn how to take their language into the real world beyond the classroom
◊ teachers help learners to learn useful language and to become better learners
◊ teachers provide models of the language they are learning and share their knowledge of real-word tasks
◊ teachers actively cooperate in providing a varied program of instruction
◊ teachers continuously assess learners' performance and provide a detailed profile of their skills

In short, task-based language teaching helps learners to learn real language for use in the real world. Learners are assessed on what they can communicate and on their skills as language learners, as solvers of problems, and as communicators in groups. As a result, teachers, parents, and employers know what skills learners have, and can match learners' abilities to the demands of particular tasks and jobs. Task-based language teaching is more than just a means of learning a language. It's a way of becoming a better communicator in the workplace, and in the social world beyond the classroom.

Table 3.2 summarizes the major shifts that have taken place in language pedagogy over the last thirty years.

In summary, the ideology driving the view of education presented

Table 3.2   The traditional and the contemporary in language education

Traditional	*Contemporary* *In addition to the features set out in the left-hand column,..*
SYLLABUS DESIGN Content & methodology decided with reference to the classroom rather than with reference to learners' real communicative needs.	Content & methodology match learner needs beyond the classroom. Process and content are integrated.
APPROACH TO TEACHING (METHODOLOGY) Learners are taught about language and its rules, learning facts about language rather than how to use it communicatively.	Learners are actively involved in using language.
ROLE OF THE LEARNERS Learners spend their time copying and reproducing language written down by others.	Learners learn how to use language creatively, responding in novel and authentic communicative situations.
APPROACH TO LANGUAGE Grammar is taught as rules to be memorized.	Grammar and vocabulary are taught communicatively so learners can use the grammar to express different communicative meanings.
USING LANGUAGE TEXTS Learners listen to and read specially written classroom texts. They have difficulty comprehending authentic language outside the classroom.	Learners study authentic texts and learn to use genuine language outside the classroom.
RESOURCES FOR LEARNING Learners have to rely only on the textbook as an aid to language learning.	Learners use a specially written, well-illustrated textbook plus self-study workbooks, cassette tapes, and videotaped materials.
APPROACH TO LEARNING Learners don't learn how to become better language learners on their own.	Learners learn a range of effective language learning strategies and are shown how to apply these strategies to their own learning outside the classroom.
CLASSROOM ORGANIZATION Learners sit in rows facing the teacher and spend most of their time repeating what the teacher says. They don't learn how to express their own ideas.	Learners work in small groups and pairs, learning skills of cooperating with others and how to express their own opinions, ideas, and feelings.
ASSESSMENT Teacher alone assesses the student's progress. Learners do not develop ability to assess what they have learned.	Learners are trained to assess their own learning progress, and can identify their own strengths and weaknesses.

here is that learners have a right to be involved in curriculum decision making, that is, selecting content, learning activities, and tasks. It is also predicated on a belief that learners learn best if the content relates to their own experience and knowledge. At the level of implementation, there is a belief that learners who have developed skills in "learning how to learn" are the most effective students, and that learners have different learning styles and strategies that need to be taken into consideration in developing learning programs.

◆ CONCEPT MAP OF CHAPTER 3

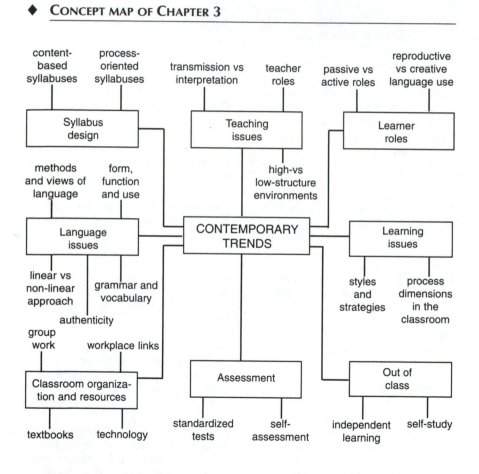

◆ QUESTIONS AND TASKS

1. What was the major conceptual shift brought about by Stenhouse to the field of syllabus design?
2. List three characteristics of a "high-structure" classroom, and three characteristics of a "low-structure" classroom.

3. What is the essential difference between a "reproductive" and a "creative" learning task?
4. Why is it desirable to introduce learners to authentic data? List ten sources or, potential sources, of authentic data in your current teaching situation.
5. What media, in addition to commercial texts, are you using/do you have the potential to use in your current teaching situation?
6. Identify three ways in which learning strategies could be integrated into your current teaching situation.
7. Identify three impediments to group work in your teaching situation, and brainstorm solutions to these.
8. List and discuss three ways in which your students can activate their language skills out of class.
9. Collect samples of authentic texts and use them as the basis for designing tasks for low-level learners. If possible, introduce the tasks in the classroom, and evaluate their strengths and weaknesses.

◆ REFERENCES

Biggs, J., and R. Telfer. 1987. *The Process of Learning*. 2nd ed. Sydney: Prentice-Hall.

Breen, M. 1984. Process syllabuses for the language classroom. In C. Brumfit (ed.), *General English Syllabus Design*. Oxford: Pergamon.

Brindley, G. 1989. *Assessing Achievement in a Learner-Centred System*. Sydney: National Centre for English Language Teaching and Research.

Gardner D., and L. Miller (eds.). 1996. *Tasks for Independent Language Learning*. Alexandria, Va.: TESOL.

Huizenga, J., and M. Thomas–Ruzic 1990. *Writing Workout: A Program for New Students of English*. Boston: Heinle & Heinle.

Larsen–Freeman, D. (ed.). 1995. *Grammar Dimensions*. Boston: Heinle & Heinle.

Molinsky, S. J., and B. Bliss. 1989. *Side by Side Second Edition*. Book 1. Englewood Cliffs, N.J.: Prentice-Hall.

Moulton, W. 1963. Linguistics and language teaching in the United States 1940–1960. *International Review of Applied Linguistics*, 1, 21–41.

Nunan, D. 1989. *Syllabus Design*. Oxford: Oxford University Press.

Nunan, D., and C. Lamb. 1996. *The Self-Directed Teacher*. Cambridge: Cambridge University Press.

Oxford, R. 1990. *Language Learning Strategies: What Every Teacher Should Know*. New York: Newbury House.

Pemberton, R., E. S. L. Li, W. Or, and H. Pierson (eds.). 1996. *Autonomy and Language Learning*. Hong Kong: Hong Kong University Press.

Pinker, S. 1994. *The Language Instinct*. London: Penguin.

Stenhouse, L. 1975. *An Introduction to Curriculum Research and Development*. London: Heinemann.

Richards, J. C., and T. Rodgers. 1986. *Approaches and Methods in Language Teaching*. Cambridge: Cambridge University Press.

Tyler, R. 1949. *Basic Principles of Curriculum and Instruction*. New York: Harcourt Brace.

van Lier, L. 1988. *The Classroom and the Language Learner*. London: Longman.

Warschauer, M. 1995. *E-Mail for English Teaching*. Washington, D.C.: TESOL.

Wright, T. 1987. *Roles of Teachers and Learners*. Oxford: Oxford University Press.

PART II

Language, Learners, and the Learning Process

Introduction

The three essential elements in any successful language learning experience are language, learners, and the learning process. Note that I have omitted teachers from my list. While teachers obviously play a crucial role in thousands of language learning contexts around the world, they are not essential to the learning process. Many people have managed to acquire fluency in a second language without ever going near a teacher. (In any case, I have written extensively about teachers in other books.) In this section of the book, I take a detailed look at these three critical elements.

In Chapter 4, I look at language in context, focusing in particular on those aspects of language that can provide teachers with insights for developing materials and pedagogical procedures. In fact, in Section Three of the book, I shall draw on the ideas developed here to present some of my own ideas for teaching spoken and written language.

Chapter 5 considers the learner. It elaborates on the concept of learner-centeredness presented in Chapter 1, and looks at the practical implications of a view of learning that places learners themselves in the center of the process.

Chapter 6 takes a detailed look at learning processes. As processes and learners are inseparable, the division between Chapters 5 and 6 is, to a certain extent, arbitrary, and, as you read the chapters, you will find key issues revised from slightly different perspectives. The main concern of the chapter is to pick up on and elaborate some of the issues emerging from the research literature on learning styles and strategies.

CHAPTER 4

Focus on Language

This chapter reflects my quest for a view of language consistent with the ways in which I have observed languages being tackled (with varying degrees of success) and used. When I began teaching, audiolingualism was at the height of its fashion, and students were often taught unrelated structures unrelated to their context of use. This seemed inconsistent with my social science training in which I had been indoctrinated to believe that human behavior could only be understood in the contexts in which it occurred, because context would affect behavior. It seemed to me that language, undeniably a form of human behavior, could only be understood in the contexts in which it occurred.

It was this contextual view of language use that led me to search for instances of authentic language to take into my classrooms long before authenticity was fashionable, and when artificial models and sample sentences, concocted for the purposes of grammatical display, were the norm in classrooms. In this chapter, I shall spell out why I think that much language teaching has been relatively unsuccessful. The chapter covers the following issues and concepts:

Grammar and grammaticality
◇ defining grammar
◇ grammar—a problematic concept
◇ grammar and discourse
◇ three dimensions of grammar: form, meaning, and use

Vocabulary
◇ vocabulary and grammar
◇ the status of vocabulary within the curriculum
◇ concordancing

Pronunciation
◇ age and the critical period
◇ segmental and suprasegmental phonology
◇ pronunciation and listening

Metaphors for language development
◇ the building block metaphor
◇ the organic metaphor
◇ "growing their own grammar": Some data from learners

Language as discourse
◇ the relationship between sentences and texts
◇ textual connectivity

95

Creating cohesion
◇ reference
◇ substitution and ellipsis
◇ conjunction
◇ lexical cohesion
◇ rhetorical patterns in text

Making sense
◇ functional coherence
◇ the negotiation of meaning

Speech acts

Background knowledge
◇ interpreting discourse
◇ schema theory
◇ background knowledge and functional interpretation

Pedagogical implications
◇ teaching language as sets of choices
◇ encouraging learners to become active explorers of language
◇ encouraging learners to explore relationships between form, meaning, and use

GRAMMAR AND GRAMMATICALITY

For most people, the essence of language lies in grammar. When someone is said to "lack skills in language," or when the popular press decries what it sees as the declining standard of English, they are generally referring to an actual or perceived decline in the ability of individuals to express themselves grammatically. It is therefore fitting that this exploration of language should begin with an examination of the notions of *grammar* and *grammaticality*.

◆ DEFINING GRAMMAR

Notions of grammar and grammaticality have changed over the years. Early last century, Cobbett wrote:

> Grammar . . . teaches us how to make use of words; that is to say, it teaches us how to make use of them in the proper manner . . . to be able to choose the words which ought to be placed, we must be acquainted with certain principles and rules; and these principles and rules constitute what is called Grammar.

> *Cobbett, 1819*

Twenty-five years after Cobbett's pronouncement, a grammar for schools appeared that reinforced the notion that grammar had principally to do with correctness. Published in 1856, the *English Grammar for the Use of Schools* asserted that the object of English Grammar was to teach those who use the English language to express their thoughts correctly, either in speech or writing. For most of the history of language teaching, grammar has had to do with correctness, and the role of the teacher was to impart the rules that would result in correct usage. In terms of the contrast drawn in Chapter 1, the focus was on transmission rather than interpretation.

These days, at least, grammarians are a little more careful than in Cobbett's day to focus on describing language as it is used, rather than prescribing how it should be used. This is evident in the following entries from a recent dictionary of linguistic terminology.

Grammar.   (1) An analysis of the structure of a language, either as encountered in a corpus of speech or writing (a performance grammar) or as predictive of a speaker's knowledge (a competence grammar). A contrast is often drawn between a descriptive grammar, which provides a precise account of actual usage, and a prescriptive grammar, which tries to establish rules for the correct use of language in society. (2) An analysis of the structural properties which define human language (a universal grammar). (3) A level of structural organization which can be studied independently of phonology and semantics.

Grammaticality.   The conformity of a sentence or part of a sentence to the rules defined by a particular grammar of the language (Crystal 1992: 35–36).

Grammar.   *n* a description of the structure of a language and the way in which linguistic units such as words and phrases are combined to produce sentences in the language (Richards, Platt and Weber, 1985).

Grammar: A Problematic Concept

Research over the last few years suggests that many of the assumptions that are made about grammar and grammaticality are essentially problematic. This can be demonstrated by simple introspective tests of grammaticality (Langunoff 1992, cited in Celce–Murcia and Olshtain forthcoming; Odlin, 1994; Nunan, 1993). In their investigation of the notion of grammaticality, Nunan and Keobke (1997) presented eighty native and non-native teachers of English as a foreign language with the following sentences, and asked them to indicate which were grammatically acceptable and which were grammatically unacceptable.

> *The gang were plotting a takeover.*
> *Everybody is ready now, aren't they?*
> *Neither Fred nor Harry had to work late, did they?*
> *Someone has deliberately made themselves homeless.*

Anyone running a business should involve their spouse.
My hair needs washed.
What the cat did was ate the rat.

The results, which are set out in Table 4.1, are interesting. They indicate a large measure of disagreement between both the native and non-native teachers, although the majority believe that most of the sentences are acceptable despite the fact that they violate a range of grammatical rules.

Given this uncertainty among native speakers, the appropriate course of action might seem to be to turn to the experts for guidance. Should we not seek advice from professional linguists and language educators? After all, linguistic analysis and teaching are their bread and butter. In actual fact, levels of disagreement among linguists can be just as pronounced as those among ordinary native speakers. In a study carried out by Ross (1979) there was considerable disagreement as to the grammaticality of the following question:

What will the grandfather clock stand between the bed and?

Among nine native English-speaking linguists, two found the question completely acceptable, two found it marginally acceptable, and five found it to be completely unacceptable.

A similar picture emerges when the views of language educators are sought. Schmidt and McCreary (1977) presented ESL teachers with pairs of sentences such as the following:

Table 4.1

Native Speakers = NS Non-native Speakers = NNS	*Acceptable* NS	*Not Acceptable* NS	*Acceptable* NNS	*Not Acceptable* NNS
The gang were plotting a take-over.	34	6	30	9
Everybody is ready now, aren't they?	32	8	23	16
Neither Fred nor Harry had to work late, did they?	34	6	31	8
Someone has deliberately made themselves homeless.	24	16	24	15
Anyone running a business should involve their spouse.	33	7	25	14
My hair needs washed.	8	32	8	31
What the cat did was ate the rat.	10	30	15	24

a. *There's about five minutes left.*
b. *There are about five minutes left.*

In a test of spontaneous usage, a large majority of the subjects used (a). However, in a later test, when asked which form they used, most reported using (b). In a subsequent test, the informants were asked to judge the correctness of the probes. Only a small minority considered (a) to be correct. One can imagine students, hearing their teachers using forms that they have been told are unacceptable, asking themselves "why can't they get it right?"

Odlin (1994) in an investigation of grammaticality and acceptability, concluded that there are important limitations on the ability of "experts" to provide reliable judgments.

> Few, if any, linguists or teachers have irrefutable intuitions about grammaticality, even though many of their judgments are reliable. Both competence and performance limitations affect expert judgments of grammaticality, and these limitations can likewise affect judgments of acceptability. In linguistics, there is a growing awareness of such limitations, even if some grammarians continue to dodge the epistemological question *What is a linguistic fact?* [posed by William Labov (1975)] (Odlin 1994: 284).

◆ GRAMMAR AND DISCOURSE

In fact, it makes little sense to talk about linguistic facts at the level of the isolated sentence because, with few exceptions, these will be conditioned by the linguistic and experiential context in which the utterance occurs. From a functional perspective, we need to reverse the usual order of things, giving priority to discourse, and looking at grammatical features within the grammatical contexts in which they occur. Without reference to context, it makes little sense to speak of "facts," "correctness," or "propriety."

Discourse
Discourse is any naturally occurring stretch of language occurring in context (Carter, 1993: 22).

The adoption of such a discourse perspective is central to our understanding of language acquisition and use, and, without such a perspective, our understanding of other dimensions of language, such as *grammaticality*, will be piecemeal and incomplete, as will any attempt at understanding and interpreting utterances in isolation from the contexts in which they occur. Grammar and discourse are tied together in a fundamentally hierarchical relationship with lower-order grammatical choices being driven by higher-order discoursal ones. This view has major implications for applied linguistic research as well as language pedagogy, and, in the final section of this chapter, we look at some of the practical implications of this view of language. It also underpins the approach to pedagogy taken in the four chapters that make up the final section of the book. Later in this chapter, when we look at language as discourse, we will see that effective communication involves achieving harmony between functional interpretation and formal appropriateness.

The problems that arise when we separate sentence level and discourse level analysis are not new. As far back as 1952, Harris argued that grammar and discourse are systematically related, although his claim that grammar provides the building blocks for creating discourse (Harris 1952) would seem to accord primacy to grammar, a primacy I have challenged. More recently, McCarthy (1991: 62) has taken a similar position, arguing that ". . . grammar is seen to have a direct role in welding clauses, turns and sentences into discourse . . ."

The notion that we can derive grammatical principles and rules from the study of isolated sentences has also been attacked from various quarters in recent years. Not surprisingly, this attack has come from those who view language as a tool for the creation of meaning. Advocates of grammatical analysis within meaningful, discoursal contexts include specialists in pragmatics, such as Levinson (1983), who argues that there are very few grammatical rules that are not influenced by the wider contexts in which they are used, and who points out that the vast majority of grammatical choices that a language user makes are context dependent. Language educators such as Celce–Murcia and Olshtain (forthcoming) also maintain that there are very few grammatical elements that are not sensitive to, and affected by, the discoursal contexts in which they occur. Celce–Murcia and Olshtain argue that the following represents a fairly comprehensive list of those grammatical features that are completely context-free. (They also argue that even sentence level rule "violations" can be explained with reference to context.)

> subject-verb agreement
> determiner–noun agreement
> use of gerunds after prepositions
> reflexive pronominalization within the clause
> *some/any* suppletion in the environment of negation

These examples point to the essential problematicity and complexity of grammatical "rules" once actual use is taken into account. I believe that the implications of all this for pedagogy are fairly significant, and shall spell these out in the concluding section of the chapter. Before I do so, however, I should like to look briefly at two other important linguistic subsystems, that concerned with the study of words, and that concerned with the study of sounds.

Three Dimensions of Grammar: Form, Meaning and Use

The most comprehensive recent conceptualization of grammar has been provided by Larsen–Freeman (1995). She sees grammar as a higher-order concept within linguistics, arguing that it has three interrelated dimensions: form, meaning and use. Her model thus attempts to integrate three aspects of linguistics that have traditionally been kept separate: syntax (study of form), semantics (the study of meaning), and pragmatics (the study of use). It therefore shares a great deal in common with the model of systemic–functional linguistics developed by Halliday (see, for example, Halliday 1985).

> **Grammar**
> The study of how syntax (form), semantics (meaning), and pragmatics (use) work together to enable individuals to communicate through language.

VOCABULARY

◆ VOCABULARY AND GRAMMAR

Vocabulary is more than lists of target language words. As part of the language system, vocabulary is intimately interrelated with grammar. In fact, it is possible to divide the lexical system of most languages into "grammatical words," such as prepositions, articles, adverbs, and so on, and content words. The "grammaticality" of vocabulary also manifests itself in word morphology, that is, the grammatical particles that we attach to the beginning and ends of words in order to form new words. The following task is designed to focus learners on this aspect of language.

Task 1:

What is the meaning of the following prefixes?

Prefix	Examples	Meaning	Additional Example
a, ab, abs	abnormal, absent	away, from, off	_____
ad, ac, as	advance, advantage	to, towards, up	_____
ambi	ambivalent, ambidextrous	_____	_____
co, co, cor	correspond, correlate	_____	_____
contra	contradict, contrary	_____	_____
ex, e	external, exit	_____	_____

Prefix	Examples	Meaning	Additional Example
in	*internal*	_____	_____
in, il, im, un	*illegal, unhelpful*	_____	_____
inter	*international, interval*	_____	_____
mis	*mislead, misunderstand*	_____	_____
ante	*antecedent*	_____	_____
post	*postgraduate*	_____	_____
sub	*submarine*	_____	_____
super	*superman, supersonic*	_____	_____

Task 2:

Pair Work. Now come up with an additional example for each prefix and write it in the column headed "additional example."

Task 3:

What do the following suffixes mean? What does each suffix tell you about the word? How many words can you think of that end in these affixes?

-ate _____

-tion _____

-less _____

-ness _____

-er _____

-or _____

(Source: Adapted from M. Hill. *Learning Vocabulary*. The English Centre, University of Hong Kong.)

◆ *THE STATUS OF VOCABULARY WITHIN THE CURRICULUM*

In terms of the subsystems of language, in most language teaching approaches, vocabulary has played second fiddle to grammar. This was particularly true during the days when structural linguistics and audiolingualism were at their most popular. (In fact audiolingualism is still possibly the most influential method around the world today.) Proponents of audiolingualism argued that foreign language learning would be most

effective if learners concentrated their efforts on mastering the basic sentence patterns of the language. Once these patterns had been memorized,
new vocabulary could be "slotted in."

In recent years, the teaching of vocabulary has assumed its rightful
place as a fundamentally important aspect of language development. This
is partly due to the influence of comprehension-based approaches to
language development, partly due to the research efforts of influential
applied linguists (see, for example, Carter and McCarthy (1988), and
partly due to the exciting possibilities opened up by the development of
computer-based language corpora (Sinclair and Renouf 1988).

Proponents of comprehension-based approaches to language acquisition argue that the early development of an extensive vocabulary can
enable learners to "outperform their competence." In other words, if one
has an extensive vocabulary, it is posible to obtain meaning from spoken
and written texts, even though one does not know the grammatical structures in which the texts are encoded. (This is true only to a limited extent,
of course, and probably only in the early stages of learning.)

Interestingly, learners themselves have never questioned the importance of vocabulary. Most of us who live and work in a foreign country,
and who attempt to function in the target language, find that we can get
by more readily by learning vocabulary than grammatical structures,
although, once again, this is true only in the early stages of the learning
process. In order to communicate beyond the most rudimentary level, it
is necessary to develop a knowledge of grammar. In a survey of student
attitudes towards vocabulary, Morgan and Rinvolucri (1986:4–5) found
that:

> Two thirds of [those surveyed] said they were not taught enough
> words in class, words they needed when talking to people, watching TV,
> and reading. They felt their teachers were very keen on teaching them
> grammar and on improving their pronunciation, but that learning vocab-
> ulary came a poor third.

Another aspect of vocabulary learning is that, unlike the acquisition of
other aspects of language (particularly pronunciation), it does not seem
to be impeded by age. In fact Rivers (1983:125) argues that, in contrast
with other aspects of language, the ability to learn new vocabulary appears
to get easier as one gets older.

♦ CONCORDANCING

The development of computerized data bases has, in recent years, facilitated a great deal of fascinating vocabulary research. These data bases
consist of thousands of texts containing millions of words in context. In
addition to enabling researchers to do frequency counts, they also reveal

fascinating patterns in language. For example, concordancing programs enable researchers to explore the contexts in which particular words and phrases occur, and the other words with which they co-occur. The following example has been taken from the corpus developed by Birmingham University in the United Kingdom, the largest corpus of its type in the world. This particular example, for the noun *way*, is taken from Willis (1990:28), who points out that it is the third most common noun in English after *time*, and *people*.

These data bases enable linguists to identify patterns in language that are not immediately apparent. In the case of *way*, above, even with this limited sample of the 7,000 occurrences, it is possible to identify collocations and patterns.

Another advantage of these large data bases is that they enable researchers to identify the functions performed by particular words. In many cases the ways in which words actually function are at odds with the intuitions of teachers and textbook writers. The following example for the words *certain* and *certainly* are taken from the Birmingham corpus.

Table 4.2

ing on; fewer still had premises in any	way	suitable; some turned out to be sch
assertively un-urban that we affected a	way	of dressing quite unsuited to Unive
attention if he became too excitable, a	way	whose success was, I think, due to
hanged, and a manned craft was the best	way	of preserving flexibility. Photogra
ed to the idea very gradually. The best	way	to do this, I decided, was to intro
burn and the island beaches. I went by	way	of my family home in the south of s
ts, but not in the seemingly calculated	way	that is born of deprivation. The spa
le lifeless, and I began in a desultory	way	to review in my mind various animal
the bath; it had become an established	way	of quieting him when he was obstrep
nd the retaliatory strategy had to give	way	to the flexible response, with its
o be thrown. Such pebbles that came his	way	seem mainly to have been on the que
h strip of garden from the road. On his	way	home, but never on his way out, Mij
road. On his way home, but never on his	way	out, Mij would tug me in the direct
ed in his small body. He would work his	way	under them and execute a series of
converse with them. <p 124> "It was his	way	for the most part to wander in thos
uch panic that he could hardly make his	way	home, tottering on us feet: and ear
that he could not even turn to make his	way	back, and with a fifty-foot sheer d
bearings if he were trying to make his	way	homeward through it. I put a light
upstart. But I soon found an infallible	way	to distract his attention if he bec
e Fleet as and when it had to fight its	way	against Soviet sea and air oppositi
e chick while he went on in a leisurely	way	with his underwater exploration. It
d on the rock west of Canna, by a long	way	the nearest to me of their colonies
ozen occasions, and most of them a long	way	off. No doubt they have often been
e had to be. Camusfearna is a very long	way	from a vet.; the nearest, in fact,
No strange sea monster has ever come my	way	since I have been here, though in t

Table 4.3

certain
Function 1. (60% of occurrences) Determiner as in:
            /a certain number of students/ in certain circles/
Function 2. (18% of occurrences) Adjective as in:
            /I'm not awfully certain about . . . ./We've got to make
            certain/
Function 3. (11% of occurrences) Adjective, in phrase "A + *certain* +
            noun," as in:
            /. . . has a certain classy ring/there is a certain evil in all
         lying/

certainly
Function 1   (98% of occurrences) as in:
            /it will certainly be interesting/He will almost certainly
            launch into a little lecture . . ./
                        Sinclair and Renouf 1988: 147–148. See also Renouf 1984

PRONUNCIATION

◆ AGE AND THE CRITICAL PERIOD

In this section, we look at aspects of the phonological system of language. From a language teaching perspective, the phonological system has tended to be viewed somewhat differently from the grammatical and lexical systems. This is probably due to the fact that the influence of the first language seems to be more apparent in the case of pronunciation than for grammar or vocabulary. There is also the fact that learners who begin studying another language after the onset of puberty rarely, if ever, achieve native-like levels of fluency. This is so, even for those gifted learners who approach native-like levels of mastery of other aspects of the language. A number of researchers have suggested that the inability of learners to acquire a flawless pronunciation supports the notion of a "critical period" for language acquisition. (See the discussion in Chapter 2.)

The Critical Period
The critical period is a biologically determined period of life when language can be acquired more easily and beyond which time language is increasingly difficult to acquire. The critical period hypothesis claims that there is such a biological timetable. (Brown 1987: 42)

◆ SEGMENTAL AND SUPRASEGMENTAL PHONOLOGY

Textbooks on phonetics and phonology typically distinguish between *segmental* and *suprasegmental* features of language. *Segmental phonology* has to do with the individual sounds of the language. *Suprasegmental phonology* has to do with stress, rhythm, and intonation patterns in the language. In language teaching, at the level of segmental phonology, tasks are designed that help learners discriminate, and, ultimately produce, words that differ only in a single contrasting sound. These are known as *minimal pairs*. Examples of minimal pairs in English are *bit/pit*, *breach/beach*, and *back/bag*. The following is a typical exercise for teaching minimal pair sound discrimination.

Read each sentence twice, choosing one of the alternative words. Ask the students to mark the word they hear.

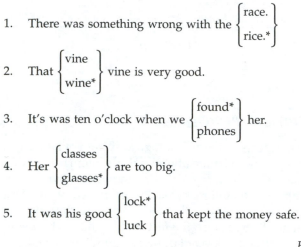

1. There was something wrong with the ⎧ race. ⎫
                                        ⎩ rice.* ⎭

2. That ⎧ vine ⎫ vine is very good.
        ⎩ wine* ⎭

3. It's was ten o'clock when we ⎧ found* ⎫ her.
                                ⎩ phones ⎭

4. Her ⎧ classes ⎫ are too big.
       ⎩ glasses* ⎭

5. It was his good ⎧ lock* ⎫ that kept the money safe.
                   ⎩ luck ⎭

Byrne and Walsh 1973: 138

◆ PRONUNCIATION AND LISTENING

While tasks such as that above are designed to help learners identify differences of meaning based on differences in individual sounds, suprasegmental tasks teach differences of meaning based on stress, rhythm, and intonation. The following task, for example, shows learners how different stress and intonation patterns signal differences of function (in this case, distinguishing between requests for information and checking for understanding).

From these tasks, it can be seen that pronunciation and listening are in a complementary relationship. In fact, in Chapter 7, we revisit some of the issues covered here from the perspective of listening.

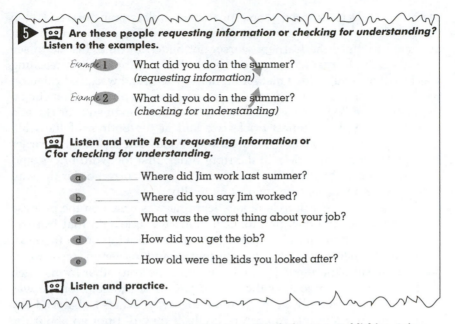

5 🔲 **Are these people *requesting information* or *checking for understanding*? Listen to the examples.**

Example 1 ▶ What did you do in the summer?
          (requesting information)

Example 2 ▶ What did you do in the summer?
          (checking for understanding)

🔲 **Listen and write *R* for *requesting information* or *C* for *checking for understanding*.**

  a _____ Where did Jim work last summer?

  b _____ Where did you say Jim worked?

  c _____ What was the worst thing about your job?

  d _____ How did you get the job?

  e _____ How old were the kids you looked after?

🔲 **Listen and practice.**

Figure 4-1   *Listen In* - Book 2, © International Thomson Publishing Asia

For most of its history, the teaching of pronunciation has been biased toward segmental apsects of the sound system. However, with the development of communicative approaches to language teaching, the importance of stress, rhythm, and intonation has been acknowledged. In a key survey article published in 1986, Pennington and Richards argue in favor of a suprasegmental approach on the grounds that "teaching isolated forms of sounds and words fails to address the fact that, in communication, many aspects of pronunciation are determined by the positioning of elements within long stretches of speech." Other commentators have pointed out that faulty stress, rhythm, and intonation patterns cause greater difficulty for hearers than the inaccurate pronunciation of individual sounds.

METAPHORS FOR LANGUAGE DEVELOPMENT

♦ *THE BUILDING BLOCK METAPHOR*

As a novice teacher, when I developed the courage to take a step back, mentally, from the learning/teaching process, and observe my students in action. I found that this was not a particularly comfortable thing to do. The first thing I noticed was the alarming gap between what I was trying to teach my learners and the things that they actually appeared to be learning. I also found that the effect of my pedagogical effort sometimes seemed to make my learners worse, not better. In classroom quizzes, I often noticed that on discrete grammatical items, the effect of my instruction appeared to make the learners worse, not better. In time, I came to see (or rather, my learners forced me to see), that my approach to teaching was based on a misguided metaphor, that my teaching was predicated on the assumption that learning another language was a process of erecting a linguistic "building" in a step-by-step fashion, one linguistic "brick" at a time. The easy grammatical bricks are laid at the bottom of the wall, providing a foundation for the more difficult ones. The task for the learner is to get the linguistic bricks in the right order: first the word bricks, and then the sentence bricks. If the bricks are not in the correct order the wall will collapse under its own ungrammaticality.

This linear approach to language learning was based on the premise that learners acquire one grammatical item at a time, and that learners should demonstrate mastery of one item before moving on to the next. For example, in learning English, a student should master one tense form, such as the simple present, before being introduced to other forms, such as the present continuous or the simple past. The problem for me was that my learners simply didn't behave this way. When I observed my learners in their struggle to acquire English, they did not go about the process in the step-by-step, building block fashion suggested by the linear model. The idea that language learners acquire one target item, perfectly, one at a time, as implied, for example, by programmed learning, audiolingual methodology, and a "systems" approach to instructional design, was simply not supported by the facts.

If we test a learner's ability to use a particular grammatical form (for example, the simple present) several times over a period of time, we find their accuracy rates varying. The accuracy does not increase in a linear fashion, from 20% to 40% through to 100%, but, at times, actually decreases. It appears that, rather than being isolated bricks, the various elements of language interact with, and are affected by, other elements to which they are closely related in a functional sense. This interrelationship accounts for the fact that a learner's mastery of a particular language item is unstable, appearing to increase and decrease at different times during the learning process. For example, mastery of the simple present deteriorates (temporarily) at the point when learners are beginning to acquire the present continuous. (Rutherford, 1987, describes this process as a kind of linguistic metamorphosis.)

◆ THE ORGANIC METAPHOR

Johnston (1987), whose work was reviewed in Chapter 2, and who developed one of the largest computerized SLA data bases ever compiled, provides an eloquent case for an organic view. In the following quote, he discusses the way in which negation in English is acquired in stages as the learner moves from formulaic usage through a series of progressive approximations towards native-like mastery.

> . . . the case of 'don('t)' shows that formulaic language can serve as what we might call the seedbed of propositional language. While it may still be necessary to use terms like formula in some kinds of linguistic discussion, the way in which a chunk like 'don't' is reanalysed by application of the rules for its production in a widening range of verbal environments makes it clear that the progression from formulaic language to productive language involves no hard and fast distinctions.
>
> *Johnston 1987: 24*

The adoption of an organic perspective can greatly enrich our understanding of language acquisition and use. Without such a perspective, our understanding of other dimensions of language, such as the notion of *grammaticality*, will be piecemeal and incomplete, as will any attempt at understanding and interpreting utterances in isolation from the contexts in which they occur. The organic metaphor describes second language acquisition as more like growing a garden than building a wall. From such a perspective, learners do not learn one thing perfectly one item at a time, but learn numerous things simultaneously (and imperfectly). The linguistic flowers do not all appear at the same time, nor do they all grow at the same rate. Some even appear to wilt, for a time, before renewing their growth. The rate and speed are determined by a complex interplay of factors related to speech processing constraints (Pienemann and Johnston 1987); pedagogical interventions (Pica 1985); acquisitional processes (Johnston, 1987); and the influence of the discourse environment in which the items occur (Levinson, 1983; McCarthy, 1991; Nunan, 1993). For comprehensive reviews of work in second language acquisition, you are referred to Larsen–Freeman and Long, 1991, and Ellis, 1994.

In a linear approach to instruction, the grammar is very often presented out of context. Learners are confronted with decontextualized structures at a sentence level, and are expected to internalize these structures through exercises involving repetition, manipulation, and grammatical transformation. While these exercises might provide learners with formal, declarative mastery, ultimately they make the task of developing procedural skill (being able to use the language for communication) more difficult than it need be because learners are denied the opportunity of seeing the systematic relationships that exist between form and function.

In proposing an alternative to the linear metaphor, care needs to be taken not to overstate the case. I would not wish to deny that some items are acquired before others, nor that there is an aspect of "linearity" in their development. What I am asserting here is that language acquisition is an extremely complex, multifaceted phenomenon in which items are acquired both hierarchically (that is, some items are acquired before others) and developmentally (that is, the acquisition of a particular element, be it grammatical, lexical, or phonological, will be gradual and will occur over time). These complex developmental and hierarchical processes are most accurately captured by the metaphor of organic development.

As teachers, we need to help learners understand that effective communication involves achieving harmony between functional interpretation and formal appropriacy (Halliday 1985). As Johnston, and others, have shown, it is particularly important to establish the correct pedagogical relationship between grammatical items and the discoursal contexts in which they occur. Grammar and context are so closely related that appropriate grammatical choices can often only be made with reference to the context and purpose of the communication. In addition, as Celce–Murcia and Olshtain (forthcoming) point out, there is only a handful of grammatical rules that are free from discourse constraints. This, by the way, is one of the reasons why it is often difficult to answer learners' questions about grammatical appropriateness. In many instances, the answer is: "It depends on the attitude or orientation that you the speaker want to take towards the events you wish to report." Recently, one of my graduate students who was preparing to submit his dissertation asked me whether he should use the simple past or the simple present when citing the work of others. I pointed out that the choice was up to him. If he were citing the study by way of background (or to demonstrate to his supervisor that he had actually read it), then the simple past was the appropriate choice. If, however, the study were still pertinent to his own research, then he ought to consider using the simple present.

If learners are not taught grammar in context, that is, from a functional perspective, it will be difficult for them to see how and why alternative forms exist to express different communicative meanings. This will make it very difficult for them to make appropriate choices. For example, exercises in which learners are required to read a set of sentences in the active voice, and then, transform these into passives following a model, deal with language at the level of form without showing learners that the different forms have different functional values. Exercises such as these convey to learners that the alternative forms are simply different ways of saying the same thing, and that they exist to make the process of acquiring another language even more difficult than it already is.

An organic approach to grammar dramatizes to learners the fact that different forms enable the learners to express different meanings in different contexts of use. Such an approach shows learners how grammar enables them to make meanings of increasingly sophisticated kinds, how it enables them to escape from the tyranny of the here and now, how it enables them, not only to report events and states of affairs, but to editorialize, and to communicate their own attitudes towards these events and affairs. Unfortunately, many coursebooks teach grammar as form, without making clear the relationship between form and function. Learners are taught about the forms rather than how to use the forms to communicate meaning. For example, through exercises such as the one referred to in the preceding paragraph, learners are taught how to transform sentences from the active voice into the passive, and back into the active voice, without being shown that passive forms have evolved to achieve certain communicative ends: to enable the speaker or writer to place the communicative focus on the action rather than the performer of the action, and to avoid referring to the performer of the action. If the communicative value of alternative grammatical forms is not made clear to learners, they come away from the classroom with the impression that the alternative forms exist merely to make things difficult for them. Through an organic methodology, learners learn both how to form structures correctly, and also how to use these structures to communicate meaning. Such a methodology shows learners how to use grammar to get things done, to socialize, to obtain goods and services, and to express their personality through language. In other words, it shows learners how to achieve their communicative ends through the appropriate deployment of the grammatical resources that exist in the language.

◆   "GROWING THEIR OWN GRAMMARS": SOME DATA FROM LEARNERS

The organic notion that learners "grow their own grammars" is readily demonstrated by tasks such as the following in which learners are asked to identify and explain the differences between closely related grammatical items, such as simple past/present perfect or the active and passive voices.

In groups of 3 or 4, study the following conversational extracts. Focus in particular on the parts of the conversation in italics. What is the difference between what Person A says and what Person B says? When would you use one form, and when would you use the other?

1. A: *I've seen* Romeo and Juliet *twice.*
    B: Me too. *I saw it last Tuesday, and again on the weekend.*
2. A: Want to go to the movies?
    B: No. *I'm going to study tonight.* We have an exam tomorrow, you know.
    A: Oh, in that case, *I'll study as well.*
3. A: Looks wet outside. I'm supposed to go to Central, but I don't have an umbrella. *If I went out without one, I'd get wet.*
    B: Yes, I went out a while ago. *If I'd gone out without an umbrella, I'd have gotten wet.*
4. A: *I finished my essay* just before the deadline for submission.
    B: Yes, *mine was finished* just in time as well.
5. A: *My brother, who lives in New York, is visiting me here in Hong Kong.*
    B: What a coincidence! *My brother, who is visiting me in Hong Kong, lives in New York,* too.
6. A: I need you to look after the kids. You'll be home early tonight, *won't you?*

B: Oh, you'll be late tonight, *will you?*

7. A: I won *a prize* in the English-speaking competition.
    B: Yeah? I won *the prize* in the poetry competition.

8. A: *The baby was sleeping* when I got home.
    B: So, *he'll be sleeping* when I get home, then?

9. A: Are you hungry?
    B: No, *I've already eaten.*
    A: Well, *I'll have already eaten* by the time you get home.

Compare explanations with another group. What similarities and differences are there in your explanations?

Here are some of the responses that I got from a group of high-intermediate-level learners who had been studying grammar formally for over ten years, and who completed the above task.

Student A (on the present perfect/simple past contrast)
"A use present perfect because something happened in the past, but affecting things happening now."

Student A (on the *going to/will* contrast)
"A is talking about a future action which has no planning. For B, the action has already planned."

Student A (on the active voice/passive voice contrast)
"They're the same meaning, but just use under different circumstances. In active voice, it means that the subject is doing something about the object. In passive voice, the subject is being affected by the object. This is a reciprocal of the relationship between the subject and the object."

Student B (on the present perfect/simple past contrast)
Present perfect tense is used only to describe a certain incidence in the past without describing the exact time of happening. However, it is necessary to describe the time of happening when using the simple past tense."

Student B (on the *going to/will* contrast)
"A is expressing something he want to do immediately. B is expressing something he want to do in the future."

Student B (on the active voice/passive voice contrast)
"A stressed on 'I finished' something. B stress on 'something is finished,' not on 'who' finished the job."

Student C (on the present perfect/simple past contrast)
"Simple past is more past than 'have seen.'"

Student C (on the *going to/will* contrast)
"For A, the action will do in a longer future. For B, the action should be done within a short future."

Student C (on the active voice/passive voice contrast)
"A emphasize the time when the work done. B emphasis work done."

Student D (on the present perfect/simple past contrast)
"We use present perfect tense when the action happen many times. B focus on actual date and use past."

Student D (on the *going to/will* contrast)
"A doesn't tell the exact time. B confirmed the studying time will be tonight. We use verb *to be* plus *going* means must do something."

Student D (on the active voice/passive voice contrast)
"A, active, clearly specify the essay was written by A. B, passive, maybe the essay was written by others."

Student E (on the present perfect/simple past contrast)
"A use present perfect to show how many times A has seen the film. B use simple past to show how much he love the film."

Student E (on the *going to/will* contrast)
"A is more sure to study than B tonight."

Student E (on the active voice/passive voice contrast)
"A is used when finished the essay the day before the deadline. B is used when finish the essay a minute before hand in."

From these responses, it can be seen that learners do not simply regurgitate the rules they are taught, but do indeed "grow their own grammars." The data show that learners' conceptualizations of grammatical principles are intimately tied to the contexts in which the rules are made salient. Understanding of grammar is integrated with knowledge of the world, experiential aspects of learning, and so on. While all learners are roughly at the same level of language proficiency, their ability to conceptualize and articulate rule and usage differences varies widely, Student A coming closest to the kinds of explanations that might typically be given by a teacher or a textbook, and Student E being furthest away. The gap between declarative and procedural knowledge (see Chapter 1) is also apparent in several of the responses. For example, several of the students who took part in the study used the passive voice appropriately in the course of giving an incorrect explanation of the different uses of active and passive voice.

LANGUAGE AS DISCOURSE

◆ *THE RELATIONSHIP BETWEEN SENTENCES AND TEXTS*

So far, in this chapter, I have built a case for the adoption of an organic, discourse-driven perspective to the teaching of language. In the next few sections, I shall explore the question of what we mean by *discourse* before concluding the chapter with a discussion of some of the practical implications of this view of language.

In a practical introduction to discourse analysis, which I wrote several years ago, I presented readers with the following extracts, and asked them to read the texts and rank order them from most to least sensible.

Extract 1

BUJUMBURA - It said in a statement on Sunday that 135 people were killed in the capital Bujumbura and surrounding areas and 137 more in the northern provinces of Citiboke and Bubanza. The government said order had been restored but security forces were still on alert for attacks from rebels of the party for the Liberation of the Hutu People. Burundi has said 272 people were killed in clashes between security forces and rebels which flared a week ago in the central African nation.

Extract 2

LIMA - At least 20 members of the Shining Path rebel organization were killed over the weekend by rural vigilantes armed by the government, police said on Monday. Police also said that two people had been killed by rebels—a rancher who had refused to give them money and another man accused of being an informer. The rebels said they planned to enforce what they called an ''armed strike'' yesterday and today to mark the 57th birthday of Abimael Guzman, the former university professor who founded Shining Path.

Extract 3

At least 14 people died on Saturday after drinking a cheap alcoholic beverage, raising to 20 the number of people killed by the poisonous brew in two days, news reports said. The quake measured 5.7 on the Richter scale and was felt shortly before 10.50 am (0850 GMT) Bucharest radio quoted an official report as saying. Judge Neil Dennison said Robert Phee, 23, a technician on the hit musical ''Miss Saigon'' was ''gripped by the excitement and theatricality'' of his eight robberies which netted him 15,000 pounds.

All of the sentences in the above extracts come from the same source (*The Nation*, Bangkok, Wednesday, December 4, 1991). In fact, they all come from the same column (World Roundup). However, most readers agreed that, in terms of their coherence, the texts are very different. In fact, many dispute that Extract 3 is a text at all. First and second language readers also have greater difficulty in processing extract three. In tests in which readers were timed as they read the three extracts, Extract 3 took significantly longer to process than Extracts 1 and 2, and Extract 1 took longer than Extract 2.

What is the source of this difficulty? What knowledge do readers require in order to make sense of these extracts? In the first place, they need to understand the grammar and vocabulary used in constructing the sentences that make up each extract. However, they need more than this, because, taken by themselves, each of the sentences in the three extracts is grammatically unexceptional, so it is obviously not the grammar that accounts for the oddity of the text. Of course, the sentences that make up a text need to be grammatical, but grammatical sentences alone will not ensure that the text itself makes sense.

In addition to the structure and meaning of the individual sentences, readers need to know how the sentences relate to each other. The sentences in Extract 3 do not seem to relate to each other at all. While the sentences in Extract 1 do seem to relate to each other in some way, the way they are arranged appears to be rather odd. In the first sentence, for example, there does not seem to be any way of determining what *it* refers to. In addition to sentence-level knowledge, then, the reader also needs to be able to interpret the sentences in relation to one another.

◆ TEXTUAL CONNECTIVITY

The interconnections between sentences in discourse and the contributions they make to coherence have been studied by Hoey (1983, 1994). In one study, he presented over 200 undergraduates with the following sentences, which had been jumbled up from their original order, and asked them to reorder the sentences to make a coherent passage. You might like to see whether you can place the sentences in their original order by numbering the brackets.

[ ] In England, however, the tungsten-tipped spikes would tear the thin tarmac surfaces of our roads to pieces as soon as the protective layer of snow or ice melted.

[ ] Road maintenance crews try to reduce the danger of skidding by scattering sand upon the road surface.

[ ] We therefore have to settle for the method described above as the lesser of two evils.

[ ] Their spikes grip the icy surfaces and enable the motorist to corner safely where non-spiked tyres would be disastrous.

[ ] Its main drawback is that if there are fresh snowfalls the whole process has to be repeated, and if the snowfalls continue, it becomes increasingly ineffective in providing some kind of grip for tyres.

[ ] These tyres prevent most skidding and are effective in the extreme weather conditions as long as the roads are regularly cleared of loose snow.

[ ] Such a measure is generally adequate for our very brief snowfalls.

[ ] Whenever there is snow in England, some of the country roads may have black ice.

[ ] In Norway, where there may be snow and ice for nearly seven months of the year, the law requires that all cars be fitted with special spiked tyres.

[ ] Motorists coming suddenly upon stretches of black ice may find themselves skidding off the road.

Hoey 1983:4

The results demonstrated that there was close agreement between the students as to what was an acceptable ordering of the sentences. In addition, when students did provide an order that differed from the original, the differences were limited to only a small number of variations. The order in which these sentences originally appeared was as follows: 8, 10, 2, 7, 5, 9, 6, 4, 1, 3.

What is it about the sentences that enables the competent reader to order them into a coherent passage? According to Hoey, it is the existence within the sentences of certain "text-forming devices." Most of the sentences can be connected to preceding ones by what are called anaphoric or "backward pointing" devices, for example *such, its, this.* The meaning of these words can only be determined by words or phrases in the preceding sentences. The remaining sentences are linked by the simple repetition of words and phrases (Hoey 1983: 6).

These "text-forming devices" are presented in Figure 4.1.

From studies such as these, it has been argued that the difference between coherent pieces of discourse (such as Extract 2) and disconnected sentences (such as Extract 3) is to be found in these words and phrases, which serve to connect each sentence with one or more of the sentences that come before it.

However, that is not the end of the story. As we shall see, in addition to what we might call "linguistic knowledge," that is, knowledge of how sentences are formed internally, and combined with each other externally, there is also "nonlinguistic knowledge," that is knowledge of the subject matter or content of the text in question. Later, we shall consider evidence that suggests that subject matter knowledge plays an important part in enabling the reader (or listener) to interpret texts. We shall also look at the views of a number of linguists who disagree with the idea that it is these connecting words and phrases that create discourse.

Sentence 8		black ice
Sentence 10	black ice	skidding
Sentence 2	skidding	scattering sand on the road surface
Sentence 7	such a measure	
Sentence 5	Its	
Sentence 9		tyres
Sentence 6	these tyres	
Sentence 4	Their	spikes
Sentence 1	spikes	
Sentence 3	method described above	

Figure 4.1   Text-forming devices in the Hoey sentences

From what I have already said, it would seem that discourse can be defined as a stretch of language consisting of several sentences that are perceived as being related in some way. In the next section, we shall see that sentences can be related, not only in terms of the ideas they share, but also in terms of the jobs they perform within the discourse, that is, in terms of their functions.

CREATING COHESION

In the preceding section, we saw that coherent texts (that is, sequences of sentences or utterances that seem to "hang together") contain what were called "text-forming devices." These are words and phrases that enable the writer or speaker to establish relationships across sentence or utterance boundaries, and that help to tie the sentences in a text together. In this section we shall look at these text-forming devices in greater detail.

The most comprehensive description and analysis of these devices is to be found in Halliday and Hasan (1976). They identified five different types of cohesion. These are reference, substitution, ellipsis, conjunction, and lexical cohesion. In Halliday (1985) these have been further refined and the five categories have been reduced to four, with substitution being seen as a subcategory of ellipsis.

The different types of cohesion to be discussed in this section are set out in the following figure. In each instance, the underlined words can only be interpreted with reference to prior information.

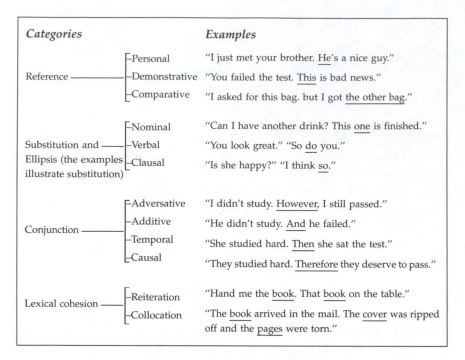

Categories		Examples
Reference	Personal	"I just met your brother. He's a nice guy."
	Demonstrative	"You failed the test. This is bad news."
	Comparative	"I asked for this bag. but I got the other bag."
Substitution and Ellipsis (the examples illustrate substitution)	Nominal	"Can I have another drink? This one is finished."
	Verbal	"You look great." "So do you."
	Clausal	"Is she happy?" "I think so."
Conjunction	Adversative	"I didn't study. However, I still passed."
	Additive	"He didn't study. And he failed."
	Temporal	"She studied hard. Then she sat the test."
	Causal	"They studied hard. Therefore they deserve to pass."
Lexical cohesion	Reiteration	"Hand me the book. That book on the table."
	Collocation	"The book arrived in the mail. The cover was ripped off and the pages were torn."

Figure 4.2 Cohesion in English

◆ REFERENCE

If a single sentence is taken out of context and presented in isolation, it is likely to contain elements that are difficult, if not impossible, to interpret. Consider the following fragment:

> He is near the end of the *Cape Fear* shoot, in front of a grocer's stand just outside Fort Lauderdale, Florida. . . . He used to have Armani make his jeans, but he felt guilty wearing them.

Who is this mysterious figure on the outskirts of Fort Lauderdale, who suffers guilt over the wearing of jeans by a particular designer? In the above fragment, the pronoun *he* is uninterpretable. However, if we have access to the context in which the sentence appears, the question is quite straightforward.

> Martin Scorsese is killing time, waiting for the sun to go behind a cloud so the next shot will match the last one. He is near the end of the *Cape Fear* shoot, in front of a grocer's stand just outside Fort Lauderdale, Florida. With him are Nick Nolte, Jessica Lange and Juliette Lewis, playing a married couple and their daughter fleeing from a psycho. Scorsese's

hand rarely leaves the side pocket of his custom-made jeans, where he works his watch chain like worry beads. He used to have Armani make his jeans, but he felt guilty wearing them.

The Australian magazine, December 21–22, 1991

In the above text the words *Martin Scorsese, he, him, his, he, his, he, his,* and *he* all refer to a single individual whose identity is established in the opening sentence. The subsequent items can only be interpreted with reference to the initial phrase of sentence one. This type of device is known as *cohesive reference.*

Halliday and Hasan identify three types of cohesive reference: personal, demonstrative, and comparative reference. Personal reference items, such as those in the above text, are realized by pronouns and determiners, and, as in the above text, they serve to identify individuals and objects that are named at some other point in the text. *Demonstrative reference* is realised by determiners and adverbs. This class of reference items can represent a single word or phrase, or much longer chunks of text ranging across several paragraphs or even several pages. *Comparative reference* is realized through adjectives and adverbs and serves to compare items within a text in terms of identity or similarity. These various devices enable the writer or speaker to make multiple references to people and things within a text. Examples of each type are provided below. (The first part of the referential relationship is <u>underlined,</u> the second is in **bold.**)

Personal Reference:
<u>Roni Size</u> peers down from the top floor of a midtown Manhattan hotel at a skyscraper across the street. 'You could fit the whole of Bristol in that,' **he** exclaims. (*Rolling Stone* magazine, Issue 775, December 1997).

Demonstrative Reference:
Roni Size peers down from the top floor of a midtown Manhattan hotel at <u>a skyscraper across the street</u>. 'You could fit the whole of Bristol in **that,**' he exclaims. (*Rolling Stone* magazine, Issue 775, December 1997).

Comparative Reference:
A: Would you like <u>these seats</u>?
B: No, as a matter of fact, I'd like **the other seats**.

These devices exist in both spoken and written discourse, as the following conversation illustrates. The cohesive devices in the extract are featured in **bold.**

A: **That'**s a funny looking **bottle**.
B: Yes, **it** is, isn't **it**. **It'**s **beautiful**. **Beer'**s nice **too**.

A: Oh, gosh, **that's** **lovely**. Where'd you buy **that**?
B: Oh, there's a little **bottle shop** in the city called the **Wine** . . .
City Wines. maybe we'll go **there** tomorrow and have a look.
A: **That'd** be good. I'd love to keep **this bottle**. Wish we could keep **it**.

Nunan, 1993

There are two different ways in which reference items can function within a text. They can refer back to previously mentioned entities and states of affairs (as in the above examples), or they can refer to things that are to come. References that point backwards are known as "anaphoric," while those that point forward are known as "cataphoric." While anaphoric reference reminds readers or listeners of what has gone before, cataphoric reference points them forward. It therefore draws them further into the text in order to identify the elements to which the items refer. In the conversation above, the initial *that* serves to point the listener forward. Authors sometimes employ cataphoric reference for dramatic effect, as in the following extract from the beginning of a novel by Tom Wolfe, and the use of forward-pointing reference items entices us to keep reading to find out who "the others" are, and where "out there" is.

> Within five minutes, or ten minutes, no more than that, three of the others had called her on the telephone to ask her if she had heard that something had happened out there.
> "Jane, this is Alice. Listen, I just got a call from Betty, and she said she heard that something had happened out there. Have you heard anything?" That was the way they phrased it, call after call. She picked up the telephone and began relaying this same message to some of the others.
>
> *Wolfe, 1979*

◆ SUBSTITUTION AND ELLIPSIS

In their 1976 work on cohesion, Halliday and Hasan deal with substitution and ellipsis separately, although they point out that these two types of cohesion are essentially the same. Ellipsis is described as a form of substitution in which the original item is replaced by zero. In a later publication Halliday (1985) combines substitution and ellipsis into a single category.

There are three types of substitution: nominal, verbal, and clausal substitution. Examples of each are as follows:

Nominal Substitution:
I'll get you some more bread rolls. These **ones** are stale. (*ones* = bread rolls)

Verbal Substitution:
A: I think you work too hard.
B: So **do** you! (*do* = work too hard)

Clausal Substitution:
A: Are we going to land soon?
B: I think **so**. (*so* = we're going to land soon)

In each of these examples, part of the preceding text has been replaced by *ones, do,* and *so,* respectively (these replacements are indicated in parentheses). Each of these words can only be interpreted with respect to what has gone before.

Ellipsis occurs when some essential structural element is omitted from a sentence or clause and can only be recovered by referring to an element in the preceding text. Consider the following discourse fragment and comprehension question.

> Mary: "I prefer the green."
> Question: Select the correct alternative: Mary prefers the green:
> (a) hat, (b) dress, (c) shoes.

As it stands, the question is impossible to answer. However, if we know what was said before, it becomes a relatively straightforward matter to answer the question.

> Sylvia: I like the blue hat.
> Mary: I prefer the green.

As with substitution, there are three types of ellipsis: nominal, verbal, and clausal ellipsis. Examples of each of these follow (the point at which material has been omitted from the second sentence of each text is marked by (0)). In each example, the second sentence or utterance can only be interpreted with reference to the one that precedes it.

Nominal Ellipsis:
My kids play an awful lot of sport. Both (0) are incredibly energetic.

Verbal Ellipsis:
A: Have you been working?
B: Yes, I have (0).

Clausal Ellipsis:
A: Why'd you only set three places? Paul's staying for dinner, isn't he?
B: Is he? He didn't tell me (0).

These elements are all cohesive in that they require other aspects of the discoursal contexts in which they occur to be present in order to be interpretable. Without context, interpretation is impossible.

♦ CONJUNCTION

Conjunction differs from reference, substitution, and ellipsis because it is not a device for reminding the reader of previously mentioned items. In other words, it is not what linguists call an *anaphoric relation*. However, it is a cohesive device because it signals relationships that can only be fully understood through reference to other parts of the text. There are four different types of conjunction, and they signal the following semantic relationships: temporality, causality, addition, and adversity. Examples of each type of relationship follow:

Adversative:
"I'm afraid I'll be home late tonight. <u>However,</u> I won't have to go in until late tomorrow."
"I quite like being chatted up when I'm sitting in a bar having a drink. <u>On the other hand</u>, I hate it if . . . you know . . . if the guy starts to make a nuisance of himself."

(The relationships signaled by *however* and *on the other hand* are adversative because the information in the second sentence of each text mitigates or qualifies the information in the first.)

Additive:
"From a marketing viewpoint, the popular tabloid encourages the reader to read the whole page instead of choosing stories. <u>And</u> isn't that what any publisher wants?"

(Here *and* signals the presentation of additional information.)

Temporal:
"Brick tea is a blend that has been compressed into a cake. It is taken mainly by the minority groups in China. <u>First</u>, it is ground to a dust. <u>Then</u> it is usually cooked in milk."

(Temporal relationships exist when the events in a text are related in terms of the timing of their occurrence.)

Causal:
Chinese tea is becoming increasingly popular in restaurants, and even in coffee shops. This is <u>because</u> of the growing belief that it has several health giving properties.

(In this final type of conjunction, the relationship is one of cause and consequence.)

◆ LEXICAL COHESION

The final category of cohesion is *lexical cohesion*. Lexical cohesion occurs when two words in a text are semantically related in some way. In other words, they are related in terms of their meaning. In Halliday and Hasan (1976), the two major categories of lexical cohesion are *reiteration* and *collocation*. Reiteration includes repetition, a synonym or near synonym, superordinate, and general words.

Repetition:
What we lack in a <u>newspaper</u> is what we should get. In a word, a "popular" <u>newspaper</u> may be the winning ticket.

Synonym:
You could try reversing the car up the <u>slope</u>. The <u>incline</u> isn't all that steep.

Superordinate:
<u>Pneumonia</u> has arrived with the cold and wet conditions. <u>The illness</u> is striking everyone from infants to the elderly.

General Word:
A: Did you try the <u>steamed buns</u>?
B: Yes, I didn't like the <u>things</u> much.

The second underlined word or phrase in each of these texts refers back to the previously mentioned entity. Reiteration thus fulfills a similar semantic function as cohesive reference.

The second type of lexical cohesion is collocation. Collocation can cause major problems for discourse analysis because it includes all those items in a text that are semantically related. In some cases this makes it difficult to decide for certain whether a cohesive relationship exists or not. In the extract below, we could say that the following items are examples of lexical collocation because they all belong to the scientific field of biology.

plants . . . synthesize . . . organic . . . inorganic . . . green plants
. . . energy . . . sunlight . . . plants . . . energy . . . green pigment
. . . chlorophyll . . . photosynthesis . . . light synthesis . . . self
feeding . . . autotrophic

Plants characteristically synthesize complex organic substances from simple inorganic raw materials. In green plants, the energy of this process is sunlight. The plants can use this energy because they possess the green pigment chlorophyll. Photosynthesis or "light synthesis," is a "self-feeding," or autotrophic process.

Animals, on the other hand, must obtain complex organic substances by eating plants and other animals. The reason for this is that they lack chlorophyll. Among these "other feeders" or phagotrophs, are "liquid feeders" or osmotrophs. Whereas phagotrophic organisms take in solid and often living food, osmotrophic ones absorb or suck up liquid food. This is usually from dead or rotting organisms.

Pearson 1978

Most linguists who have written about cohesion admit that lexical collocation is a problem, and some refuse to deal with it because of this. Martin (1981: 1) points out that, while there are problems in defining collocation, "its contribution to coherence in text is so significant that it cannot be ignored." The problems arise because, in contrast with other categories, lexical cohesion is realized through open rather than closed class items. *Closed lexical items* include pronouns, conjunctions, prepositions, and other grammatical categories, membership of which is fixed. In contrast, there is no limit to the items that can realize lexical relationships. This makes the establishment of lexical sets of items that regularly co-occur an extremely tentative business as new items will constantly be added to the sets.

An additional problem is the fact that many lexical relationships are text- as well as context-bound. This means that words and phrases that are related in one text may not be related in another. For example, the terms *neighbor* and *scoundrel* are not related at all. However, in the following text they are synonyms.

> My neighbor has just let one of his trees fall into my garden.
> And the scoundrel refuses to pay for the damage he has caused.

Given this text-bound nature of many lexical relationships, it is impossible to develop a finite list of relatable lexical items in English. At best, such a list could provide only a partial analysis of lexical cohesion in English.

Despite its problematic nature, lexical cohesion is, in many ways, the most interesting of all the cohesive categories. The background knowledge of the reader or listener plays a more obvious role in the perception of lexical relationships than in the preception of other types of cohesion. Collocational patterns, for example, will only be perceived by someone who has the requisite knowledge for the subject at hand. The text-bound nature of many lexical relations, and the role of the language user in perceiving these, creates a problem for the linguist concerned with providing a semantic account of lexical cohesion. However, concordancing programs and the creation of massive computerized text databases such as the Collins Cobuild database at the University of Birmingham in the United Kingdom are beginning to provide insights into the co-occurrence of words that are useful for researchers and teachers

One problem that arises in analyzing these relations in text has to do with how many "steps" away an item can be in a taxonomy and still contribute to cohesion. For example, *rose* and *flower* seem more closely related than *rose* and *plant*, and though one would accept *mosquito* and *insect* one wonders about *mosquito* and *animal*. Are the latter items too many steps apart in the taxonomy to be related?

As I have already suggested, text or context-free taxonomies can only be partial, and the test of whether many items are cohesive or not will be determined by the text in which they occur. In addition, our ability to identify a collocational relationship will depend on our familiarity with the content of a text.

Recent work by Hoey (1991) has advanced our understanding of lexical cohesion. Hoey argues that lexical cohesion is the single most important form of cohesion, accounting for something like forty percent of cohesive ties in texts. His work is too complex for us to deal with in any detail here. However, it is worth considering his central idea.

Hoey argues that various lexical relationships between the different sentences making up a text provide a measure of the cohesiveness of the text. The centrality and importance to the text of any particular sentence within the text will be determined by the number of lexical connections that sentence has to other sentences in the text. He illustrates this point with an analysis of the following text.

DRUG CRAZED GRIZZLIES

A drug known to produce violent reactions in humans has been used for sedating grizzly bears *Ursus arctos* in Montana, USA, according to a report in The New York Times. After one bear, known to be a peacable animal, killed and ate a camper in an unprovoked attack, scientists discovered it had been tranquillized 11 times with phencyclidine or 'angel dust', which causes hallucinations and sometimes gives the user an irrational feeling of destructive power. Many wild bears have become 'garbage junkies', feeding from dumps around human developments. To avoid potentially dangerous clashes between them and humans, scientists are trying to rehabilitate the animals by drugging them and releasing them in uninhabited areas. Although some biologists deny that the mind-altering drug was responsible for uncharacteristic behaviour of this particular bear, no research has been done into the effects of giving grizzly bears or other mammals repeated doses of phencyclidine.

BBC Wildlife, *1984, 2, 3: 160*

Hoey's analysis consists, first, of counting the number of repetition links between the different sentences in the text. In the above text, sentence 1 has four links with the sentences 2, 3, 4, and 5. These are highlighted below:

1. produce	humans	used	sedating grizzly bears
2. bear	tranquilized	user	
3. bears	human		
4. them	humans	animals	drugging
5. drug responsible for		grizzly bears	

(Note that while *known to* appears in both sentences 1 and 2, they are not treated as repetition as they refer to different events.)

Using this procedure, it is possible to identify the number of connections between each of the sentences in a text. Hoey uses a more complicated version of the procedure to determine the cohesiveness of a text, and also to indicate the degree to which different sentences contribute to the cohesiveness of the text.

It is important for anyone involved in the teaching of reading and writing to have some understanding of cohesion and the ways in which it serves to make textual relationships explicit. As we shall see, learning to read and write involves developing control of these various devices, and it has been shown that young children can benefit from explicit instruction in using these in reading and writing.

♦ RHETORICAL PATTERNS IN TEXT

Textual coherence is also related to the ways in which information is printed in a text. In his book on patterns of organization in texts, Hoey (1983), argues that the ordering of information in discourse can be accounted for in terms of certain rhetorical relationships such as cause–consequence, problem–solution. He uses the following four sentences to illustrate the ways in which these relationships function in discourse.

> *I opened fire.*
> *I was on sentry duty.*
> *I beat off the attack.*
> *(and) I saw the enemy approaching.*

These four sentences can be sequenced in twenty-four different ways. However, not all of these sequences will be acceptable as coherent discourse, for example "I beat off the attack. I opened fire. I saw the enemy approaching. I was on sentry duty." In fact the twenty-four different versions could probably be graded on a continuum from completely unacceptable to completely acceptable. According to Hoey, only one sequence is completely acceptable: "I was on sentry duty. I saw the enemy approaching. I opened fire. I beat off the attack."

Constraints on the ordering of information within a text, which determine levels of acceptability, are due in part to the relationships that exist between these elements. In the texts we have been considering, there are two particular types of relationship. These are cause–consequence and instrument–achievement relationships.

I was on sentry duty.

cause → I saw the enemy approaching. → consequence → I opened fire.

instrument → I opened fire. → achievement → I beat off the attack.

There are in fact grammatical devices that can be employed to change the sequencing of the information in the text in acceptable ways. These include subordination ("While I was on sentry duty, I opened fire, because I saw the enemy approaching. I (thereby) beat off the attack.") and conjunction ("I opened fire because I saw the enemy approaching when I was on sentry duty. By this means I beat off the attack.").

MAKING SENSE

So far, we have looked at some of the linguistic elements that help to establish the coherence of language. However, these devices do not always guarantee that a speaker or writer will be understood. Nor does their absence mean that a speaker or writer will not be understood. Consider, for example, the following conversation.

> **A:** *Where's Rebecca?*
> **B:** *The rehearsals started tonight.*
> **A:** *Oh, OK.*

Although the conversational fragment does not contain any of the cohesive devices described earlier in the chapter, most people agree that it makes sense. (The verb *make* illustrates the active, constructive nature of the process, in which the reader or listener has to "work" to interpret the writer or speaker's meaning.) The above conversational fragment demonstrates that it is possible to have pieces of coherent discourse that do not contain overt cohesive links. It makes sense, because it is possible to create a context in which it fits together at a functional level.

Utterance	*Function*
A: *Where's Rebecca?*	Request
B: *The rehearsals started tonight.*	Explanation
A: *Oh, OK.*	Acceptance

In creating a meaningful context and identifying the functions of each utterance, coherence is established. As a result, the missing bits of conversation, which would make it cohesive as well as coherent, could be restored. Such a cohesive conversation might run as follows:

> **A:** *Where's Rebecca? I want to give her her allowance.*
> **B:** *She's out. You remember that she successfully auditioned for* The Jungle Book—*well, the rehearsals started tonight.*
> **A:** *Oh, OK. I'll leave the money here and she can get it when she comes home.*

The conversation works because, as competent users of the language we expect the function "request" to be followed by the function "explanation," in much the same way as we expect a transitive verb to be followed by an object. Initially, this insight led to the belief that discourse could be explained and predicted in the same way as sentences, in terms of rules that specified optional and obligatory conditions determining whether or not they were "well formed."

◆ FUNCTIONAL COHERENCE

It is certainly possible to identify regularly recurring patterns and elements within discourse, particularly within contexts such as the classroom, the courthouse, and the consulting room, where the communicative situation encourages highly predictable, even ritualistic use of language. It is also apparent in other contexts, particularly transactional encounters involving the exchange of goods and services. This is exemplified in the following extract.

> *Cabin attendant:* Are you having salad?
> Passenger: Yes, I am.
> *Cabin attendant:* Caesar or regular?
> Passenger: Regular.
> *Cabin attendant:* Would you like dressing on that?
> Passenger: Yes, please.
> *Cabin attendant:* Blue cheese or ranch?
> Passenger: Blue cheese, please.

The following extract is very different from the one above. Here, the speakers have to "negotiate" at certain points to ensure mutual understanding.

> **A:** *How do I get to Kensington Road?*
> **B:** *Well you go down Fullarton Road . . .*
> **A:** *. . . what, down Old Belair, and around . . . ?*
> **B:** *Yeah. And then you go straight . . .*
> **A:** *. . . past the hospital?*
> **B:** *Yeah, keep going straight, past the racecourse to the roundabout. You know the big roundabout?*
> **A:** *Yeah.*
> **B:** *And Kensington Road's off to the right.*
> **A:** *What, off the roundabout?*
> **B:** *Yeah.*
> **A:** *Right!*
>
> Nunan, 1993

In this extract, the negotiation done by the interlocutors pays off. This is not always the case when people converse, however. Cases of pragmatic failure, in which conversations and people fail one another, abound. This is illustrated in the following samples:

1. Context: the upper, nonsmoking deck of a 747 aircraft
    Passenger: I've been smoking for 28 years, and I gave up so I could travel up here.
    Cabin attendant: Sorry?
    Passenger: I said, I've been smoking for 28 years, and I gave up so I could sit up here.
    Cabin attendant: So?
    Passenger: So, I gave up smoking.
    Cabin attendant: What do you want?
    Passenger: I don't want anything. (Turns to partner). Well, I won't be traveling with this outfit again.

2. Context: at the end of a shift in a factory
    Native speaker: See you later.
    Non-native speaker: What time.
    Native speaker: What do you mean?

3. Context: during a coffee break at work
    A: *I have two tickets for the theatre tonight.*
    B: *Good for you. What are you going to see?*
    A: *Measure for Measure.*
    B: *Interesting play. Hope you enjoy it.*
    A: *Oh, so you're busy tonight. (Widdowson, 1984)*

4. Context: A is addressing her husband who is clearing out the garden shed.
    A: *Are you wearing gloves?*
    B: *No.*
    A: *What about the spiders?*
    B: *They're not wearing gloves either.*

5. Context: in an elementary school classroom
    A: *Tony, are you talking?*
    B: *Yes, I am.*
    A: *Don't be cheeky.*

6. Context: University of Hong Kong campus
    A: *Did you enjoy your Christmas?*
    B: *I was in Beijing.*

7. Context: overheard in the hallway at a conference
    It was just like whatever, exactly.

In none of these interactions is miscommunication caused by the interlocutors getting their linguistic facts wrong. The miscommunication occurs at the level of discourse. Communication breaks down because one person misinterprets the function of the other person's utterance.

In situation 1, the cabin attendant thought that the passenger wanted something (because this is typically why they are addressed by passengers), and assumed the discourse was part of a transactional encounter. In this case, however, the passenger was simply trying to engage in a piece of social interaction.

In situation 2, Speaker B, an immigrant worker, interprets "See you later" as an invitation. In many situations it would be. In this particular cultural context, however, it is a formulaic way of saying "Good-bye." I have been the victim of similar misinterpretations. The first time that someone in the United States said that they would "Check me later," my immediate reaction was to inquire why I should be subjected to scrutiny, whether it would be physical or painful, and why it was deemed necessary. On another occasion, when the person on the check-out desk of a hotel, someone I had never met before, told me she was "Missing me already," the possibility occurred that I might possess some sort of magnetic personality that had been hidden all these years.

In Situation 3, B, deliberately or otherwise, takes A's utterance as a statement of fact, rather than an invitation.

In 4, the husband, presumably in an attempt at humor, misinterprets the wife's utterance as a simple question rather than a warning.

In Situation 5, the schoolchild, perhaps deliberately, misinterprets the teacher's utterance as a question, when in fact it is a command.

What do these situations have in common? All of the participants are either native speakers of English or highly competent users of the language. It is not at the level of grammar or vocabulary that communication breaks down, but at a discoursal/functional level. Granted that grammar is a central, critical, element in functional communication, but it is not the only element. What we need, in teaching grammar, is a functional approach that demonstrates to learners, not only how structures are formed in English but why one form is to be preferred over another in a given context.

The second to last example underlines this point perfectly. It was part of a conversation I overheard on the University of Hong Kong campus shortly after Christmas. While I understood every word perfectly, as someone who had at that time never been to Beijing, I was unable to assign an functional value to the response "I was in Beijing," and had no idea whether the speaker enjoyed her Christmas or not. The final utterance was overheard in the hallway at a conference. The meaning escapes me entirely.

It is clear from these examples that interpreting discourse, and thus establishing coherence, is a matter of readers/listeners using their linguistic knowledge to relate the discourse world to entities, events, and states of affairs beyond the text itself. While any piece of language is ultimately interpretable with reference to extralinguistic context, it is going too far to conclude that the language itself is somehow irrelevant or unnecessary.

SPEECH ACTS

In the preceding section, we saw that explicit, cohesive links between utterances were insufficient to account for the coherence of discourse, that such coherence depends on the ability of the language users to recognize the functional role being played by different utterances within the discourse. In the next section, we shall look at the role of background knowledge in the interpretation of discourse. Before turning to the role of background knowledge, however, I should like to explore the issue of language functions, or speech acts, a little further. Speech acts are simply things people do through language, for example, "apologizing," "complaining," "instructing," "agreeing," and "warning." The term *speech act* was coined by the linguistic philosopher Austin (1962) and developed by another philosopher, Searle (1969). The essential insight developed by these philosophers was that, when using language, we not only make propositional statements about objects, entities, states of affairs, and so on, but we also fulfill functions such as requesting, denying, introducing, apologizing, and so on. Identifying the speech act being performed by a particular utterance can only be done if we know the context in which the utterance takes place. What the speaker actually wants to achieve in functional, communicative terms is known as the *illocutionary force* of the utterance.

However, as we also saw in the preceding section, functions are rarely explicitly marked on the surface of discourse. A given utterance or sentence can fulfill a multiplicity of functions, and these functions can very often only be recovered from the context in which the piece of language occurs.

During the seventies, some language specialists began to argue that teaching learners the formal elements of second and foreign languages was insufficient, that, following the work of people such as Austin and Searle, teachers should also teach language functions. Accordingly, language teachers began to incorporate the insights provided by speech act theory into teaching materials and procedures. The ability of a listener or reader to identify the function of a particular piece of language will often depend on how much he or she knows of the context in question. We shall look a little further at this in the next section.

BACKGROUND KNOWLEDGE

♦ INTERPRETING DISCOURSE

Earlier in the chapter, we looked at the debate over the nature of discourse coherence, and concluded that the language user's knowledge of language and also of content were needed for the interpretation of discourse. In this section, we look in greater detail at the ways in which things we know about the world assist us in the interpretation of discourse. The inadequacy of linguistic knowledge (that is, knowledge of the vocabulary, grammar and discourse features) for interpreting discourse is demonstrated by the following text.

```
If the balloons popped, the sound wouldn't be able to
carry since everything would be too far away from the
correct floor. A closed window would prevent the sound
from carrying, since most buildings tend to be well
insulated. Since the whole operation depends on a
steady flow of electricity, a break in the middle of
the wire would also cause problems. Of course, the
fellow could shout, but the human voice is not loud
enough to carry that far. An additional problem is
that a wire could break on the instrument. Then there
could be no accompaniment to the message. It is clear
that the best situation would involve less distance.
Then there would be fewer potential problems. With
face-to-face contact, the least number of things could
go wrong.
```

Most native speakers have no trouble comprehending the grammatical structures and vocabulary items in this story. Despite this, they have a great deal of trouble understanding what the text is all about, and even greater difficulty in providing an oral or written summary.

The passage is from a well-known study by Bransford and Johnson (1972) that demonstrated the importance of context and background information for the interpretation of discourse. They found that subjects who were asked to listen to the text and recall it had a great deal of difficulty. However, another group of subjects who were provided with a picture were able to recall virtually all of the text. This picture showed a man serenading his girlfriend. The girl was leaning out of the window of an apartment, and the sound was carried to her through some speakers that were suspended by a bunch of balloons.

The studies showed that discourse comprehension requires more than a knowledge of the words and grammatical structures used by the writer or speaker. It also requires the listener or reader to relate the content of the text to their knowledge of the world, that is, to entities, states of affairs, and so on that exist in the world outside the text.

This interaction between the world within the text and the world outside the text is exploited by writers in many different ways. For example, humorists and satirists often create fictional worlds that parallel the real world, and they obtain their humorous or satirical effect by juxtaposing the real and imaginary worlds. The following text illustrates this process. To someone unfamiliar with events in the former Soviet Union, the following text would make as little sense as the "serenade" text above.

> The former Comrade Chairman of the former Communist Party, former president of the former empire and former photo opportunity slogged up the last six flights of stairs to his office. The stairs were well worn, particularly in the centre of each step where two deep grooves commemorated the heel-marks of generations of politically incorrect thinkers who had been dragged to the basement by men with no necks. Later, they had been released as politically correct mulch. Somewhere in the basement was a room full of their hats, sorted and labelled. The former Comrade Chairman wondered what had happened to them. The former re-education staff had probably opened a shop, he decided. There wasn't much call for trained interrogators who could correct political error while forcing the miscreants' kneecaps down their throats, outside the more progressive Western universities. He hoped the shop was doing well. Everyone needed a hat, if only to gather up stray potatoes down at the shunting yards, and it was just the kind of entrepreneurial spirit he knew lurked beneath the coarse woollen exterior of the former Soviet people, even the horrible ones.
>
> *Cook, 1991: 194*

With the insight that there is more to comprehending discourse than knowing the words on the page, have come attempts to provide theoretical models that can explain the ways in which our knowledge of the world guides our efforts to comprehend discourse. Much of this work has been carried out by researchers in the field of artificial intelligence. Their aim is to develop programs that will enable computers to comprehend and produce natural discourse. Terms used to explain how we make sense of the world include *frames, scripts, scenarios,* and *schemata.*

◆ SCHEMA THEORY

The most widely used term in the psychological and applied linguistics literature is *schema,* a term that was coined as long ago as 1932 by the psychologist Bartlett in his classic study of how human memory works. Like frame theory, schema theory suggests that the knowledge we carry around in our heads is organized into interrelated patterns. These are constructed from all our previous experiences of a given aspect of the experiential world, and they enable us to make predictions about future experience. Given the fact that making sense of discourse is a process of using both our linguistic knowledge and our content knowledge, these schemata or "mental film scripts" are extremely important.

The central insight provided by researchers using mental models such as frame and schema theory is that meaning does not come neatly prepackaged in aural and written texts. Widdowson (1978) has suggested that texts are little more than elaborate "signposts" to the speaker or writer's original meanings, and that the reader or listener must use their linguistic and content knowledge to reconstruct the original meanings of the creator of the discourse.

In a later work, Widdowson (1984) provides a novel reinterpretation of schema theory from the perspective of discourse comprehension. He argues that there are two dimensions or levels to any given discourse, a systemic level and a schematic level. The systemic level includes the reader or listener's linguistic knowledge, while the schematic level relates to background content knowledge. In making sense of a given piece of discourse, we try and match up our own schematic knowledge to that of the writer or speaker. In doing so, we have to interpret what we read or hear. (Cicourel [1973] was one of the first researchers to point out the importance of interpretation to comprehension. He showed that we use procedures of interpretation to supply meanings that do not actually appear in the discourse itself.)

Widdowson (1984) has shown how these interpretative procedures might work in making sense of discourse. He argues that a major task for someone listening to or reading a piece of discourse is to keep track of the various things and events that are referred to within the discourse. In doing so, they can make use of the various cohesive devices that we looked at in Chapter 2. It is often assumed that the ability to track cohesive relationships through a text is a fairly straightforward business. Consider the following text:

```
I saw John yesterday. He gave me his hat.
```

Most people would assume that the hat belongs to John. However, Widdowson demonstrates that the ability to establish and track such relationships often involves more than simple identification. There are cases in which we need to interpret what we see or hear. Widdowson illustrates this point through a number of rather bizarre texts, the first of which is as follows (as you read it, consider what the underlined reference items refer to).

```
    Statistical probability was discovered in a tea-
pot. A postman saw it there and connected it to a
petrol pump. He was wearing silk pajamas at the time.
They were old and dusty.
```

As Widdowson rightly points out, while the reader might be surprised by this surrealistic piece of prose, there is no difficulty in identifying *it* with *statistical probability,* *he* with *postman,* and *there* with *teapot.* Other cases are more difficult. What, for instance, does *it* refer to in the following text?

```
    Statistical probability was discovered in a tea-
pot. A postman saw it and connected it to a petrol
pump. It was old and dusty.
```

Determining what *it* refers to now becomes more difficult as there are two possible antecedents for the first *it* (*statistical probability* and *a teapot*), and three for the third (*statistical probability, a teapot,* and *a petrol pump*). Because we cannot use our background knowledge to help us, we are unable to say what *it* refers to.

Consider now a third text:

```
    Statistical probability was discovered in a tea-
pot. A postman rinsed it out. He had no idea what it
was of course.
```

In this text we can appeal to our knowledge of the world to determine what *it* refers to. We know that teapots are occasionally rinsed out, and therefore assume that the first *it* refers to *teapot*. As we also assume that postmen are familiar with teapots, we would assign the second *it* to statistical probability. The point of all this is that in many cases discourse processing depends, not only on the identification of cohesive relationships, but also on our knowledge of the world.

We engage in these interpretative procedures more frequently than might be imagined. Consider the following textual fragment from a popular magazine.

```
    I believe all children have a mystical empathy
with nature. We come into this world 'trailing clouds
of glory' as the poet Wordsworth put it.
```

Clyne 1991

Here, there are no direct links between the first sentence and the second, and so we need to use our background knowledge to create the links and establish a relationship between the metaphorical phrase "clouds of glory," and the mystical empathy that children are claimed to have with nature. Most native speakers have little difficulty in identifying the relationship.

◆ BACKGROUND KNOWLEDGE AND FUNCTIONAL INTERPRETATION

So far, I have discussed the ways in which listeners and readers might need to use their background knowledge to work out what various reference items might refer to. Here we are dealing with the propositional level of language. Let us now look at how background knowledge might help us interpret discourse on a functional level. When studying functions, the question is not "what is the speaker/writer trying to tell us about events and things in the world?" but "what is the speaker/writer trying to achieve through language?" Once again, Widdowson provides a lively piece of (fictional) interaction to demonstrate the points he wishes to make.

> **A:** *I have two tickets to the theater tonight.*
> **B:** *My examination is tomorrow.*
> **A:** *Pity.*

What are our fictional speakers trying to do here? According to Widdowson, there are implicit assumptions on both sides that A's first statement is an invitation. B's response, which, on the surface, has little to do with A's statement, is taken as a refusal of the invitation. This is recognized in A's final remark. Of course, the encounter may not have gone quite as smoothly as this. Consider the following exchange, in which A's opening gambit is intended as an invitation. What do you think the speakers are trying to do in the other utterances in the exchange?

> **A:** *I have two tickets for the theater tonight.*
> **B:** *Good for you. What are you going to see?*
> **A:** Measure for Measure.
> **B:** *Interesting play. Hope you enjoy it.*

The negotiation is not going to plan, and A has to renegotiate to return to his original discourse strategy.

> **A:** *Look, are you free tonight?*
> **B:** *I'm not sure, why?*

The message is still not getting across, so he tries again.

> **A:** *Well, I'd like to invite you to come to the theater with me.*
> **B:** *Well, actually my examination is tomorrow.*

Now Widdowson allows A to be obtuse.

> **A:** *I know, so is mine. What's that got to do with it?*
> > *Widdowson 1983: 44–45*

Notice how these negotiating procedures depend crucially on the participants knowing what each utterance stands for functionally (that is as "invitation," "polite refusal," etc.).

PEDAGOGICAL IMPLICATIONS

In the rest of the chapter, I shall spell out some of the practical implications of the ideas on language set out here. These are taken up and elaborated on in Section 3 of the book, where I shall focus more closely on pedagogical concerns.

There are many different ways of activating organic learning, and many traditional exercise types can, with a slight twist, be brought into harmony with this approach, particularly if they are introduced into the classroom as exploratory and collaborative tasks. (For examples, see Wajnryb's [1990] "grammar dictation" tasks, and Woods's [1995] gap and cloze exercises.)

In my own classroom, I activate an organic approach by:

teaching language as a set of choices;
encouraging learners to become active explorers of language;
encouraging learners to explore relationships between grammar and discourse.

◆ TEACHING LANGUAGE AS A SET OF CHOICES

As indicated in the preceding section, one of the reasons why it is difficult to give learners hard-and-fast grammatical rules is because once grammar is pressed into communicative service the choice, in many instances, will be determined by the meanings learners themselves wish to make. Ultimately, the answer to the question "Which form should I use here?" will be: "It depends on the message you wish to convey." For example, if learners wish to give equal weight to two pieces of information, then they can present the information in a single sentence using coordination. If they wish to give one of these pieces of information greater weight, then they can use subordination.

In order to help learners see that alternative grammatical realizations exist and enable them to make different kinds of meanings, and that ultimately it is up to them to decide exactly what they wish to convey, I often begin my language courses with "ice-breaker" tasks such as the following.

[Note: Each of the following sentences is typed on to a separate piece of paper. The pieces of paper are randomly distributed around the class.]

Task 1:

Without looking at another student's paper, find the person who has a sentence or question containing information that is almost identical to your own.

1. a. In his 1925 study, Smith asserts that grammar and discourse are closely linked.
   b. In his 1925 study, Smith asserted that grammar and discourse are closely linked.
2. a. Mr. Patten, a former governor of Hong Kong, was warmly greeted when he arrived in London.
   b. Mr. Patten, the former governor of Hong Kong, was warmly greeted when he arrived in London.
3. a. You'll be late tonight, won't you?
   b. You'll be late tonight, will you?
4. a. The team are playing in Nagoya, tonight.
   b. The team is playing in Nagoya, tonight.
5. a. You should call your parents, tonight.
   b. You could call your parents, tonight.
6. a. The passive voice should be avoided in academic writing.
   b. Academic writers should use the passive voice.
7. a. I'm going to study for the exam tonight.
   b. I'll study for the exam tonight.
8. a. Alice saw a white rabbit.
   b. Alice saw the white rabbit.
9. a. My brother lives in New York, but he is visiting me in Hong Kong at present.
   b. My brother, who lives in Hong Kong, is visiting me in Hong Kong at present.
   c. My brother, who is visiting me in Hong Kong at present, lives in New York.

Task 2:

Decide (a) whether or not one of the items is ungrammatical, and (b) whether there is any difference in the meaning of the two (or three) items.

♦ ENCOURAGING LEARNERS TO BECOME ACTIVE EXPLORERS OF LANGUAGE

By exploiting this principle, teachers can encourage their students to take greater responsibility for their own learning. (A striking example of this principle, in an ESL setting, can be found in Heath, 1992.) Students can bring samples of language into class, and they can work together to formulate their own hypotheses about language structures and functions. I sometimes give my students a Polaroid camera, and get them to walk around the campus and take photographs, either of signs and public notices that they believe are ungrammatical, or of signs that they think are interesting, or puzzling, or which contain language they would like to know more about. They bring the photos back to class, and these become the raw material for our next language lesson. In fact, the last time I did this, the lesson culminated in the students writing a letter to the office responsible for signs and public notices pointing out the errors and suggesting amendments to them.

Classrooms in which the principle of active exploration has been activated will be characterized by an inductive approach to learning in which learners are given access to data and are provided with structured opportunities to work out rules, principles, and applications for themselves. The idea here is that information will be more deeply processed and stored if learners are given an opportunity to work things out for themselves, rather than simply being given the principle or rule. (For excellent, practical examples, see Woods, 1995.)

The example on page 140 is taken from a unit of work from the *ATLAS* textbook series. In the task chain preceding these language focus exercises, students carry out a series of tasks based on authentic spoken and written advertisements for a range of goods and services. In the authentic listening and reading texts, modifying words are particularly salient, and these become the focus of the language focus exercises. Students work through a series of exercises focusing on this particular feature, and are then asked to formulate a rule or principle relating to word order.

◆ ENCOURAGING LEARNERS TO EXPLORE RELATIONSHIPS BETWEEN FORM, MEANING, AND USE

Tasks exploiting this principle show learners that form, meaning, and use are inextricably interlinked, and that grammatical choices (for example, whether to combine two pieces of information using coordination or subordination) will be determined by considerations of context and purpose. Such tasks help learners to explore the functioning of grammar in context, and assist them in using their developing grammatical competence in the creation of coherent discourse.

Consider the following pieces of information about nursing.

◆ The nursing process is a systematic method.
◆ The nursing process is a rational method.
◆ The method involves planning nursing care.
◆ The method involves providing nursing care.

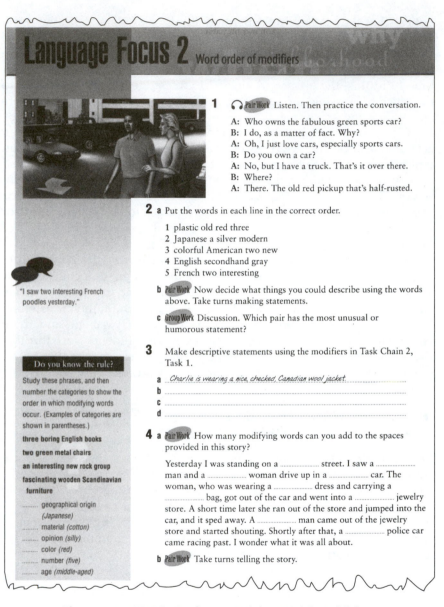

Language Focus 2 Word order of modifiers

1 🎧 **Pair Work** Listen. Then practice the conversation.

A: Who owns the fabulous green sports car?
B: I do, as a matter of fact. Why?
A: Oh, I just love cars, especially sports cars.
B: Do you own a car?
A: No, but I have a truck. That's it over there.
B: Where?
A: There. The old red pickup that's half-rusted.

2 a Put the words in each line in the correct order.

1 plastic old red three
2 Japanese a silver modern
3 colorful American two new
4 English secondhand gray
5 French two interesting

"I saw two interesting French poodles yesterday."

b **Pair Work** Now decide what things you could describe using the words above. Take turns making statements.

c **Group Work** Discussion. Which pair has the most unusual or humorous statement?

3 Make descriptive statements using the modifiers in Task Chain 2, Task 1.

a *Charlie is wearing a nice, checked, Canadian wool jacket.*
b ....
c ....
d ....

Do you know the rule?

Study these phrases, and then number the categories to show the order in which modifying words occur. (Examples of categories are shown in parentheses.)

three boring English books

two green metal chairs

an interesting new rock group

fascinating wooden Scandinavian furniture

.... geographical origin
(Japanese)
.... material (cotton)
.... opinion (silly)
.... color (red)
.... number (five)
.... age (middle-aged)

4 a **Pair Work** How many modifying words can you add to the spaces provided in this story?

Yesterday I was standing on a .... street. I saw a .... man and a .... woman drive up in a .... car. The woman, who was wearing a .... dress and carrying a .... bag, got out of the car and went into a .... jewelry store. A short time later she ran out of the store and jumped into the car, and it sped away. A .... man came out of the jewelry store and started shouting. Shortly after that, a .... police car came racing past. I wonder what it was all about.

b **Pair Work** Take turns telling the story.

Figure 4-2 *ATLAS* - Book 3, © Heinle & Heinle Publishers

These can be packaged into a single sentence by using grammatical resources of various kinds.

> *"The nursing process is a systematic rational method of planning and providing nursing care."*

Task 1

Using the above sentence as the topic sentence in a paragraph, produce a coherent paragraph incorporating the following information (you can rearrange the order in which the information is presented):

◆ The goal of the nursing process is to identify a client's health status.
◆ The goal of the nursing process is to identify a client's health care problems.
◆ A client's health care problems may be actual or potential.
◆ The goal of the nursing process is to establish plans to meet a client's health care needs.
◆ The goal of the nursing process is to deliver specific nursing interventions.
◆ Nursing interventions are designed to meet a client's health care needs.
◆ The nurse must collaborate with the client to carry out the nursing process effectively.
◆ The nurse must collaborate with the client to individualize approaches to each person's particular needs.
◆ The nurse must collaborate with other members of the health care team to carry out the nursing process effectively.
◆ The nurse must collaborate with other members of the health care team to individualize approaches to each person's particular needs.

Task 2

Compare your text with that of another student. Make a note of similarities and differences. Can you explain the differences? Do different ways of combining information lead to differences of meaning?

Task 3

Now revise your text and compare it with the original. [This is supplied separately to the students.]

[Adapted from D. Nunan. 1996. *Academic Writing for Nursing Students*. The English Centre, University of Hong Kong.]

◆ CONCLUSION

In this chapter, I have attempted to articulate a view of language that is consistent with what we currently know about language learning and use. In the first part of the chapter, I drew on the research described in Chapter 2 to argue the case in favor of an organic view of language acquisition. I then explored in some detail a view of language that is consistent with this organic view. This is a view of language in context. In the body of this section, I teased out some of the complex links and interrelationships between grammar, discourse, context, and background knowledge. In the final section, I argued that a pedagogy underpinned by an organic, discoursal view of language development will be characterized by the following features:

◇   learners are exposed to authentic samples of language so that the grammatical features one is trying to teach are encountered in a range of different linguistic and experiential contexts

◇   it is not assumed that once learners have been drilled in a particular form they have acquired it, and drilling, if it is used, is seen only as a first step toward eventual mastery

◇   there are opportunities for recycling of language forms, and learners are engaged in tasks designed to make transparent the links between form and function

◇   learners are given opportunities to develop their own understandings of the grammatical principles of English by progressively structuring and restructuring the language through inductive learning experiences that encourage them to explore the functioning of grammar in context

◇   over time, learners encounter target language items in an increasingly diverse and complex range of linguistic and experiential environments.

The persistence of a strictly linear approach to language development in different parts of the world is intriguing. In teacher development seminars and workshops, teachers are generally ready to admit that their students do not learn in a linear step-by-step fashion. However, the usual reaction to this is an uneasy feeling that perhaps, they, the teachers, "aren't doing it right." One reason for the persistence of an approach that does not adequately reflect ways in which learners acquire language is the pervasiveness of the "three Ps" (presentation, practice, production) methodology that has dominated language teaching for many years. In fact, many teachers define teaching in terms of this model, and, for them, activities not fitting into the three Ps approach are simply not recognized as language teaching. This was stated to me recently by a teacher who was required to use a textbook underpinned by an organic approach. This teacher could not believe it when her students actually progressed more rapidly than learners in parallel classes who were still using materials based on a three Ps approach. When asked why she was surprised, she replied that it was not the way that languages were supposed to be learned!

In seeking to explore alternative ways of achieving our pedagogical goals, it is important not to overstate the case for one viewpoint rather than another, or to discount factors such as cognitive style, learning strategy preferences, prior learning experiences, and the cultural contexts in which the language is being taught and learned. However, while there are some grammatical structures that may be acquired in a linear way, it seems clear from a rapidly growing body of research that the majority of structures are acquired in an organic, complex, multilinear way.

◆ **CONCEPT MAP OF CHAPTER 4**

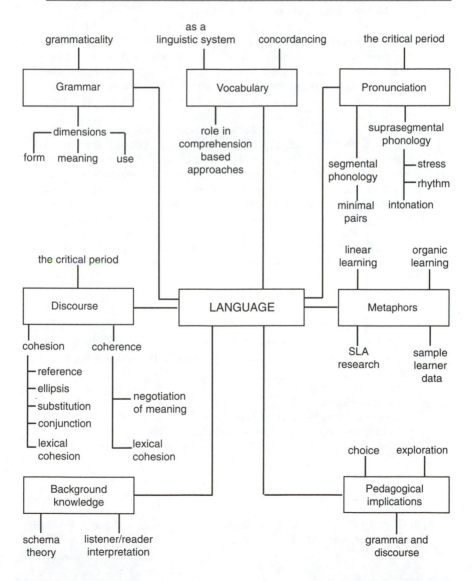

◆ **QUESTIONS AND TASKS**

1. Why is the concept of grammaticality problematic?
2. Do the grammaticality judgment test on page 3 of the set reading. How do your results compare with those reported in the chapter?
3. What are the essential characteristics of an organic approach to second language acquisition? In what ways does an organic approach differ from a linear approach? What are the practical implications for teaching an organic approach?
4. Identify three examples of referential cohesion, three of lexical cohesion, and three conjunctions in the following passage. Use your analysis to develop a lesson for teaching these items.

> A common criticism of the simple alternative-response type item is that a pupil may be able to recognize a false statement as incorrect but still not know what is correct. For example, when pupils answer the following item as false, it does not indicate that they know what negatively charged particles of electricity are called. All it tells us is that they know they are not called neutrons.
>
> T/F Negatively charged particles of electricity are called neutrons.
>
> This is a rather crude measure of knowledge, because there is an inestimable number of things that negatively charged particles of electricity are not called. To overcome such difficulties, some teachers prefer to have the pupils change all false statements to true. When this is done, the part of the statement it is permissible to change should be indicated. However, unless the key words to be changed are indicated in the correction-type true-false item, pupils are liable to rewrite the entire statement. In addition to the increase in scoring difficulty, this frequently leads to true statements which deviate considerably from the original intent of the item.
>
> *Gronland 1981: 165*

5. What are speech acts? Why are they important in language teaching?
6. What is the role of background knowledge in discourse comprehension?
7. Find examples of (or design your own) tasks to incorporate the following principles:
   ◇ teaching language as choice
   ◇ using authentic data
   ◇ showing form/function relationships
   ◇ learners as active explorers of language
   ◇ exploring relationships between grammar and discourse

◆ **REFERENCES**

Bartlett, F. C. 1932. *Remembering: A Study in Experimental and Social Psychology.* Cambridge: Cambridge University Press.

Bransford, J., and M. Johnson. 1972. Contextual prerequisities for understanding: Some investigations of comprehension and recall. *Journal of Verbal Learning and Verbal Behaviour*, 11.

Brown, H. D. 1987. *Principles of Language Learning and Teaching*. Englewood Cliffs, N.J.: Prentice Hall.

Byrne, D., and G. Walsh. 1973. *Listening Comprehension 1*. London: Longman.

Carter, R. 1993. *Introducing Applied Linguistics*. London: Penguin.

Carter, R., and M. McCarthy (eds.). 1988. *Vocabulary and Language Teaching*. London: Longman.

Celce–Murcia, M., and E. Olshtain. (forthcoming) *Discourse and Context in Language Teaching*. New York. Cambridge: Cambridge University Press.

Clyne, D. 1991. *The Bulletin Magazine*, December 1991.

Cobbett, W. 1819. *A Grammar of the English Language*. Oxford: Oxford University Press.

Cook, P. 1991. *The Bulletin Magazine*. December 1991.

Crystal, D. 1992. *An Introduction to Linguistics*. London: Penguin.

Ellis, R. 1994. *The Study of Second Language Acquisition*. Oxford: Oxford University Press.

Gronlund, N. 1981. *Measurement and Evaluation in Education*. New York: Macmillan.

Hall, N., & J. Shepheard. 1991. *The Anti-Grammar Grammar Book*. London: Longman

Halliday, M. A. K. 1985. *An Introduction to Functional Grammar*. London: Arnold.

Halliday, M. A. K., and R. Hasan. 1976. *Cohesion in English*. London: Longman.

Harris, Z. 1952. Discourse analysis, *Language* , 28, 4.

Heath, S. B. 1992. Literacy skills or literate skills? Considerations for ESL / EFL learners. In D. Nunan (ed.) *Collaborative Language Learning and Teaching*. Cambridge: Cambridge University Press.

Hoey, M. 1983. *On the Surface of Discourse*. London: Allen and Unwin.

Hoey, M. 1991. *Patterns of Lexis in Text*. Oxford: Oxford University Press.

Johnston, M. 1987. Understanding learner language. In D. Nunan (ed.), *Applying Second Language Acquisition Research*. Adelaide: NCRC.

Kellerman, E. 1983. If at first you do succeed . . . In S. Gass and C. Madden (eds.), *Input in Second Language Acquisition*. Rowley, Mass.: Newbury House.

Larsen–Freeman, D. 1995. *Grammar Dimensions: Form, Meaning and Use*. Boston: Heinle & Heinle.

Larsen–Freeman, D., and M. Long. 1991. *An Introduction to Second Language Acquisition Research*. London: Longman.

Levinson, S. 1983. *Pragmatics*. Cambridge: Cambridge University Press.

Martin, J. R. 1981. Lexical cohesion. Mimeograph, Linguistics Department, University of Sydney.

McCarthy, M. 1991. *Discourse Analysis for Language Teachers*. Cambridge: Cambridge University Press.

Morgan, J., and M. Rinvolucri. 1986. Vocabulary. Oxford: Oxford University Press.

Nunan, D. 1993. *Introducing Discourse Analysis*. London: Penguin.

Nunan, D. 1995. *ATLAS: Learning-Centered Communication*. Boston: Heinle & Heinle.

Nunan, D., and K. Keobke. 1997. Growing their own grammars: learners and language acquisition. Paper presented at the International Language in Education Conference, University of Hong Kong, December 1997.

Odlin, T. (ed.). 1994. *Pedagogic Grammar*. Cambridge: Cambridge University Press.

Pearson, I. 1978. English in Medical Science.

Pennington, M., and J. C. Richards. 1986. Pronunciation revisited. TESOL Quarterly, 20, 2, 207–225.

Pica, T. 1985. The selective impact of classroom instruction on second language acquisition. *Applied Linguistics*, 6, 3, 214–222.

Pienemann, M., and M. Johnston. 1987. Factors influencing the development of language proficiency. In D. Nunan (ed.), *Applying Second Language Acquisition Research*. Adelaide: NCRC.

Renouf, A. 1984. Corpus development at Birmingham University. In J. Aarts and W. Meijs (eds.), *Corpus Linguistics: Recent Developments in the Use of Computer Corpora in English Language Research*. Amsterdam: Rodopi.

Richards, J. C., J. Platt, and H. Weber. 1985. Dictionary of Applied Linguistics. London: Longman.

Rivers, W. 1983. *Interactive Language Teaching*. Cambridge: Cambridge University Press.

Ross, J. 1979. Where's English? In C. Fillmore, D. Kempler, and W. Wang (eds.), *Individual Differences in Language Ability and Language Behavior*. New York: Academic Press.

Rutherford, W. 1987. *Second Language Grammar: Teaching and Learning*. London: Longman.

Schmidt, R., and C. McCreary. 1977. Standard and superstandard English: Recognition and use of prescriptive rules by native and non-native speakers. *TESOL Quarterly*, 11, 271–288.

Searle, R. 1962. *Speech Acts*.

Sinclair, J. McH., and A. Renouf. 1988. A lexical syllabus for language learning. In R. Carter and M. McCarthy (eds.) *Vocabulary and Language Teaching*. London: Longman.

Wajnryb, R. 1990. *Grammar Dictation*. Oxford: Oxford University Press.

Widdowson, H. G. 1978. *Teaching Language as Communication*. Oxford: Oxford University Press.

Widdowson, H. G. 1984. *Learning Purpose and Language Use*. Oxford: Oxford University Press.

Willis, D. 1990. *The Lexical Syllabus*. London: Collins.

Woods, E. 1995. *Introducing Grammar*. London: Penguin.

Wolfe, T. 1979. *The Right Stuff*. New York: Farrar, Straus & Giroux.

CHAPTER 5

Focus on the Learner

This chapter, and the one that follows, are closely related. In this chapter, we look at learners, while in the one that follows we look at learning processes. As learners and learning processes are two sides of the same pedagogical coin, the issues we visit in both chapters will be similar. However, they will be looked at from slightly different perspectives.

In this chapter, the following concepts and issues are covered:

Learner needs
◇ defining needs
◇ objective and subjective needs
◇ techniques and procedures for identifying needs
◇ integrating needs analysis into the instructional process
◇ critiquing needs analysis

Learner roles and contributions
◇ role diversity
◇ learner contributions

Learner choices
◇ learning to make informed choices
◇ classroom techniques

LEARNER NEEDS

In Chapter 1, I traced the disintegration of a unitary approach to syllabus design. In such an approach, learners were fed an undifferentiated linguistic diet regardless of their communicative ends. This view was challenged on several fronts, but most particularly by the emergence of communicative approaches to language teaching. Proponents of such approaches argued that the content of language courses should reflect the purposes for which the students were learning the language in the first place. Rather than fitting students to courses, courses should be designed to fit students. Thus was born the English for Specific Purposes movement, and the appearance of courses such as *English for Science and Technology, English for Medical Students, and English for Tourism.*

♦ DEFINING NEEDS

The most comprehensive system for analyzing learner needs was that developed by Munby (1978). Munby based his model on prevailing views

> **Needs analysis**
> Sets of tools, techniques, and procedures for determining the language content and learning process for specified groups of learners.

of language as communication. He developed his model at the time when linguists such as Hymes and Halliday and applied linguists such as Widdowson, Breen, Candlin, Sinclair, and Coulthard were creating the conceptual universe out of which the so-called communicative revolution was spun, and the model itself was an ambitious attempt to atomize the various components of communicative competence. The model itself consists of a huge number of linguistic and nonlinguistic variables, and it is difficult to see how it could be applied in any comprehensive fashion to curriculum design. Certainly, I am not aware of any curriculum that has been fully derived from the model. Nonetheless, it is a useful reminder of the daunting number of variables that, potentially at least, need to be taken into consideration in developing needs-based curricula.

◆ OBJECTIVE AND SUBJECTIVE NEEDS

Some of the most practical work in needs analysis was carried out by Brindley (1984). In the mid-1980s, Brindley elaborated on a distinction drawn by Richterich (1972, Richterich and Chancerel, 1978) between "objective" needs and "subjective" needs. He also drew a distinction between initial and ongoing needs, a distinction of some importance to teachers, many of whom are only in a position to engage in ongoing needs analysis.

The "objective" needs are those that can be diagnosed by teachers on the basis of the analysis of personal data about learners along with information about their language proficiency and patterns of language use (using as a guide their own personal experience and knowledge, perhaps supplemented by Munby-type specifications of macro-skills), whereas the "subjective" needs (which are often wants, desires, expectations, or other psychological manifestations of a lack) cannot be diagnosed easily, or, in many cases, even stated by learners themselves. (Brindley 1984: 31). Brindley suggests that the data set out in Table 5.1 can be useful for program planning purposes. The reasons for collecting the data are set out in the right-hand column.

While Brindley's distinction is a useful one, I prefer to draw a distinction between "content" needs and "process" needs. *Content needs* includes the selection and sequencing of such things as topics, grammar, function, notions, and vocabulary—traditionally the domain of syllabus design—while *process needs* refers to the selection and sequencing of learning tasks and experiences—traditionally seen as the domain of methodology. Another useful distinction is that between initial and ongoing needs analy-

Table 5.1

Type of Data	*Rationale*
1. Learners' life goals	So that teachers have a basis on which to determine or predict learners' language goals, communicative networks, and social roles
2. Language goals, communicative networks and social roles	So learners can be placed in a group based on common social roles; so teachers can make preliminary decisions about course content appropriate to learners' social roles
3. Objective needs, patterns of language use, personal resources (including time)	So learners can be grouped according to their needs and/or interests
4. Language proficiency and language difficulties	So learners can be grouped according to their language proficiency
5. Subjective needs, including learning strategy preferences, affective needs, learning activity preferences, pace of learning, attitude towards correction	So that teachers may adapt learning activities to individual needs
6. Information about learners' attainment of objectives	So that the teacher can monitor performance and modify programs accordingly
7. Information about developmental processes in second language learning, including learners' communicative strategies	So that teacher can gear language content and materials to learners' stage of development

Adapted from *Brindley, 1984*

sis. Initial needs analysis is that carried out before a course begins. In most educational systems, this is very often beyond the control of the teacher, being determined by curriculum specialists, subject panels, and the like. Ongoing needs analysis refers to the often relatively informal analysis carried out by teachers once a course has begun.

◆ TECHNIQUES AND PROCEDURES FOR IDENTIFYING NEEDS

A wide range of instruments and techniques is available for carrying out needs analysis. One family of techniques is used for collecting and analyzing information about the target language situation. These techniques are largely, although not exclusively, used for initial content analysis. The key question addressed here is: What are the skills and linguistic knowledge needed by students to comprehend and produce language for communicating successfully in target language situations? The second set of techniques is designed to obtain information about and from learners themselves. This information can relate to both content and process, and is usually carried out through some form of questionnaire. The three-part questionnaire included as Appendix 5.1, page 324 is a comprehensive instrument designed to yield both content and process information. As you look through the questionnaire, think about how you might modify it for the kinds of learners that you have.

As far as possible, I like to make needs analysis part of the learning process itself. I do this by incorporating into my lessons activities that require my learners to contribute ideas about what should be learned and how. From the very first lesson, I get learners used to the idea that they will contribute to their own own learning through techniques such as the following. This procedure, or a version of it, forms the basis of the first lesson that I have with students at an intermediate level or above. (With beginning students, the questionnaire used in the first part of the procedure can be administered in the students' first language.)

1.   Students are told that the content and procedures in the class will be partly derived from their own views on what they like to learn and how they like to learn. They are asked to indicate their attitude by circling a number according to the following key.

Key

1.   I don't like this at all
2.   I don't like this very much
3.   This is OK.
4.   I quite like this
5.   I like this very much

I. Topics

In my English class, I would like to study topics...................

1. about me: my feelings, attitudes, beliefs, etc.	1 2 3 4 5
2. from my academic subjects: psychology, comp. lit., etc.	1 2 3 4 5
3. from popular culture: music, film, etc.	1 2 3 4 5
4. about current affairs and issues	1 2 3 4 5
5. that are controversial: underage drinking, etc.	1 2 3 4 5

II. Methods

In my English class, I would like to learn by ....

6. small group discussions and problem-solving	1 2 3 4 5
7. formal language study, e.g., studying from a textbook	1 2 3 4 5

8.	listening to the teacher	1 2 3 4 5
9.	watching videos	1 2 3 4 5
10.	doing individual work	1 2 3 4 5

III. Language Areas

This year, I most want to improve my.....................................

11.	listening	1 2 3 4 5
12.	speaking	1 2 3 4 5
13.	reading	1 2 3 4 5
14.	writing	1 2 3 4 5
15.	grammar	1 2 3 4 5
16.	pronunciation	1 2 3 4 5

IV. Out of Class

Out of class, I like to...

17.	practice in the independent learning center	1 2 3 4 5
18.	have conversations with native speakers of English	1 2 3 4 5
19.	practice English with my friends	1 2 3 4 5
20.	collect examples of English that I find interesting/ puzzling	1 2 3 4 5
21.	watch TV/read newspapers in English	1 2 3 4 5

V. Assessment

I like to find out how much my English is improving by ....

22.	having the teacher assess my written work	1 2 3 4 5
23.	having the teacher correct my mistakes in class	1 2 3 4 5
24.	checking my own progress/correcting my own mistakes	1 2 3 4 5
25.	being corrected by my fellow students	1 2 3 4 5
26.	seeing if I can use the language in real-life situations	1 2 3 4 5

2. Students are then asked to get into five groups, and introduce themselves to their fellow students (While the students are doing this, I cut up the completed questionnaires into five sub-sections. each group is then given a designation: There is a "topic" group, a "methods" group, etc.)

3. In groups, students analyze the section of the questionnaire that they have been given, and provide a summary of the results on an overhead projector transparency. (Here, I encourage students to be as creative as possible, encouraging them to use pie charts, tables, even cartoons, to represent their data.)

4. In groups, they are then asked to provide an interpretation of the information, answering the question: Why do you think that the class as a whole has responded as they have to this section of the questionnaire?

5. Students then prepare a report for the class as a whole based on the data that they have collected and analyzed.

This lesson has a number of benefits. It provides me with an instant "snapshot" of group interests and preferences, it gets learners thinking about the course and its rationale, it forces them to work collaboratively in small groups, and it gets them actively practicing their English. To illustrate the active involvement of the learners, here is a transcript from one group that had been assigned the task of analyzing and interpreting the class response to the assessment questions. We pick up the interaction as the students are discussing the relative unpopularity of item 25 ("I like to be corrected by my fellow students").

F1   *Question 25. Being corrected by my fellow students. Also O.K.*

F2   *[How about talking about usage?] The, ah, classmates, [like], maybe they, they, they need the fellow students in our class as why don't we actually find?*

F1   *Because we're, we're having equal footing, ah, and my ability is almost [ ]. So, ah, the classmate do not really rely on the, the other classmate's ability. And//*

F2   *Why?*

F1   *Because we are the same, we are the same kind.*

F2   *You mean that they're not native speaker so we're should not really believe in other people saying English.*

F1   *I don't mean that, but you have to understand this, and you are a undergraduate, so do I. So, I don't, that means the classmates do not think that your ability is greater than my ability. They don't rely on, on a certain kind. But, but the result of that said we really rely on teachers because they, they're of patient, is teaching others. And//*

M1   *Ha.*

F1   *as well they're the native speaker.*

F2   *What's your opinion about it, don't you think that it's . . . . (background noise is too loud.) [the good idea to have exchange] The study to the student, you see ah, I, I understand that you may get ah, we're not very good in English, but we all have made mistakes in English, so we may know more about the mistakes, maybe we're more aware of the mistakes we usually make.*

F1   *Sometimes we know the mistake, but we don't know how to correct the mistakes, so we have to rely on teachers.*

M2:   *Well, to sum up, I think that ah, all of us think that may be our ability to correct other fellow students work. Agree? Maybe our English is not good enough to correct their work.*

M1   *So students are prefer to the native teachers//*
F1&M1 *Yes.*
M1   *to correct it.*
F1   *Data do reflect this.*

One of the students who took part in this group discussion reported back to the whole class as follows (Groups are given a choice as to how they report back, the only stipulation being that all members of the group are required to contribute.):

F1 *I'll talk about number 25 that item ah, being corrected by my fellow students. And it is ah, the least popular one may be. Ah, only four of us, only four of us choose this item. And only four of us show their positive per-, preference in this item. There're several reasons in, in this area. Firstly, mmm, we believe we are, we are e-, we are having equal footing, ah, we are admitted by the University, ah, that means we have the same ability in most areas. So, we don't believe our classmates can help us to correct these. And they don't have, ah, besides ah, the students show that they don't have enough confidence in correcting ah, other's people work. And they're, they think that they're, they're incapable of doing so. And it also reflects that mmm, they don't think what they have learnt in the past can help themselves in correcting other's work. Ah, the, that result reinforce, reinforce the result of number 22 and number 24 that is, that means we don't have confidence in English. And in the number 26 will be, will be explained by Fiona.*

◆ CRITIQUING NEEDS ANALYSIS

The development of needs-based courses did not escape criticism. One of the most articulate critics was Henry Widdowson (1984), who argued that attempting to atomize and teach a series of discrete skills was basically a training endeavor that would result in a limited communicative repertoire. In effect, learners would end up with little more than "phrase book" English. According to Widdowson, for language education to be effective, learners needed to develop a communicative capacity. In other words, they needed to be able to use the skills taught in the classroom to do things other than those that they had been specifically taught. He suggests that, in needs-based course design,

> we have an assumption that ESP is simply a matter of describing a particular area of language and then using this description as a course specification to impart to learners the necessary restricted competence to cope with this particular area. In other words, it is assumed the ESP is essentially a training exercise. Now in some kinds of ESP, training, as I have defined it, may well be appropriate, since it services a restricted

repertoire of behaviour where formulae and problems to be solved correspond quite closely. This would presumably be the case with the communication of air traffic control. But it will obviously not do when the English taught is intended to be auxiliary to aims which are fundamentally educational. And here we can make a first move towards a comprehensive theoretical view of the field. We can suggest that the purposes in ESP are arranged along a scale of specificity with training at one end and education at the other. As one moves along the scale in the direction of education, one has to account increasingly for the development of capacity and, at the same time, one has to take into consideration the pedagogic problem of establishing objectives which are projections of final aims. At the training end of the scale, objectives and aims will converge into close correspondence and will seek to impart restricted competence. At the education end of the scale will cluster courses of English for academic purposes which require the development of communicative capacity and which will call for pedagogic decisions in the formulation of objectives. At this end of the scale, ESP shades into GPE.

Widdowson, 1984: 10–11

My own view is that Widdowson is right in pointing to the need for language education to develop generalized capacities in learners. Whether or not courses achieve this however, would seem to have more to do with how instruction was realized at the level of classroom action than in the prior specification of content. In other words it is more a matter of methodology than syllabus design. Whether or not courses developed to teach learners skills related to specific situations and events do result in language that learners are unable to transfer to other situations is a matter for empirical investigation, as is the question of whether GPE courses result in language that learners can use in communicative situations for which they have not been specifically prepared. My teaching and research experiences lead me to believe that the ability of students to transfer what they have learned to solve unpredictable communication problems is much more restricted than is usually assumed by course designers and materials developers. In any case, the educational potential or otherwise of a given course would seem to rest more with the types of learning experiences provided than with the types of content selected. (For a discussion on this point, see Nunan, 1988.)

The other criticism that might be made of needs analysis techniques is that they are irrelevant in most foreign language contexts because learners have no immediate communicative ends in view. In such situations, the only possible rationale for language courses must be an educational one. In other words, learners engage (or more usually are required by the system to engage) in the learning of a foreign language, not because there is any likelihood that they will actually use the language, but because it will foster the development of cognitive, affective, interpersonal, and intercultural skills, knowledge, and attitudes.

LEARNER ROLES AND CONTRIBUTIONS

◆ *ROLE DIVERSITY*

One of the things that makes teaching a source of endless fascination is the fact that no two classes are ever the same. The complex interpersonal chemistry between teacher and student and between student and student sees to that. As I write this book, I am teaching two sections of an advanced level writing course. One class is held on Monday morning, the other on Wednesday morning. Despite the fact that the course objectives, materials, teacher, room, and time of day are the same, the classes themselves are quite different. The difference has to do with the different interpersonaal dynamics that have developed within each group, and the different role expectations that the participants (including myself) have of themselves and others in the group.

In his fascinating book on role relationships in the classroom, Tony Wright identifies two aspects to roles. The first relates to social and inter-personal factors. These include views about status and position, attitudes and values held by individuals, and group and individuals' personalities. The second aspect relates to the learning tasks themselves, particularly teacher and learner expectations about the nature of the learning tasks, and the ways that they are dealt with in the classroom (Wright 1987: 12).

In any given classroom, these two factors will be in constant interaction, creating a dynamic, unstable environment that can either facilitate the learning process or seriously impair it. The role expectations of both teacher and learners will be conditioned by individual personality factors such as introversion/extroversion, cognitive style, prior learning and teaching experiences, and cultural factors. These factors are also what makes teaching fun, because we can never be entirely sure how these complex sets of factors will play out on any particular occasion. When the unexpected happens in the classroom, the cause can usually be traced back to role diversity and conflict.

From time to time, claims appear that communicative language teaching, with its experiential learning-by-doing philosophy, and assumptions about learners as active constructors of their own knowledge, is inappropriate in many non-Western contexts. Such contexts are characterized by high-structure, transmission modes of learning, in which teachers control the action, and where it is considered inappropriate for pupils to speak up in front of the class. Many of my own students come into my classes from schools where high-structure, transmission modes of teaching and learning are the norm, and it is a challenge for me to create a climate in which different role expectations are articulated to the students and ac-cepted by them. In fact, my learners generally want to adopt a more active role. The problem for them is that they do not know how.

Several solutions have been explored to meet this challenge with varying degrees of success. One of the classroom variables that has had a marked effect on student participation in oral activities has been group size. Students who remain silent in groups of ten or more will contribute actively to discussions when the size of the group is reduced to five or three. Type of communicative task can also influence students' willingness to speak. My own students greatly enjoy formal debates, and many, who would be reluctant to contribute in other kinds of oral tasks, will participate enthusiastically in debates, particularly when they have had the opportunity to determine the topic of debate themselves.

♦ LEARNER CONTRIBUTIONS

At the beginning of a new course, my first concern is to find out about students attitudes, prior learning experiences, and expectations for the future. I then monitor their changing attitudes and expectations during the course through learner journals, surveys, and conversations. The following conversations were recorded with one group of students several weeks into the course. I had asked them to compare their school experiences with learning at a university, and this is what they had to say:

Tony: *I learn English in school by, just by doing some exercises . . .*

Mandy: *. . . on the class or homework. And when Cert. Level or A Level, we just do all the past paper and that's all, no special learning. We have different approach if we have different teachers, some teacher will take primary school approach. (The rest of the students laugh together.)*
She will let you read a text and then tell you to underline some difficult words and then you have to jot them in a book and we did not like this way because we are not primary student, for some teachers they will just give you, we have a textbook and then she will tell us to do the exercise inside that.

Teacher: *Do you like that way?*

Mandy: *No, (laughing) because we don't know what we are doing. (The others agree.) In fact, I'm in, I was in the same school as Paula (who had spoken earlier) and all more less the same. Drills every day, no fun at all.*

Paula: *No fun at all, yes. Yeah, I am at the same school as Mandy. (All laugh.) Even in English lesson, we don't speak English. (laughing)*

As the students talked about their secondary school experiences, it became clear that, while there was a cultural overlay to what goes on in the classroom, what was considered as "legitimate" activity was also conditioned by a range of other factors, particularly by the attitudes, beliefs, and practices of individual teachers. This was so even for practices that were critical to successful language development, such as the extent to which use of the target language in class was encouraged or even permitted. In some English classes, English itself was rarely used. In others, students reported being fined if they used Cantonese. This had (predictably) negative consequences, as the following conversation reveals.

Steve: *While I was in secondary one, if we are heard speaking Cantonese in class, you will be fined.*
Teacher: *Ah!*
Steve: *Yeah.*
Teacher: *What?*
Steve: *Fifty cents.*
Teacher: *Did you find that useful?*
Steve: *Ya. But I keep on . . .*
Tony: *. . . Silent.*
Steve: *trick them try to speak in Cantonese to earn the money for the class, but then I don't concentrate in class.*
Teacher: *Mmm.*
Steve: *I don't think it's work. This tragedy because, not tragedy, strategy, because if you, when you say Cantonese you must give fifty cents then very often no one will speak in class, so they don't learn English, they cannot learn English.*

In this conversation, we find an unsurprising response by Steve and his school friends to the teacher strategy of fining students for using their native language. The students lapsed into silence. The strategy thus has the opposite effect from what had been intended by the teacher.

In systemic terms, Hong Kong has an extremely examination-driven educational system, and, not surprisingly, this is reflected in what happens in the classroom, and has a major influence on the perpetuation of a transmission-mode of teaching. Many of the students I interviewed reported that their secondary level English language learning experiences were dominated by preparation for examinations. This is illustrated in the following conversation.

Julia: *In secondary school, the English lesson is quite boring because we student just sit in the classroom and listen to what teachers tell us, and I'm afraid that I seldom practice English outside classroom because I can't find anyone who can practice with me. And so I have to find other ways to practice my English, so I just watch television in order to practice, to improve my listening skill and things like that.*

Teacher: *Mmm Mmm.*

Martin: *In my experience, my secondary teacher only sent out the papers to us, to only do the exercise without teaching anything. They are just follow the textbook and just read out again and again without teaching us grammar or the style of composition or the normal conversation in English, so I think my secondary school English lesson is very boring . . . and not very useful.*

Julia: *Yes, I agree with Martin. In secondary school, in the lesson we only do exercise in order to meet the examination requirement.*

Cindy: *In secondary school I hate English very much because I have to re-sit for various examination. And I also need to sit for the HKCE English examination and HKAL. [These are externally administered government examinations.] And then I always ask a question is why must I learn English because I am a Chinese.*
(laughing together)

In the final conversational extract, the students compare their school experiences with the demands of university study. Here we see that students are ready to adjust to changing contextual expectations about the role of the learner.

Tim: *The approach is obviously difference. In secondary school we only strive for high marks.*

Paul: *But in University, we will concerning something, we have to do in the future, maybe learn something could help in the career. Something like that or studies.*

Tim: *I think in University, we don't do much exercises with our English because it's not a test, but we have to concern how we can use English effectively in our studying. For example, learn more vocabulary or read more quickly, or oral skill in tutorial, so the approach is different.*

Trudy: *I think the lecturer, most of them speak in English, this includes my listening because we have to familiarize . . .*

Amanda: *Different accents.*

Trudy: *Yes.*

Teacher: *So you find that in University, your way of learning English is of different approach. How about how often do you use English? Do you use English outside English class? Do you speak English with other students or peers? Do the lecturers use English in class?*

Tim: *All my lecture and tutorial are spoken in English, especially in tutorial when we are discussing, we all use English, so I think the chance is more to practice English.*

Teacher: *But do you use it outside the class?*

Tim: *No.*

In addition to talking to my students about their learning experiences, I get illuminating, and often surprising, insights into their reactions to the learning process by reading the journals that they keep. (I give my students ten minutes at the end of most of my two-hour classes to record their reactions to the course in general and the class they have just had in particular.) The following extracts were collected midway through an academic writing course. At the beginning of the course, students had indicated a desire for some "fun" oral interactive tasks to counterbalance what they saw as the rather heavy academic diet offered by the course. These journal entries were collected at the end of a two-hour class in which I tried to balance the academic writing requirements of the course with the less academic desires of the students. In the first hour, students completed a series of writing tasks. In the second hour, they watched a short video clip, and then completed a small group, problem-solving task based on the material in the video. (One problem with this class was that it met in the late afternoon, when student energy levels were low, a fact commented on by several of the students.)

> I think this lesson is quite useful since its focus on the academic issue. But, the most interesting part in this lesson is I can meet new classmates in every time. Moreover, through reading articles and watching television in the class, the atmosphere is rather relax and not too much feel boring since in the afternoon, much of our energy is exhausted.

> Sorry, I could not follow you for many times because you speak quite fast to me! Anyway, I do enjoy this lesson even though we have so-called "dead air". I think the big problem about this class is that we are very passive and maybe, shy to speak a word! Moreover, I think opportunities should be given to us to let us know each other well, as it is important to let us say more/give more opinion/have good discussion during the class.

> I think this lesson is more interesting than the last one because of conversations with other students in the group and the chance to watch video. These two things make the lesson less boring. I think it would be better still if we can be given more similar tasks in the coming lessons e.g. watching television and discussing topics that are related to youngsters daily lives. Moreover, I would like to point out that listening skill is as important as oral one. So, it would be better if emphasis can put on this also.

> I found that this lesson was really interesting. I
> felt relaxed and enjoyed it very much. It's so funny
> to have discussion on this topic since we (most of
> us) could express our opinions and share our feel-
> ings. Also, the TV program gave me more chances to
> listen to English spoke by native speakers, so that I
> could familiarize with different accents. I felt very
> satisfactory and happy with what we did this lesson.
> I hope I can continue this feeling in the whole EAS
> [English for Arts Students] program!

These journal entries demonstrate the tension between attempting to be responsive to students' needs and interests (which are often related to nonacademic things such as watching videos and having fun) on the one hand, and meeting the objectives of the course; that is, to prepare students for university-level study in English. Although many of these students find lessons on academic writing "boring," this is the central requirement of the course, and cannot be jettisoned. The extracts reveal the tension that often occurs between the interests of the students and the requirements of the course. They also show the diversity of interests among members of the class, although they show quite clearly that all students enjoy active, interactive learning.

In his book on classroom roles, Tony Wright suggests that learners' expectations about the nature of learning tasks and the way in which individuals and groups deal with learning tasks will be an important aspect of the dynamics of the classroom. One way of getting at student attitudes and opinions at the beginning of a course is to administer a questionnaire. I find it interesting to administer questionnaires such as the following at the beginning and again towards the end of a course. At the beginning of the course, this enables me to get an idea of the interests and preferences of the students. Collecting data towards the end of the course lets me see whether, as a result of the course, there has been a shift in attitude on the part of the students.

What kinds of classroom tasks do you like?

A. Study the following descriptions of small group tasks and evaluate them according to the following key. (Write a number where it says "task rating.") React to the task type, not just to the example.

1. I don't like this type of task at all
2. I don't like this type of task very much
3. I don't mind this type of task
4. I like this type of task very much

Task A. Information Sharing

Example: The class is split into two groups, A and B. You listen to a discussion between three people talking about aspects of their lifestyle: where they go on vacation, what they like to do on the weekend, their favorite hobby. The other half of the class listens to a discussion between three people talking about other aspects of their lifestyle: their favorite forms of entertainment, their favorite kinds of food, the kinds of sports they play. You then work in pairs with a student from the other group to complete the following form.

	PERSON 1	PERSON 2	PERSON 3
Vacations			
Entertainment			
Weekends			
Food			
Hobbies			
Sports			

Task Rating:

Task B. Decision Making/Problem-Solving

Example: You work in pairs. You are given a job description and three job applications. You have to decide which person should get the job.

Task Rating:

Task C. Grammar Practice

Example: You read a short passage containing a number of grammatical errors. You have to correct the errors and say what rules have been broken.

Task Rating:

Task D. Dialogue Practice

Example: You listen to a conversation and then practice it with another student.

Task Rating:

Task E. Authentic Reading

Example: You bring an English language newspaper to class. You work with three or four other students to select an article, and prepare a set of reading comprehension questions to accompany the article. You exchange the article and questions with another group. They read your article and answer your questions. You read their article and answer their questions.

Task Rating:

Task F. Gap Filling

Example: You read an passage in which every fifth word has been deleted. You have to work out which words were deleted and replace them.

Task Rating:

Task G. Small Group Discussion

Example: Working with several other students, you carry out a discussion task. You record the discussion. At the conclusion of the discussion, you listen to the tape and identify your errors.

Task Rating:

Task H. Role Play

Example: You take part in a role play with three or four other students. One of you pretends to be someone who is being interviewed for a job. The other students pretend to be the interviewing panel.

Task Rating:

B. Compare responses with three or four other students and note similarities and differences. Rank the tasks from most to least popular.

Most   Least
Popular ____   ____   ____   ____   ____   ____ Popular

C. Based on the responses you gave to Tasks 1 and 2, decide what makes a "good" classroom task. (List up to five characteristics.)

1. _____

2. _____

3. _____

4. _____

5. _____

The last time I administered this questionnaire, I obtained the following results.

Most popular	1. Role Play
	2. Small group discussion
	3. Dialogue practice
	4. Information sharing
	5. Decision-making/Problem-solving
	6. Gap filling
	7. Grammar practice
Least popular	8. Authentic reading

LEARNER CHOICES

♦ *LEARNING TO MAKE INFORMED CHOICES*

The difference between an effective and an ineffective language user is that effective language users make the appropriate choices when it comes to the linguistic options available to them. (This applies to native speakers as well as to second language learners.) Similarly, one important difference between effective and ineffective language learners is that effective learners make appropriate choices when it comes to the means through which they learn language. We help learners develop skills in making appropriate choices by giving them practice in doing so in the security of our classrooms. Learning to make informed choices, then, is an important skill for all learners to develop to some degree. When one is working with learners who have learned to make such choices, a negotiated classroom such as I described in Chapter 1 can become a reality.

As I indicated in Chapter 1, negotiation and choice points exist in all classrooms, although their potential significance is not always recognized by those involved. In a single week with the class I am teaching at the moment, I was involved in negotiating with the students over the following issues:

whether to work in groups or pairs for a particular task;

whether to do the reading task before the listening task or vice versa;

who should operate the cassette recorder;

whether the visit to the self-access center should happen today or tomorrow;

how long a series of group reports should go on for;

whether a particular writing task should be done in or out of class;

whether a series of reflection sheets should be completed every week or every two weeks;

whether we should conclude the lesson early on Monday evening to allow
   some of the class to watch an important (to them!) football match;

whether a particular task would be completed individually and then shared
   in groups, or whether it should be done as a group task from scratch.

This list might seem modest, even rather pedestrian, the sort of things
that teachers and learners might potentially make at any time. This is the
point that I am trying to make. By highlighting these points for discussion,
and by looking for opportunities to weave them into the fabric of one's
teaching, the whole climate of the classroom can be gradually transformed.

◆ CLASSROOM TECHNIQUES

If the idea of making choices is unfamiliar to your learners, you can
introduce them to this important dimension to their learning gradually
by building choice points into your lessons. Negotiation can take the form
of decisions about the management of learning (most of the illustrations
above from my own classroom are of this type), or it can involve making
substantive decisions about which tasks to complete. In the following
task, for example, learners have to choose whether to practice speaking
or writing.

   In the next illustration, both tasks involve reading. However, they are
practicing different types of reading strategy. The first focuses on reading
for detail, while the second requires skimming the text for the main idea.

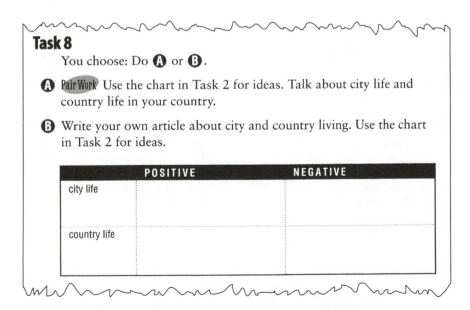

Task 8

   You choose: Do **Ⓐ** or **Ⓑ**.

Ⓐ Pair Work Use the chart in Task 2 for ideas. Talk about city life and
   country life in your country.

Ⓑ Write your own article about city and country living. Use the chart
   in Task 2 for ideas.

	POSITIVE	NEGATIVE
city life		
country life		

Figure 5-1   *ATLAS* - Book 2, © Heinle & Heinle Publishers

Initially, students may be a little uncomfortable with the idea of making individual choices. If this is the case, they can look quickly at both tasks and then take a class vote on which one they will do. Alternatively, students who want to do both tasks can decide on the order in which the tasks are done. It is the act of taking responsibility and making a choice, rather than the choice itself, that is the significant thing.

◆ CONCLUSION

In this chapter, I have explored language learning from the perspective of the learners. I looked at the development of needs-based courses, which emerged out of communicative language teaching, as well as the importance of learner roles, learner contributions, and learner choices in the language learning process. I would argue that these elements are important, even in contexts where decisions about how and what are out of the hands of the learner and even the teacher, as well as situations where it is considered culturally inappropriate for learners to be given active roles in making decisions about how and what to learn. My argument here would be based on the simple fact that, ultimately, if learners are to learn, then they have to do the learning for themselves.

In the next chapter, we look at these issues from a slightly different perspective, that is, from the perspective of the learning processes that underlying what happens in the language classroom.

◆ CONCEPT MAP OF CHAPTER 5

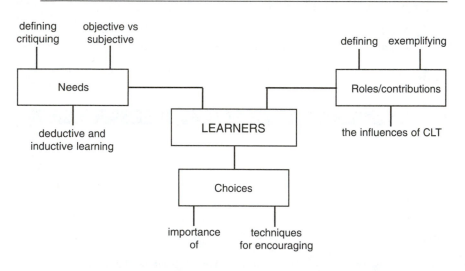

◆ QUESTIONS AND TASKS

1. What is the difference between objective needs and subjective needs? Which would be easier for the classroom teacher to deal with?
2. What assumptions about language underpin a needs-based approach to course design?
3. What learner roles are implicit in the interview data with learners presented in the body of the chapter?
4. What learner roles are implicit in your own classroom or a classroom with which you are familiar?
5. What arguments in favor of learner choices are made in the set reading?
6. If possible, observe a lesson or record and review one of your own lessons. Make a list of the choices offered to students. What other opportunities are there for learners to make choices that are not exploited by the teacher?
7. Develop a needs assessment instrument for a specified group of learners using some of the sample resources provided in the chapter. Use your instrument to conduct a needs analysis with a group of learners of your choice. Based on the data you collected, formulate a series of recommendations for a course designer who plans to develop a course for these learners.
8. Study the following learner diary entries collected as parts of the evaluation of a writing class. What emerge as the positive and negative aspects of the lesson? What changes would you make to your teaching/this lesson, as a result of feedback such as this?

> It is quite boring to watch the video and answer the questions about the video. But I enjoy talking with my classmates about the people they think important, and also discussing some questions. From these activities, I know the experience and opinions of other classmates.

> I found this lesson much interesting than the previous one. But I can't tell what I have learnt from this lesson, but I enjoy it. I think discussing topics which are more relevant to us or having some personal experiences are interesting. P.S. I learnt some vocabularies maybe.

> The topic about marriage is not so interesting to me. Most of us have not yet think of this issue. We still study in university. It seem boring to read some paragraph. And most people do not change his/her mind easily by just reading few sentence. And the reading material is not convicing that it seem just a new idea rather than a fact. Second part of EAS seem more fun. And we can't to sit in a stabilized place/ chair. It is interesting and happy to talk about my

idea to the other classmate. And it can improve our communication skill.

I think that the 1st part of the lesson is quite boring, though the topic is quite attracting. It's mainly because we have less chance to speak out our opinions with the classmates. The 2nd part is good, esp. the sharing part. We can be more familiar with our classmates by having more sharing and conversation.

In the first part, the atmosphere of discussion in my group is not very well. Maybe due to exhaustion of energy, classmates cannot brainstorm many ideas. But, the break is very helpful to regain energy and relax the mind. In the end of the tasks (sharing the important persons), the effect is obviously good. We can share our experience in life and we can be more awake to walk around and talk to each other. It gets us to know each other more. The "vocabulary filling-in" task is also helpful for the later tasks.

It is great that I have the chance to take a break. The workload (better say task) is okay and I can manage them. But it seems to me that the first part is quite boring. After the refreshment, I find the class becomes quite active and the use of videos can arouse our interest in the class in a short period of time. I hope we can do more on watching videos especially movies and then come along with a discussion time. That will be great. Generally speaking, I had the chance to talk with my classmates, and do group discussion. This might be beneficial to me.

Today's lesson is quite interesting since it provides me chances to think of what is a good relationship. Through the discussion, I can have a better understanding of "relationship". Also, I can get the main idea of how to write a good essay.

Today's discussion is very interesting because we can share ourselves to our classmates and we can know more about each other. We can have more chances to speak in English through discussion. Besides, the topic is more interesting than AIDS [the topic in last week's class-DN]. I do enjoy today's discussion.

Today is a rather "academic" lesson i.e. academic writing, it's boring for me. I think it's better to let us discuss among each other rather than look at the sheets. I enjoy the TV programme although it's short but I like watching and listening to the TV/tape more than looking at the articles. The atmosphere during class is rather serious. I hope next time there will be more fun and smiles/laughs.

I think that it is boring to identify the purpose/audience and title of paragraph. But the passage "Choosing Mates—The American Way" is interesting. We can have a chance to practise our listening and oral skill in the second part of the EAS. The interviews/questionnaire part is quite interesting but some of us haven't got enough time to ask questions to find out how other students answer this questionnaire.

Talking with other people about their vital persons in their life is wonderful. Through this, I can know more about them. I think it is better to spend more time on Task 2. The questions listed in Task 2 are controversial and worthwhile to discuss. Perhaps, we can have a debate about these controversial questions. The topic of this lesson is a little bit boring, I think. In fact, I want to have a more concentrated topic or activity. Perhaps we can have one activity, e.g. debate, throughout the lesson.

Today's lesson is very interesting in that it enables us the opportunity of learning, comparing and appreciating different introduction paragraphs with different purposes and audiences, yet under the same topic—"relationship". In addition, the article written by Whyte could help us to develop our critical thinking, i.e. we ought to think before we believe. Whether it have enough evidences, or whether the writer has contradictions among himself, or whether we decided to stick to our own believes even though it might not be the fact.

9. If you have access to a group of students, try out some of the classroom techniques described in this chapter. Record and review the lesson. What worked well? What was not so successful? Why? What would you do differently next time?

◆ **REFERENCES**

Brindley, G. 1984. *Needs Analysis and Objective Setting in the Adult Migrant Education Program*. Sydney: AMES.

Brindley, G. 1986. *The Assessment of Second Language Proficiency: Issues and Approaches*. Adelaide: NCRC.

Munby, J. 1978. *Communicative Syllabus Design*. Cambridge: Cambridge University Press.

Nunan, D. 1988. *The Learner-Centred Curriculum*. Cambridge: Cambridge University Press.

Richterich, R. 1972. *A Model for the Definition of Learner Needs*. Strasbourg: Council of Europe.

Richterich, R., and J–L. Chancerel. 1978. *Identifying the Needs of Adults Learning a Foreign Language*. Strasbourg: Council of Europe.

Widdowson, H. G. 1984. *Learning Purpose and Language Use*. Oxford: Oxford University Press.

Wright, T. 1987. *Roles of Teachers and Learners*. Oxford: Oxford University Press.

CHAPTER 6

The Learning Process

In the last chapter, we looked at the role of the learner in the learning process. In this chapter, we take a closer look at learning processes themselves. The chapter also has strong connections with Chapter 2. There, I summarized some of the key research that has been conducted into learning styles and strategies. In this chapter, I explore the pedagogical applications of this work to the classroom. In this chapter, the following issues and concepts are dealt with:

What are learning strategies?
◇ defining strategies
◇ the importance of strategies to the learning process
◇ direct and indirect strategies

Introducing strategies in the classroom
◇ a sample lesson
◇ sample classroom tasks

Learning strategies and tasks
◇ a typology of learning strategies

Encouraging learner independence
◇ goal setting
◇ self-assessment and evaluation
◇ learner choice

WHAT ARE LEARNING STRATEGIES?

◆ DEFINING STRATEGIES

Strategies are the mental and communicative procedures learners use in order to learn and use language. Underlying every learning task is at least one strategy. However, in most classrooms, learners are unaware of the strategies underlying the learning tasks in which they are engaged.

◆ THE IMPORTANCE OF STRATEGIES TO THE LEARNING PROCESS

Knowledge of strategies is important, because the greater awareness you have of what you are doing, if you are conscious of the processes underlying the learning that you are involved in, then learning will be more

171

effective. In Chapter 2, we looked at research that shows that learners who are taught the strategies underlying their learning are more highly motivated than those who are not. Research has also shown that not all learners automatically know which strategies work best for them. For this reason, explicit strategy training, coupled with thinking about how one goes about learning, and experimenting with different strategies, can lead to more effective learning.

Rebecca Oxford, one of the leading teachers and researchers in the language learning strategies field, argues that strategies are important for two reasons. In the first place, strategies "are tools for active, self-directed involvement, which is essential for developing communicative competence" (1990: 1). Secondly, learners who have developed appropriate learning strategies have greater self-confidence and learn more effectively. In her introduction to the field, she identifies twelve key features of strategies. According to Oxford, language learning strategies

◇ contribute to the main goal, communicative competence
◇ allow learners to become more self-directed
◇ expand the role of teachers
◇ are problem-oriented
◇ are specific actions taken by the learner
◇ involve many actions taken by the learner, not just the cognitive
◇ support learning both directly and indirectly
◇ are not always observable
◇ are often conscious
◇ can be taught
◇ are flexible
◇ are influenced by a variety of factors (p. 9)

◆ DIRECT AND INDIRECT STRATEGIES

Oxford draws a distinction between *direct* strategies and *indirect* strategies. Direct strategies include such things as memorizing, analyzing and reasoning, and guessing intelligently. As the name suggests, these are specific procedures that learners can use to internalize the language. Indirect strategies, on the other hand, include things such as evaluating one's learning, [taking steps to power one's anxiety,] and cooperating with others.

INTRODUCING STRATEGIES IN THE CLASSROOM

In this section I shall look at some of the ways in which strategies can be introduced into the classroom. As you read this section, it is important to keep in mind that, as far as possible, strategies should be integrated into the ongoing process of the language lesson. I have sometimes visited schools where strategies are presented separately from the language lessons. This is a mistake, because it makes it harder for learners to see the relevance of the strategies. It also makes it more difficult for learners to apply the strategies to language learning.

◆ A SAMPLE LESSON

Here is an extract from an ethnographic narrative I kept on my teaching a number of years ago. In this initial lesson, I wanted to do two things. In the first place, I wanted to collect information on the learning preferences of the students in the class. Secondly, I wanted to create a pedagogical climate and set of expectations among my students about the level of commitment and involvement I expected from them in this class.

> It is my first morning with my new class. As I deposit my various bits and pieces on the teacher's desk, I can feel the students shifting nervously in their seats. I tell them that this class will be a little different from the other language classes that they have had, that, while the purpose of the class is to improve their language skills, particularly the speaking skills they'll need in the workplace, the course is also intended to develop their skills as learners. I point out that in the amount of time we have together I can only teach them a tiny piece of the linguistic jigsaw puzzle that is English, and that because of this some of our time together will be spent doing tasks designed to help them become more effective language learners. They receive all this in what can only be described as watchful silence. Better get on with it. I tell them that, given goals of developing oral language skills, which was negotiated with the students the preceding week, most of our lessons would be given over to small group problem-solving tasks. I asked the students to get into groups of four and told them that eight more students would be joining the group the following day. I had interviewed these students and asked them how they liked to learn. I then distributed the following handout containing summary statements from each of these students.

> **Student A:** What helped me most to learn English? Let's see, reading all sorts of printed material, listening to native speakers on the radio, TV, and films, finding opportunities to use English out of class.

Student B: The things that helped me least, well, I would say memorizing grammar rules, reading aloud one by one around the class, doing boring grammar exercises.

Student C: Language taught inside the classroom is not sufficient to make a person a competent speaker in the real world. You need to use the language outside of the classroom.

Student D: Practising through conversations and using the media, especially TV with subtitles and newspapers. You must have someone who is proficient in the language to speak with in order to learn the language sufficiently well.

Student E: I find that motivation is vital in the success of learning a foreign language. Strong interest, sheer determination and motivation to learn a second language were the most important things for me.

Student F: I would say ''teacher talk'' helped me least. Looking back, I wish he had given me more opportunities to use the language in class, especially speaking it inside and outside the classroom. It would have been more fun and challenging if I was thrown into the deep end.

Student G: The thing I liked least was negative oral criticism and punishment for wrong answers. Dull teachers creativity or who are inactive/cannot be heard clearly.

Student H: What helped me most was constant drilling, and when I had my own textbook and made notes from teacher explanations.

I asked the groups to read the statements, discuss them, and decide (a) which of these students they would like to join their group, and (b) which they would definitely not like to have in their group. I asked if there were any questions, responded to two procedural questions, and then said that they could have 25 minutes to complete this task. There was an air of surprised silence as the students digested what had been said and began reading the handout. I signaled that the ball was now in their court by leaving the room. On my return, the atmosphere has changed dramatically. The students are all talking animatedly in small groups. I call a halt to the groupwork and begin the debriefing.

The brief classroom description illustrates the beginning of a course, the very first lesson, in fact, within which negotiation is a key element. By the third week of the course, the students were making important decisions about what they would learn and how they would go about it. However, in the first three weeks, a great deal of energy was devoted to helping them to identify and refine their own preferred learning styles and strategies as well as equipping them with other key skills they would need to negotiate the curriculum with me and with their peers. I have included the classroom snapshot to illustrate the fact that negotiation is not an all-or-nothing concept, and to show that, in the initial stages, a philosophy of negotiation can in fact be realized through a teacher-directed classroom.

◆ SAMPLE CLASSROOM TASKS

In my teaching, I try to introduce learners to the following aspects of learning-how-to-learn:

◇ the learning process in general;
◇ becoming more sensitive to the context and environment within which learning takes place;
◇ dealing with the macroskills (that is, listening, speaking, reading and writing);
◇ dealing with the linguistic systems of pronunciation, vocabulary, grammar, and discourse.

Sample tasks, illustrating each of these, are set out below.

The Learning Process in General

During the initial phases of a course, I incorporate into my classes opportunities for learners to focus on the general aspects of learning and being a learner. I have developed and adapted a range of tasks that get learners thinking about how they like to learn best, what works for them, and what does not work. I also push them to contest their own ideas, preferences, and attitudes against those of other students. The following illustrative task, adapted from Gibbs *et al.* (1989) is designed to help students identify their broad orientation to learning. You will notice that the task also involves learners in oral discussion work, as they share their ideas with other students.

What's your orientation?

Task 1

Study the following statements and decide which one describes you most accurately. (You will probably find that each one describes you partially, but try to find the one that is most like you.)

Statement A: "I am very competitive. When it comes to studying, I am well organized, and I like to do well."

Statement B: "I like to be told exactly what to do by the teacher, and I like to spend most of my study time memorizing the material provided by the teacher and the textbook."

Statement C: "I like to understand what I am learning and why I am learning it."

Task 2

Now complete the following survey. Circle a number that corresponds to the statement in the key

4 = I definitely agree
3 = I agree with reservations
2 = This statement doesn't really apply to me
1 = I disagree with reservations
0 = I definitely disagree

1. I find it easy to organize my study time effectively.   4 3 2 1 0 [A]

2. I like to be told exactly what to do in essays and other set work.   4 3 2 1 0 [B]

3. It's important for me to really well in my English course.   4 3 2 1 0 [A]

4. I start out by trying to understand thoroughly what's expected of me.   4 3 2 1 0 [C]

5. When I'm studying, I try to memorize facts that might be important later.   4 3 2 1 0 [B]

6. When I'm doing a piece of work, I try to produce what the teacher seems to want, even if it's not exactly what I think.   4 3 2 1 0 [A]

7. My main reason for taking this course is to find out more about a subject that I really like.   4 3 2 1 0 [C]

8. I'm more interested in getting the qualification that in the subject matter of the course.   4 3 2 1 0 [B]

9. When I have work to do in the evenings, I start immediately, rather than putting it off.   4 3 2 1 0 [A]

10. I put a lot of effort into trying to understand things that seem difficult to begin with.   4 3 2 1 0 [C]

11. Often I have to learn things without having a chance to really understand them.   4 3 2 1 0 [B]

12. If there are things about my course I don't like I generally do something to change them.   4 3 2 1 0 [A]

13. I often find myself questioning things I am taught in class or that I read about in my books.   4 3 2 1 0 [C]

14. I tend to do very little work beyond what is
    required by the course.   4 3 2 1 0 [B]

15. It's important for me to do better than my friends
    if I possibly can.   4 3 2 1 0 [A]

16. I spend a lot of time outside of class finding out
    more about interesting topics that came up in
    class.   4 3 2 1 0 [C]

17. I find the things we studied in class so interesting,
    I'd like to continue studying them after this
    course.   4 3 2 1 0 [C]

18. I find I have to spend a lot of time memorizing
    the things that we learned in class.   4 3 2 1 0 [B]

Task 3

	A	B	C

Find out your overall score by writing down
the numbers circled for the questions marked
A, B, or C. Then add up the totals from each
column. The column with the highest score
shows your overall orientation.

Totals _____

Task 4

Find someone who had the same response as you on Task 1. Compare
your responses to the questionnaire in Task 2, and note similarities and
differences. Does your overall highest score fall in the same column as
that of your partner?

Task 5

Work with three or four other students. Try and ensure that there are
representatives of the three different orientations in each group. Study
the following descriptions and decide whether they accurately describe
the different orientations as revealed by the questionnaire in Task 2.

If you score highest in the A column:
This is a score out of 24 on "achieving orientation." This indicates
competitiveness, well-organized study methods, and hope for success.
Students who score high on this scale are oriented toward doing well,
whatever this involves. They tend to do well.

If you scored highest in the B column:
This is a score out of 24 on "reproducing orientation." This indicates a surface approach to learning. Students who score high on this scale attempt to memorize subject matter and are not interested in studying a subject for its own sake but only out of concern to pass or gain qualifications. . . . Despite their concern to pass, they generally do badly.

If you scored highest in the C column:
This is a score out of 24 on "meaning orientation." This indicates a deep approach to learning: The intention to make sense of the subject, an interest in the subject itself, and a desire to learn. Students who score high on this scale follow up their own interests even if these are outside those parts of the course that are assessed.

Adapted from Gibbs, G., S. Habeshaw, and T. Habeshaw. 1989.

The Context and Environment of Learning

The second thing I focus on is the context and environment of the learning process. Here, I have designed tasks that help learners develop a reflexive attitude towards, and skills in working in a variety of different modes, including whole-class work, pair and group work, individualized learning, cooperative learning, self-access learning, and learning beyond the classroom.

The following sequence of tasks is designed for students who have had some exposure to independent learning, and now need a framework for formulating a learning objective, identifying appropriate procedures and resources for achieving the objective, setting a realistic time frame, and identifying the means for self-evaluating their learning.

Learning contract

Task 1

Complete the following learning contract.

1. Period of instruction. From: _____ to: _____
2. Scheduled meeting time(s): _____
3. Learning objective:

   _____

   _____

4. Procedures for achieving objective:

_____

_____

_____

5. Resources:

_____

_____

_____

6. Evaluation (How will you know if you have achieved your objective?)

_____

_____

_____

Task 2

In pairs, exchange contracts. Review your partner's contract.

Does the objective clearly state what you are to do?

Are the procedures and resources consistent with the objective?

Are the objectives, timeframe, etc. realistic?

Will the evidence satisfy an outside observer that the objective has been achieved?

Task 3

List three questions to ask your partner. Make three suggestions for improving the contract.

Questions

1. _____

2. _____

3. _____

Suggestions

1. _____

    _____

2. _____

    _____

3. _____

    _____

Task 3

Discuss your questions and suggestions with your partner.

Task 4

Revise your contract in light of the discussion with your partner.

Dealing with the Macroskills

The third area that I concentrate on is in relation to the macroskills. Here I help learners develop skills such as skimming, scanning, selective listening, notetaking, and organizing information. In other words, the tasks are designed to encourage learners to reflect on the direct strategies they can use in listening, speaking, reading, and writing. The task that follows is part of an academic listening program in which students are required to attend lectures in a language that is not their first. However, it can also be used in general English programs. The aim of the task sequence is to show learners how they can use what they already know to make listening more successful.

Predicting and confirming

Task 1

You are going to listen to a short discussion on "How to succeed in an employment interview." Write down as many words you can think of associated with the subject.

How To Succeed In an Interview

Task 2

Now pair up with two other students and add their words to your list.

Task 3

Study the following theme, and, with two other students, write down 3 to 5 ideas associated with the theme.

Theme: Success in an interview depends on being able to talk confidently about yourself, your skills, and your abilities.

Ideas:

1. _____
2. _____
3. _____
4. _____
5. _____

Task 4

Now listen to the lecture, and check off those words and ideas in the listening text that are on your list.

Task 5

Listen again, and make a list of the key words in the lecture.

_____

_____

_____

_____

Task 6

Compare your list with two other students.

Linguistic Systems

The final area where strategy training can assist learners is in approaches to dealing with pronunciation, vocabulary, grammar, and discourse. Here, I show learners how to use context to work out the meaning of unknown words, how to monitor their pronunciation, and how to develop their grammatical awareness through inductive and deductive learning experiences. One technique that works extremely well for raising learners' consciousness about the workings of grammar in context is the "dictogloss" technique. The steps involved in introducing dictogloss in the classroom are set out below. The technique is particularly good for encouraging monitoring of and reflecting on grammar.

Dictogloss

Task 1

In this task, I am going to read you a short text. I am going to read it twice. As you listen, make a note of as many words and phrases as you can.

_____

_____

_____

_____

Task 2

Now, working with 2 or 3 other students, share your notes and see whether you can come up with your own version of the text. Once you have reconstructed the text, check it carefully for spelling, pronunciation, and grammatical accuracy.

_____

_____

_____

_____

Task 3

Compare your version of the text with another group, and note similarities and differences.

Similarities	Differences
_____	_____
_____	_____
_____	_____
_____	_____

LEARNING STRATEGIES AND TASKS

◆ A TYPOLOGY OF LEARNING STRATEGIES

Underlying every task that one introduces into the classroom is a learning strategy of one kind or another. Sometimes, tasks that seem on the surface to be quite different turn out to be underpinned by the same strategy. And when they identify the strategies underlying the tasks they typically use in the classroom, teachers are sometimes surprised to find that they are based on a rather limited repertoire of strategies.

For my own teaching and textbook writing I have developed the following typology of strategies. Some of these strategies will be used more frequently than others, depending on the age and proficiency of the students, the skills being focused on, and the individual learner needs. In the rest of this section of the chapter, I set out some of the more commonly used learning strategies, saying why they are important and how they can aid the learning process. I have extracted these examples from a range of different sources. As I looked through recently published textbooks, I was gratified to find increasing numbers of authors building strategies, and strategy awareness, into their materials.

Cognitive

Classifying	Putting things that are similar together in groups Example: Study a list of names and classify them into male and female.
Predicting	Predicting what is to come in the learning process Example: Look at unit title and objectives and predict what will be learned.
Inducing	Looking for patterns and regularities Example: Study a conversation and discover the rule for forming the simple past tense.
Taking Notes	Writing down the important information in a text in your own words
Concept Mapping	Showing the main ideas in a text in the form of a map
Inferencing	Using what you know to learn something new
Discriminating	Distinguishing between the main idea and supporting information
Diagramming	Using information from a text to label a diagram

Interpersonal

Cooperating	Sharing ideas and learning with other students Example: Work in small groups to read a text and complete a table.
Role-Playing	Pretending to be somebody else and using the language for the situation you are in Example: You are a reporter. Use the information from the reading to interview the writer.

Linguistic

Conversational Patterns	Using expressions to start conversations and keep them going Example: Match formulaic expressions to situations.
Practicing	Doing controlled exercises to improve knowledge and skills Exercise: Listen to a conversation, and practice it with a partner.
Using Context	Using the surrounding context to guess the meaning of unknown words, phrases, and concepts.
Summarizing	Picking out and presenting the major points in a text in summary form
Selective Listening	Listening for key information without trying to understand every word Example: Listen to a conversation and identify the number of speakers.
Skimming	Reading quickly to get a general idea of a text Example: Decide if a text is a newspaper article, a letter, or an advertisement.

Affective

Personalizing	Learners share their own opinions, feelings, and ideas about a subject Example: Read a letter from a friend in need and give advice.
Self-Evaluating	Thinking about how well you did on a learning task, and rating yourself on a scale.
Reflecting	Thinking about ways you learn best

Creative

Brainstorming	Thinking of as many new words and ideas as you can Example: Work in a group and think of as many occupations as you can.

Classifying

Tasks such as the following that require learners to put vocabulary items into their semantic groups are classification tasks. Classifying helps learners because it is easier to memorize items that are grouped together in meaningful ways than trying to remember isolated items. Figure 6-1.

UNIT REVIEW: *Word Power*

Group these words and phrases from the unit into the categories below.

bus   drive   lack of oxygen
row   river   brilliant sunsets
fatigue   ranch   fear
subway   wildflowers   rowboat
fly   dehydration   fractured ribs
canyon   mule   ship
ocean   plane   ride
museum   imbalance   train
jet lag   dolphin   sadness
terror   cliffs   walk
bicycle   airport   stores
cacti   bighorn sheep

Travel			
Forms of Transportation	Ways to Travel (Verbs)	Things to See on Trips	Possible Problems on Trips
bus			

Figure 6-1   *Reading Workout,* © **Heinle & Heinle Publishers**

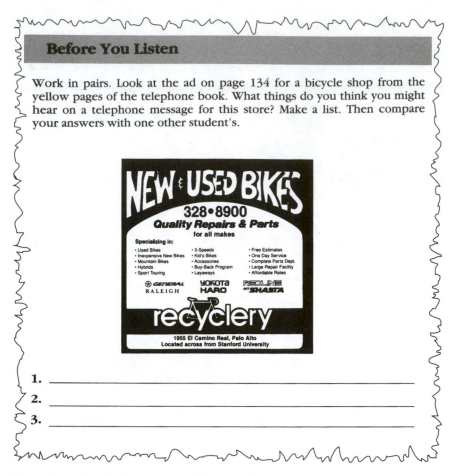

Before You Listen

Work in pairs. Look at the ad on page 134 for a bicycle shop from the yellow pages of the telephone book. What things do you think you might hear on a telephone message for this store? Make a list. Then compare your answers with one other student's.

1. _____
2. _____
3. _____

Figure 6-2 *Get It? Got It!*, © Heinle & Heinle Publishers

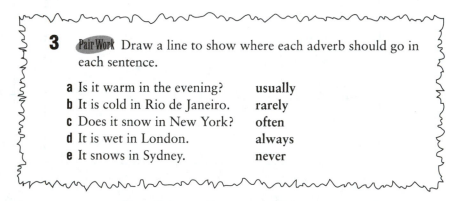

3 Pair Work Draw a line to show where each adverb should go in each sentence.

a Is it warm in the evening?   usually
b It is cold in Rio de Janeiro.   rarely
c Does it snow in New York?   often
d It is wet in London.   always
e It snows in Sydney.   never

Figure 6-3 *ATLAS* - Book 2, © Heinle & Heinle Publishers

Predicting

Predicting, or looking ahead, helps learners to anticipate what is to come. This results in more effective learning, because the learners are adequately prepared for the new material. Figure 6-2, page 186.

Inductive Reasoning

In an inductive approach to learning, students are given access to data, and are provided with structured opportunities to work out rules, principles, and so on for themselves. The idea here is that information will be more deeply processed and stored if learners are given an opportunity to work things out for themselves, rather than simply being told. Figure 6-3, page 186.

Inferencing

Inferencing involves using what you know to learn something new. Because learning is basically making links between what is new and what is already known, inferencing is an extremely important strategy. Figure 6-4.

8. **Class Work.** Writers often suggest what they mean rather than stating it directly. Readers must then make inferences, or draw logical conclusions, based on the available information. What inferences can you make about the slave traders and the Ibo people based on the information in the sentences below?

> READING STRATEGY:
> *Making Inferences*
> See page 225.

a. While the slave traders were in Africa, they went by the Ibo tribe, and they found eighteen grown people. They fooled them. They told them, "We want you to go to America to work."

What inferences can you make about the slave traders from the information in these sentences?

The slave traders weren't honest.

_____

b. When these people got to St. Simon's Island, they found out that they had been tricked and they were going to be sold as slaves. Then all eighteen of these people agreed together. They all said, "No! Rather than be a slave here in America, we would rather be dead."

What inferences can you make about the people from the Ibo tribe based on the information in these sentences?

_____

_____

Figure 6-4 *Multicultural Workshop* - Book 2, © Heinle & Heinle Publishers

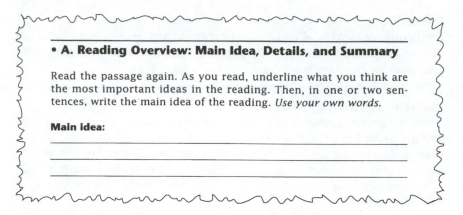

Figure 6-5a *Topics for Today,* © Heinle & Heinle Publishers

Discriminating

Discriminating means distinguishing between the main idea and supporting information in both aural and written texts. Learners who are skilled at identifying the most important information in a text are more effective listeners and readers. They can process language more quickly, and are able to identify and remember the speaker or reader's central message more effectively. Figure 6-5a and 6-5b, c. Pages 188 and 189.

Details:

Use the chart below to organize the information in the article. Refer back to the information you underlined in the passage as a guide. When you have finished, write a brief summary of the reading. *Use your own words.*

A Nuclear Graveyard

The Nuclear Repository Controversy: To Use or Not to Use the Yucca Mountain Site	
Arguments Against Using This Site	Arguments in Favor of Using This Site

Summary:

_____

_____

_____

_____

Figure 6-5b - c   *Topics for Today,* © Heinle & Heinle Publishers

PLAN A TRIP

With a group of three students, consult the information from the tables above, and choose a city that you would like to visit. Describe to your class your choice of destination and the reasons your group chose it. Next, as a group, write a letter to its tourist board (addresses below), or visit a local travel agency to get more information. When you receive the information, read it, and create a poster advertising your destination. Include information from the tables in this chapter, as well as photos or information included in the promotional literature you received in the mail.

Argentinean Tourist Information
330 West 58th Street
New York, NY 10019

Japan National Tourist Office
360 Post Street
San Francisco, CA 94108

Brazilian Consulate General
3810 Wilshire Blvd.
Los Angeles, CA 90010

Mexican Tourist Office
10100 Santa Monica Boulevard
Los Angeles, CA 90067

British Tourist Authority
40 West 57th Street
New York, NY 10019

Russian Intourist
630 Fifth Avenue
New York, NY 10111

Egyptian Tourist Authority
323 Geary Street
San Francisco, CA 94102

Singapore Tourist Board
342 Madison Avenue
New York, NY 10173

French Government Tourist Office
610 Fifth Avenue
New York, NY 10020

Spanish Tourist Office
665 Fifth Avenue
New York, NY 10022

Hong Kong Tourist Association
548 5th Avenue
New York, NY 10036

Thailand Tourism Authority
3440 Wilshire Blvd.
Los Angeles, CA 90010

Italian Government Travel Office
630 Fifth Avenue
New York, NY 10111

Figure 6-6 *Global Views,* © Heinle & Heinle Publishers

Cooperating

When we cooperate, we share ideas and learn with other students. This principle exploits the old saying that "two heads are better than one." It is particularly effective in language learning, because students are required to communicate with each other in order to cooperate. Figure 6-6, page 190.

The Sound of It: Understanding Intonation in Negative Questions

People often use statement word order to ask a negative question if they think the answer will be "no." Their intonation goes up. Here's an example from Conversation 1.

    EXAMPLE: Question: You don't have one?

In many languages, people answer "yes" because they're thinking, "Yes, that's right. I don't have one." But in English the answer is "no."

    EXAMPLE: Question: You don't have one?
                  Answer: No (I don't).

A. With a partner, take turns asking and answering these questions. In each case, answer "no" and give the correct answer. Then listen and check your answers.

  EXAMPLE: **a:**   The main language of Quebec isn't English?

           b: _No, it's French_   (French)

1. a: It's not strange to experience culture shock?

   b: _____ (normal)

2. a: Osaka isn't the capital of Japan?

   b: _____ (Tokyo)

3. a: Men don't usually talk much at home?

   b: _____ (in public)

4. a: Women don't usually talk much in public?

   b: _____ (at home)

5. a: English isn't easy?

   b: _____ (hard)

6. a: You're not from Canada?

   b: _____

Figure 6-7   *Get It? Got It!*, © Heinle & Heinle Publishers

Practicing

An essential strategy for developing skills is practicing. Practicing means doing controlled exercises to improve knowledge and skills. Figure 6-7, page 191.

Selective Listening

A key strategy for learners is listening for key information without trying to understand every word. This strategy is essential if learners are to cope effectively in genuine communicative situations outside the classroom. It

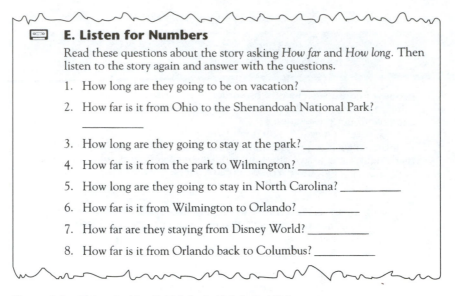

E. Listen for Numbers

Read these questions about the story asking *How far* and *How long*. Then listen to the story again and answer with the questions.

1. How long are they going to be on vacation? _____

2. How far is it from Ohio to the Shenandoah National Park? _____

3. How long are they going to stay at the park? _____

4. How far is it from the park to Wilmington? _____

5. How long are they going to stay in North Carolina? _____

6. How far is it from Wilmington to Orlando? _____

7. How far are they staying from Disney World? _____

8. How far is it from Orlando back to Columbus? _____

Figure 6-8 *Listen to Me,* © Heinle & Heinle Publishers

is important for learners to realize that native speakers use this strategy quite naturally when communicating with one another, that it is, in fact, impossible as well as unnecessary to process every single word in most listening situations. Figure 6-8.

ENCOURAGING LEARNER INDEPENDENCE

◆ GOAL SETTING

Making goals explicit to learners has a number of important pedagogical advantages. In the first place, it helps to focus the attention of the learner on the tasks to come. This enhances motivation. Research shows that a program in which goals are made explicit leads to higher performance by students than programs in which goals are implicit. Two researchers in this field concluded that: "Goal setting can have exceptional importance in stimulating L2 learning motivation, and it is therefore shocking that so little time and energy are spent in the L2 classroom on goal setting." (Oxford and Shearin 1993).

◆ SELF-ASSESSMENT AND EVALUATION

Self-evaluating involves thinking about how well you did on a learning task, and rating yourself on a scale. By having learners rate themselves against their learning goals, the teacher not only develops the learner's self-critical faculties, but also serves to remind them of the goals of the instructional process. It also prompts learners to begin making links between important links in the educational chain; for example, between their communicative goals and the grammatical and structural means of achieving those goals.

◆ *LEARNER CHOICE*

Encouraging learners to make choices is also an important aspect of learner independence. Just as the effective language user is the one who can make appropriate choices from the range of grammatical options available in the language, so the effective language learner is the one who can make effective choices in terms of learning tasks and strategies. By encouraging learners to make choices in our classrooms and in the teaching materials we provide for them, we convey to our learners the important message that they have responsibility for making decisions about and taking control of their learning.

◆ CONCLUSION

In this chapter, I have provided a theoretical and empirical rationale for placing learning strategies alongside language content in the language classroom. The chapter complements the preceding one on the role of the learner within the learning process. The bulk of the chapter is devoted to the practicalities of introducing a strategy dimension in the classroom. The points made in the chapter are illustrated with a range of sample tasks drawn from a range of sources, both published and unpublished.

◆ CONCEPT MAP OF CHAPTER 6

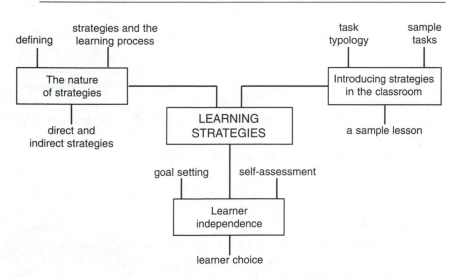

◆ **QUESTIONS AND TASKS**

1. Write your own definition of a learning strategy.
2. What is the difference between a direct strategy and an indirect strategy?
3. Analyze a chapter or unit of work from a coursebook of your choice. Identify the strategies underlying the tasks in the chapter. List and describe these. How broad or restricted is the range of strategies in the text? Produce a typology based on the strategies.
4. Teach a lesson or part of a lesson based on one of the strategies set out in the set reading. Record the session and then analyze and discuss what happened.

◆ **REFERENCES**

Bacon–Shone, J., K. Bolton, and D. Nunan. 1997. Language use, policies and support at the tertiary level. Research Report to the Committee for Research and Conference Grants, University of Hong Kong.

Barnett, M. A. 1988. Teaching reading strategies: how methodology affects language course articulation. *Foreign Language Annals*, 21/2: 109–119.

Blanton, L. L., and L. Lee. 1995. *The Multicultural Workshop*. Boston: Heinle & Heinle.

Brophy, J. 1987. Synthesis of research on strategies for motivating students to learn. *Educational Research*, 47, 40–48.

Carroll, J. B. 1981. Twenty-five years of research on foreign language aptitude. In K. C. Diller (ed.). *Individual Differences and Universals in Language Learning Aptitude* (pp. 83–118) Rowley, Mass.: Newbury House.

Cohen, A. D. 1996. Language learning strategies instruction and research. AILA '96 Symposium on Learner Autonomy, Finland, August 1996.

Cohen, A. D., and Aphek, E. 1980. Retention of second language vocabulary over time: investigating the role of mnemonic associations. *System*, 8: 221–235.

Cohen, A., S. Weaver, and T. Y. Li. 1995. The impact of strategies-based instruction on speaking a foreign language. Research Report, National Language Resource Center, University of Minnesota.

Ellis, G., and B. Sinclair. 1989. *Learning to Learn English*. Cambridge: Cambridge University Press.

Foley, B. 1994. *Listen to Me: Beginning Listening, Speaking & Pronunciation*. Boston: Heinle & Heinle.

Gardner, R. 1985. *Social Psychology and Second Language Learning: The Role of Attitudes and Motivation*. London: Arnold.

Gibbs, G., S. Habeshaw, and T. Habeshaw. 1989. *53 Interesting Ways to Appraise your Teaching*. Bristol, Avon: Technical and Educational Services Ltd.

Green, J. M., and R. Oxford. 1995. A closer look at learning strategies, L2 proficiency, and gender. *TESOL Quarterly*, 29/2: 261–297.

Hatch, E., and A. Lazaraton. 1991. *The Research Manual: Design and Statistics for Applied Linguistics*. New York: Newbury House.

Huizenga, J., and Thomas–Ruzic, M. 1994. *Reading Workout*. Boston: Heinle & Heinle.

Jones, B., A. Palincsar, D. Ogle, and E. Carr. 1987. *Strategic Teaching and Learning: Cognitive Instruction in the Content Areas*. Alexandria, Va.: Association for Supervision and Curriculum Development.

Jones, V., and L. Jones. 1990. *Classroom Management: Managing and Motivating Students*. Needham Heights, MA: Allyn and Bacon.

McVey Gill, M., and P. Hartmann. 1993. *Get it? Got it!* Boston: Heinle & Heinle.

Nunan, D. 1991. *Language Teaching Methodology*. London: Prentice-Hall.

Nunan, D. 1995a. Self-assessment as a tool for learning. In D. Nunan, R. Berry, and V. Berry (eds.), *Bringing about Change in Language Education*. Hong Kong: Department of Curriculum Studies, University of Hong Kong.

Nunan, D. 1995b. Closing the gap between instruction and learning. *TESOL Quarterly*, 29/1: 133–158.

Nunan, D. 1995c. *ATLAS: Learning-Centered Communication*. Levels 1–4. Boston: Heinle & Heinle/International Thomson Publishing.

O'Malley, J. M., A. U. Chamot, G. Stewner–Manzanares, G. Russo, and L. Kupper. 1985. Learning strategy applications with students of English as a Second Language. *TESOL Quarterly*, 19, 285–296.

O'Malley, J. M. and A. U. Chamot. 1990. Learning Strategies in Second Language Acquisition. Cambridge: Cambridge University Press.

Oxford, R. 1990. *Language Learning Strategies: What Every Teacher Should Know*. Boston: Newbury House.

Smith, L. C., & N. N. Mare. 1997. *Topics for Today*. Boston: Heinle & Heinle.

Sokolik, M. 1993. *Global Views. Reading About World Issues*. Boston: Heinle & Heinle.

Spada, N. 1990. In J. C. Richards and D. Nunan (eds.), *Second Language Teacher Education*. New York: Cambridge University Press.

Tsui, A. 1996. Reticence and anxiety in second language learning. In K. Bailey and D. Nunan (eds.), *Voices from the Classroom: Qualitative Research in Language Education*. New York: Cambridge University Press.

Willing, K. 1990. *Teaching How to Learn*. Sydney: National Centre for English Language Teaching and Research.

Willis, D. 1990. *The Lexical Syllabus*. London: Collins ELT.

PART III
Language Skills In Action

Introduction

This final section focuses on the teaching of listening, speaking, reading, and writing. I have chosen to deal with the four skills separately. This is more for organizational convenience than out of a belief that they should be taught separately. In general, I favor an integrated approach to the teaching of skills, although I recognize that in many contexts and situations, particularly when dealing with adults, learner needs dictate a primary focus on one particular skill rather than the other three. At present, I am teaching a course with a primary focus on the development of academic writing skills. However, that does not mean that students do not also do lots of reading, discussing, and listening.

In the chapters in this section, you will find many of the thematic concerns that emerged in the first two sections reappearing to support the ideas that are set out. While Section 1 of the book had a primary focus on theoretical concerns, and Section 2 an emphasis on the importance of applied research to pedagogy, the main focus of this final section is on the practice of language teaching. This does not mean that theory and research that speaks directly to the skills are not dealt with, but that the main focus is very much on issues to do with the design of courses and the development of pedagogical tasks.

Chapter 7 deals with listening, the Cinderella skill, as I call it. The first part of the chapter reviews conceptual and empirical issues before setting key considerations in the development, sequencing, and grading of listening tasks.

Chapter 8 looks at speaking, and begins with a consideration of what it is that differentiates spoken from written language. It also looks at ways of encouraging and motivating the reluctant speaker. Course design and materials/task development issues are then explored. The chapter concludes with a sample speaking lesson that is designed to illustrate some of the main points that are made in the chapter.

Chapter 9 on reading, also begins with a consideration of some of the key theoretical and empirical underpinnings of a reading program. In particular, the debate between product- and process-oriented approaches to reading are dealt with. The focus then turns to task types in a reading program, and looks in particular at tasks that help learners master and apply a range of strategies to the reading process.

Chapter 10 on writing, advocates a functional, discourse-based approach to writing pedagogy. A rationale for such an approach is presented that builds on and extends the functional view of language set out in Chapter 4. Practical ways of using the principles in the design of teaching materials are then presented.

CHAPTER 7

Listening

Listening is the Cinderella skill in second language learning. All too often, it has been overlooked by its elder sister, speaking. For most people, being able to claim knowledge of a second language means being able to speak and write in that language. Listening and reading are therefore secondary skills, means to other ends, rather than ends in themselves.

Ever so often, however, listening comes into fashion. In the 1960s, the emphasis on oral language skills gave it a boost. It became fashionable again in the 1980s, when Krashen's ideas about comprehensible input gained prominence. A short time later, it was reinforced by James Asher's Total Physical Response, a methodology drawing sustenance from Krashen's work, and based on the belief that a second language is learned most effectively in the early stages if the pressure for production is taken off the learners. During the 1980s, proponents of listening in a second language were also encouraged by work in the first language field. Here, people such as Gillian Brown (see, for example, Brown 1984, Brown *et al.* 1987) were able to demonstrate the importance of developing oracy (the ability to listen and speak) as well as literacy, in school. Prior to this, it was taken for granted that first language speakers needed instruction in how to read and write, but not how to listen and speak because these skills were automatically bequeathed to them as native speakers.

The chapter covers the following issues and concepts:

Listening in another language
◇ the nature of listening
◇ top-down and bottom-up processing
◇ schema theory
◇ types of listening

Research into listening
◇ comprehensible input
◇ task difficulty
◇ listening and general language development

The role of the learner in the listening process
◇ learner roles
◇ personalizing listening

The database for listening courses
◇ authentic data

Task types
◇ reciprocal versus non-reciprocal listening
◇ listening strategies
◇ focus on linguistic skills

LISTENING IN ANOTHER LANGUAGE

◆ *THE NATURE OF LISTENING IN ANOTHER LANGUAGE*

As already indicated, listening is assuming greater and greater importance in foreign language classrooms. There are several reasons for this growth in popularity. Later in the chapter, we will see that, by emphasizing the role of comprehensible input, second language acquisition research has given a major boost to listening. (You will recall that some of this research was reviewed in Chapter 2.) As Rost (1994:141–142) points out, listening is vital in the language classroom because it provides input for the learner. Without understanding input at the right level, learning cannot begin. He provides three other important reasons for emphasizing listening, and these demonstrate the importance of listening to the development of spoken language proficiency:

◇ Spoken language provides a means of interaction for the learner. Because learners must interact to achieve understanding, access to speakers of the language is essential. Moreover, learners' failure to understand the language they hear is an impetus, not an obstacle, to interaction and learning.

◇ Authentic spoken language presents a challenge for the learner to attempt to understand language as native speakers actually use it.

◇ Listening exercises provide teachers with the means for drawing learners' attention to new forms (vocabulary, grammar, new interaction patterns) in the language (pp. 141–142).

◆ *TOP-DOWN AND BOTTOM-UP PROCESSING*

Two views of listening have dominated language pedagogy over the last twenty years. These are the "bottom-up" processing view and the "top-down" interpretation view. The bottom-up processing model assumes that listening is a process of decoding the sounds that one hears in a linear fashion, from the smallest meaningful units (or phonemes) to complete texts. According to this view, phonemic units are decoded and linked together to form words, words are linked together to form phrases, phrases are linked together to form utterances, and utterances are linked together to form complete meaningful texts. In other words, the process is a linear one, in which meaning itself is derived as the last step in the process. In

---

Phonemes:
Phonemes are the smallest meaningful units of sound in a language.
Example: /s/ /sh/ These two sounds form meaningful contrasts in English, as in *ship* and *sheep*.

their introduction to listening Anderson and Lynch (1988) call this the "listener as tape-recorder view of listening because it assumes that the listener takes in and stores messages in much the same way as a tape-recorder, sequentially, one sound, word, phrase, and utterance at a time."

The alternative, top-down view, suggests that the listener actively constructs (or, more accurately, reconstructs) the original meaning of the speaker using incoming sounds as clues. In this reconstruction process, the listener uses prior knowledge of the context and situation within which the listening takes place to make sense of what he or she hears. (Context of situation includes such things as knowledge of the topic at hand, the speaker or speakers and their relationship to the situation as well as to each other, and prior events.)

◆ SCHEMA THEORY

An important theoretical underpinning to the top-down approach is schema theory. The term *schema* was first used by the psychologist Bartlett (1932), and has had an important influence on researchers in the areas of speech processing and language comprehension ever since. Bartlett argued that the knowledge we carry around in our heads is organized into interrelated patterns. They are like stereotypical mental scripts or scenarios of situations and events, built up from numerous experiences of similar events. During the course of our lives we build up literally hundreds of mental schemas, and they help us make sense of the many situations we find ourselves in during the day, from catching the train to work, to taking part in a business meeting, to having a meal.

> **Schema Theory**
> Schema theory is based on the notion that past experiences lead to the creation of mental frameworks that help us make sense of new experiences.

Occasionally, particularly in cross-cultural situations, when we apply the wrong or inappropriate scheme to a situation it can get us into trouble. I am indebted to Erik Gundersen for the following vignette, which eventually found its way into the ATLAS learning series.

```
    ''When I was in Taiwan, I went out to this restau-
rant for a business dinner with maybe five or six
people, and I was the least important person. There
was the manager of our Asian office, a local sales
representative, and a few other important people. Our
host offered me a seat, and I took it, and everyone
looked sort of uncomfortable, but no one said any-
thing. But I could tell somehow I had done something
```

wrong. And by Western standards I really didn't feel
I had. I simply sat down in the seat I was given. I
knew I had embarrassed everyone, and it had something
to do with where I was sitting, but I didn't know
what it was. . . . Towards the end of the evening,
our Asian manager in Taiwan said, ''Just so that you
know, you took the seat of honor, and you probably
shouldn't have.'' And I thought to myself, '' Well,
what did I do wrong?'' And I asked her, and she said,
''Well, you took the seat that was facing the door,
and in Taiwan, that's the seat that's reserved for
the most important person in the party, so that if
the seat is offered to you, you should decline it.
You should decline it several times, and perhaps on
the fourth or fifth time that someone insists that
you sit there as the foreign guest, you should, but
you shouldn't sit there right away, as you did.''

ATLAS *Level 3, Unit 7*

In this situation, Gundersen applied his Western schema, which says that when you are offered a seat by a guest, then you take it. However, in many Eastern contexts, this is the wrong thing to do, as Erik Gundersen discovered to his discomfort. However, the experience would have led him to modify his "restaurant" schemata. Seen in this way, even relatively uncomfortable learning experiences can be enriching. These mental frameworks are critically important in helping us to predict and then cope with the exigencies of everyday life. In fact, as Oller (1979) has pointed out, without these schema, nothing in life would be predictable, and if nothing were predictable, it would be impossible to function. The world would appear chaotic.

In addition to stereotypical, cultural knowledge, local knowledge of participants, events and persons is important. It is difficult to interpret the following text, for example, without knowing that Jack is a vegetarian.

> **Denise:** *Jack's coming to dinner tonight.*
> **Jim:** *I'd planned to serve lamb.*
> **Denise:** *Well, you'll have to rethink that one.*

The inadequacy of a strictly bottom-up approach has been demonstrated by research that shows that we do not store listening texts word-for-word as suggested by the bottom-up approach. When asked to listen to a text, and then write down as much as they can recall, listeners remember some bits, forget some bits, and often add in bits that were not there in the original listening. Additionally, it is highly unlikely that the pieces that are successfully recalled will be recorded in exactly the same words as the original message.

What has all this to do with listening comprehension? It suggests that, in developing courses, materials, and lessons, it is important, not only to teach bottom-up processing skills such as the ability to discriminate between minimal pairs, but it is also important to help learners use what they already know to understand what they hear. If teachers suspect that there are gaps in their learners' knowledge, either of content or of grammar or vocabulary, the listening itself can be preceded by schema building activities such as the following.

The purpose of this task is to introduce learners to some of the terms

A. Before You Listen Did anyone ever borrow one of these items from you? Who borrowed it? When did the person return it?

_____ your car

_____ money

_____ a tape or a CD

_____ clothes, for example, a dress to wear to a party

_____ your dictionary

_____ a tool, such as a power saw or a drill

B. Key Words Discuss the new vocabulary, then complete the sentences below.

several	more than two, but not many
break	a rest time at work or school
bill	a paper that tells the items bought and their prices
pay back	to return money that a person borrowed
wallet	a small case for keeping money, credit cards, etc.
(be) broke	to not have any money

1. Can I borrow five dollars? I'll _____ you _____ tomorrow.

2. Those people are renting _____ videos.

3. On their _____ , the workers usually sit and talk.

4. The _____ for lunch was ten dollars.

5. I don't have any money because I forgot my _____ .

6. I can't lend you any money. I'm _____

Figure 7-1 *Now Hear This!*, © **Heinle & Heinle Publishers**

that they will encounter in the body of the unit, which is concerned with renting an apartment.

◆ TYPES OF LISTENING

There are many different types of listening. We can classify these according to a number of variables, including listening purpose, the role of the listener, and the type of text being listened to. These variables can be mixed and matched to give many different configurations, each of which will require a particular strategy on the part of the listener.

Interpersonal versus transactional language
Interpersonal dialogues occur in the course of social interaction. Transactional language exists for the exchange of goods and services.

There are numerous ways in which texts can be classified. One common division is between monologues (for example, lectures, speeches, and news broadcasts), and dialogues. Monologues can be further subdivided into those that are planned and those that are unplanned. Planned monologues include media broadcasts and speeches. Many of these are texts that are written to be read, although this is not necessarily always the case. Unplanned monologues would include anecdotes, narratives, and extemporizations.

Dialogues can be classified according to purpose: whether they are basically social/interpersonal or transactional in nature. Interpersonal dialogues can be further classified according to the degree of familiarity between the individuals involved.

Listening purpose is another important variable. Listening to a news broadcast to get a general idea of the news of the day involves different processes and strategies than listening to the same broadcast for specific information, such as the results of an important sporting event. Listening to a sequence of instructions for operating a new piece of computer software requires different listening skills and strategies than listening to a poem or short story. In designing listening tasks, it is important to teach learners to adopt a flexible range of listening strategies. This can be done by holding the listening text constant (working, say, with a radio news broadcast reporting a series of international events), and getting learners to listen to the text several times, but following different instructions each time. They might, in the first instance, be required to listen for gist, simply identifying the countries where the events have taken place. The second time they listen they might be required to match the places with a list of events. Finally, they might be required to listen for detail, discriminating between specific aspects of the event, or, perhaps, comparing the radio broadcast with newspaper accounts of the same events and noting discrepancies or differences of emphasis.

This technique of developing flexibility in listening is exemplified in the task as shown in Figure 7-2. When engaging learners in such tasks, it is worth pointing out to them the different strategies that are inherent in each phase of the task, and getting them thinking of situations in which the different strategies might be used. In the example on page 206, learners are required to listen to a text three times, and to carry out increasingly challenging tasks each time.

Another way of characterizing listening is in terms of whether the listener is also required to take part in the interaction. This is known as reciprocal listening. When listening to a monologue, either "live" or through the media, the listening is, by definition, nonreciprocal. The listener (often to his or her frustration) has no opportunity to answer back, clarify understanding, or check that he or she has comprehended correctly. In the real world, it is rare for the listener to be cast in the role of nonreciprocal "eavesdropper" on a conversation. However, in the listening classroom, this is the normal role. In the section on the role of the learner in the listening process, I will describe a technique that can be used in the classroom for giving learners a chance to respond as they might in a conversational exchange.

RESEARCH INTO LISTENING

At beginning of this chapter I suggested that listening was the Cinderella skill, that it has been alternately overlooked and elevated to the status of a movement. Dunkel (1993), in her excellent overview of the state of the art in listening research and pedagogy, suggests that the current interest in listening comprehension research has been driven by relatively recent developments in second language acquisition theory. In Chapter 2, I reviewed work by Krashen (1982) and others that suggests that comprehensible input is an important factor in second language acquisition, and that a comprehension-before-production approach can facilitate language acquisition, particularly in the early stages.

◆ COMPREHENSIBLE INPUT

This research stimulated the development of a number of comprehension-based methods, the best known of which during the 1980s was probably James Asher's intriguingly titled Total Physical Response (TPR). Asher's methodology was also heavily influenced by the implications he derived

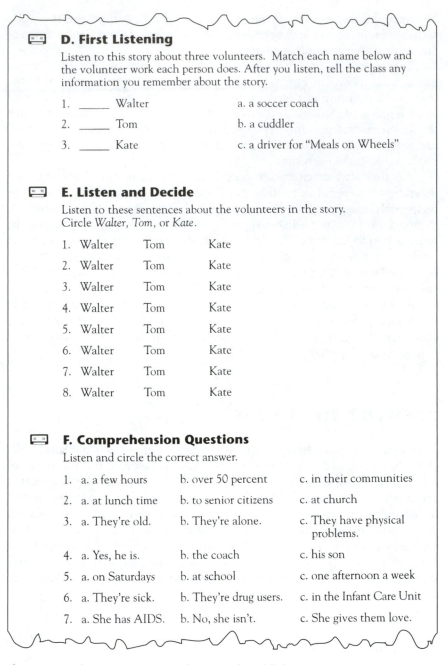

D. First Listening

Listen to this story about three volunteers. Match each name below and the volunteer work each person does. After you listen, tell the class any information you remember about the story.

1. _____ Walter   a. a soccer coach

2. _____ Tom   b. a cuddler

3. _____ Kate   c. a driver for "Meals on Wheels"

E. Listen and Decide

Listen to these sentences about the volunteers in the story.
Circle *Walter, Tom,* or *Kate.*

1. Walter   Tom   Kate

2. Walter   Tom   Kate

3. Walter   Tom   Kate

4. Walter   Tom   Kate

5. Walter   Tom   Kate

6. Walter   Tom   Kate

7. Walter   Tom   Kate

8. Walter   Tom   Kate

F. Comprehension Questions

Listen and circle the correct answer.

1. a. a few hours   b. over 50 percent   c. in their communities

2. a. at lunch time   b. to senior citizens   c. at church

3. a. They're old.   b. They're alone.   c. They have physical problems.

4. a. Yes, he is.   b. the coach   c. his son

5. a. on Saturdays   b. at school   c. one afternoon a week

6. a. They're sick.   b. They're drug users. c. in the Infant Care Unit

7. a. She has AIDS.   b. No, she isn't.   c. She gives them love.

Figure 7-2 *Listen to Me!* © Heinle & Heinle Publishers

from research into first language acquisition. Asher derived three principles from his beliefs about the nature of first language acquisition:

1. We should stress comprehension rather than production at the beginning levels of second language instruction with no demand on the learners to produce the target language.
2. We should obey the "here and now" principle, which argues that language should be associated with things that are physically present in the environment.
3. Learners should demonstrate comprehension by listening to and carrying out instructions couched in the imperative.

In the area of listening for academic purposes, Chaudron & Richards (1986) looked at the influence of discourse markers on the comprehension of academic lectures by second language learners. Although their study was beset by methodological difficulties, it did establish that knowledge of discourse markers can facilitate comprehension.

During the mid-1980s, I became interested in the effect of authentic input on listening comprehension. As with the study by Chaudron and Richards, my work was fraught with problems, although mine had to do with the difficulties of conducting a formal experiment in a naturalistic context. Nevertheless, it did establish the importance of incorporating authentic data into the teaching of listening.

◆ TASK DIFFICULTY

An important consideration for pedagogy (and a major challenge for course designers and materials writers using a task-oriented approach) concerns task difficulty. If grammatical complexity is not to be the sole determining factor in deciding the ordering of tasks within courses as a whole, and also within units of work, then what factors can be drawn on? In the first language arena, Watson and Smeltzer (1984) suggest that factors internal to the learner, such as attentiveness, motivation, interest in and knowledge of the topic, can have a marked bearing on listening success. Textual factors include the organization of information (texts in

---

What makes listening difficult?
1. The organization of information
2. The familiarity of the topic
3. The explicitness and sufficiency of the information
4. The type of referring expressions used
5. Whether the text describes a "static" or "dynamic" relationship

Anderson and Lynch, 1988

which the information is presented in the same sequence as it occurred in real life are easier to comprehend than texts in which the items are presented out of sequence), the explicitness and sufficiency of information provided, the type of referring expressions used (for example, use of pronouns rather than complete noun phrases makes texts more difficult), and whether the text is describing a "static" relationship (for example, a geometric figure) or a "dynamic" one (for example, an accident). Brown and Yule (1983) suggest that there are four principal sets of factors affecting the difficulty of listening.

1. Speaker factors: How many speakers are there? How quickly do they speak? What types of accents do they have?
2. Listener factors: What is the listener's role—eavesdropper or participant? What level of response is required? How interested is the listener in the subject?
3. The content: How complex is the grammar, vocabulary, and information structure? What background knowledge is assumed?
4. Support: How much support is provided in terms of pictures, diagrams, or other visual aids?

The tasks used by Anderson and Lynch (1988) in their research illustrate the way some of these characteristics function to facilitate or inhibit comprehension. One of these was a "trace the route" task, in which students listen to a description of a trip around a city or part of a city and then trace the route on a map. The researchers manipulated some of the features identified above, and these variations changed the difficulty of the task. Maps laid out in a rectangular grid, with all streets and features marked, were easier than those with irregular streets. Not surprisingly, completeness of information was an important factor. Texts became increasingly difficult according to the number of features mentioned in the listening that were omitted from the map. As the number of buildings and natural landmarks increased, so did the difficulty. The most difficult version of the task was one in which the listening text and the map contained contradictory information.

Another strand of research has focused on the types of classroom tasks that facilitate listening comprehension. Spada (1990) reports on an investigation demonstrating the effectiveness of structuring the listening for the learners by providing a set of predictive exercises to complete while carrying out the listening. The predictive work, plus the opportunity for students to stop the tape during the course of the listening exercise to ask questions led to greater gains in listening than in classes where the teacher launched directly into the listening without any schema-building activities, and students were not provided with the opportunity of seeking clarification during the course of the listening.

In the listening study reported in Nunan (1997), the use of a concept mapping technique also proved effective. Students were put into one of three groups, and asked to listen to an interview with a television journalist. The first group was required simply to listen to the tape, make notes, and complete a comprehension test. The second group listened, checked off key words/phrases, and completed the test. As the the third group listened, they were required to complete a concept map which showed, not only the key words and phrases, but the relationships between these. The study showed that the additional depth of processing required by the third group resulted in superior comprehension.

Difficulty is also affected by the extent to which listeners are required to extract information directly from the text, or whether they are required to make inferences. In the study described in the preceding paragraph, I found that learners had greater difficulty determining the truth value of statements requiring inferences than those in which the truth value could be determined directly from the listening text (Nunan 1997).

◆ LISTENING AND GENERAL LANGUAGE DEVELOPMENT

The value of listening to general language development has been underlined by Ross, who carried out a detailed longitudinal study of several dimensions to language teaching and its effect on student output in Japan. He found that:

> The consistent fit between the observation data and the results of the listening tests provides ample evidence to endorse an approach to TEFL at the elementary level which seeks to nurture listening comprehension and communication in the classroom at the same time. Such an approach does not necessarily require a steady stream of extemporaneous teacher talk to create on-the-spot comprehensible input. Rather, appropriate listening materials which are calibrated to the interests and abilities of the students are needed for systematic growth in listening skills.
>
> Ross 1992: 192–193

The studies reviewed in this section are summarized in Table 7.1.

THE ROLE OF THE LEARNER IN THE LISTENING PROCESS

◆ LEARNER ROLES

As we have seen, listening and reading are often characterized as "passive" or "receptive" skills. The image conjured up by these terms is of the learner-as-sponge, passively absorbing the language models provided by textbooks and tapes. However, as we saw in the preceding section, there is evidence to suggest that listening (and, as we will see in the case

Table 7.1 Research into listening

Researcher		*Results*
Krashen	(1982)	Comprehensible input is an important factor in
Asher	(1982)	second language acquisition. A comprehension-before-production approach can facilitate language acquisition, particularly in the early stages.
Brown and Yule	(1983)	Four interrelated sets of factors affect listening difficulty: 1. Speaker factors: How many speakers are there? How quickly do they speak? What types of accents do they have? 2. Listener factors: What is the listener's role—eavesdropper or participant? What level of response is required? How interested is the listener in the subject? 3. The content: How complex is the grammar, vocabulary, and information structure? What background knowledge is assumed? 4. Support: How much support is provided in terms of pictures, diagrams, or other visual aids?
Watson and Smeltzer	(1984)	Factors internal to the learner such as attentiveness, motivation, interest in and knowledge of the topic, can have a marked bearing on listening success.
Chaudron and Richards	(1986)	Knowledge of discourse markers can facilitate comprehension.
Nunan	(1987)	Students who were systematically exposed to authentic listening input outperformed those who were exposed only to nonauthentic data.
Anderson and Lynch	(1988)	Significant factors in task difficulty: 1. The organization of information 2. The familiarity of the topic 3. The explicitness and sufficiency of the information 4. The type of referring expressions used 5. Whether the text describes a static or dynamic relationship
Spada	(1990)	Students who are given schema-building tasks outperformed those who were confronted with listening texts without being prepared for listening.
Nunan	(1997)	Depth of content processing is a significant factor in listening comprehension.
Ross	(1992)	Comprehensive input is facilitated by taped listening materials.

of reading in Chapter 9), that is, making sense of what we hear, is a constructive process in which the learner is an active participant. In order to comprehend, listeners need to reconstruct the original intention of the speaker by making use of both bottom-up and top-down processing strategies, and by drawing on what they already know to make use of new knowledge.

◆ PERSONALIZING LISTENING

A challenge for the teacher in the listening classroom is to give learners some degree of control over the content of the lesson, and to personalize content so learners are able to bring something of themselves to the task. The task at the bottom of the page exemplifies one way in which this personalization can take place.

Another way of increasing learner involvement is by providing extension tasks that take the listening material as a point of departure, but which then lead learners into providing part of the content themselves. For example, the students might listen to someone describing the work they do, and then create a set of questions for interviewing the person.

A learner-centered dimension can be brought to the listening class in one of two ways. In the first place, tasks can be devised in which the classroom action is centered on the learner, not the teacher: It is the learner who does the work. In tasks based on this idea, students are actively involved in structuring and restructuring their understanding of the language and in building their skills in using the language. Secondly, teaching materials, like any other type of materials, can be given a learner-centered dimension by getting learners involved in the processes underlying their learning and in making active contributions to the learning. This can be achieved in the following ways:

◇ making instructional goals explicit to the learner
◇ giving learners a degree of choices
◇ giving learners opportunities to bring their own background knowledge and experience into the classroom

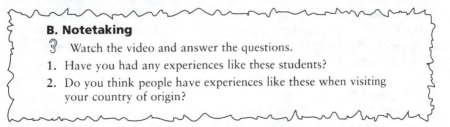

B. Notetaking

👂 Watch the video and answer the questions.

1. Have you had any experiences like these students?
2. Do you think people have experiences like these when visiting your country of origin?

Figure 7-3 *The Heart of the Matter,* © **Heinle & Heinle Publishers**

212   ♦   SECOND LANGUAGE TEACHING & LEARNING

◇ encouraging learners to develop a reflective attitude to learning and to develop skills in self-monitoring and self-assessment.

THE DATABASE FOR LISTENING COURSES

♦ *AUTHENTIC DATA*

In many language classrooms, learners listen to and read material created specifically for language learning. Such material provides security and comfort, and helps learners to see the various patterns and systems that make up the language. However, it is also essential for learners to listen to authentic texts. Exposing learners to authentic texts is important for two reasons. Firstly, nonauthentic listening texts differ in certain ways from authentic texts. They usually contain linguistic features more usually found in written rather than spoken language. There are few of the overlaps, hesitations, and false starts found in authentic texts, and there is very little negotiation of meaning. These differences do not always adequately prepare learners for dealing with genuine communication either inside or outside the classroom, because some of the features of authentic communication that rarely appear in nonauthentic texts (such as repetition, requests for clarification, and so on) actually facilitate comprehension. Also, the use of authentic sources leads to greater interest and variety in the material that learners deal with in the classroom.

In my own listening classrooms, while some use is made of specially written texts, the material is based on authentic data from the very beginning. Students will be given practice in listening to extracts from radio and television, public broadcasting announcements, conversations and discussions, telephone conversations, answering machine messages, voice mail, and other types of authentic data. This authentic material helps bring the content to life, and ultimately makes learning and using language more meaningful, and, ultimately, I believe, easier for students.

Authenticity is, of course, a relative issue. In a sense, as soon as you take language out of the context for which it was created it becomes "deauthenticated." Modifications also sometimes have to be made because speakers have used low frequency vocabulary or unusual grammatical structures that will distract or confuse the listener. Speakers also occasionally use language that is unacceptable for other reasons. In the following extract, which was designed for a commercial textbook, my editor requested that I modify the comment about the British, which she felt might be offensive to someone from Britain. (The comment, by the way, was made by someone who is British.) I have included the original transcript and the modified typescript to illustrate the kinds of changes that sometimes get made to authentic data. Despite these changes, I would argue that a large degree of linguistic and content authenticity remain.

Original Transcript

A: What do you think about tipping?

B: Oh, I find tipping very difficult and embarrassing because I never know where to, when to, and how much to.

C: Is that because Australians don't do it?

A: Yeah, basically.

B: It's not a big feature of our daily life.

C: I was talking about it to Chris Davison last week. She's Australian, but she's living in Japan, where there's no tipping, and she got very angry.

A: Well, she got chased out of a restaurant in New York by this guy who said, "Was there anything wrong with the service M'am?" And, you know, they'd left 12 percent tip instead of 15 percent or something.

B: I've heard of people having their money thrown back at them and the waiter saying "Here, you need this more than I need it."

C: Oh, well, if that were me I'd say "Fine—that's true."

B: Well, we have an argument every time we go out to a restaurant.

C: Here?

B: No, back in Australia.

C: But people don't tip there, do they?

B: Well, I don't know. You might tip for really, really good service.

A: But waitpeople there are comparatively well paid in Australia. In the States I resent it because these people are so badly exploited, you know, they

Modified Tapescript

A: (Australian) Pauline and I were talking to Angie last night about her trip to Italy. She just loved it, apart from the cost. And the tipping. Apparently, you have to tip everywhere you go.

B: (Australian) Yeah. She hated that aspect of it. I must say I find tipping very difficult and embarrassing because I never know where to, when to, and how much to.

C: (Brazilian) Is that because Australians don't do it?

B: Well, it's not a big feature of our daily life.

D: (British) I was talking about it to Yumiko, who's from Japan, of course, where there's no tipping of any kind. Anyway, she's in the States for a conference, and she got questioned by the waiter because she didn't leave a big enough tip.

B: Well, we have an argument every time we go out to a restaurant.

C: Here?

B: No, back in Australia.

C: But people don't tip there, do they?

B: Well, I don't know. You might tip for really, really good service.

A: But waiters are comparatively well paid in Australia. In the States they have to rely on tips to make a reasonable income.

B: Really? What does a waiter get?

D: There are some restaurants where waiters pay to work.

A: Yeah, in some places, you actually pay to work there.

B: To me, that seems really wrong.

Original Transcript

get two bucks an hour or whatever.

B: Is that all? What would a waiter get?

C: There are some restaurants where you pay to work there.

A: Yeah, in some places, you actually pay to work there.

B: To me, that seems really wrong.

C: Well my attitude's changed a lot since living in the States for seven years. Now I'm pretty careful to give people their 15 percent unless I really dislike the service. And if I really like it, I'll give more than 15 percent. But I hate going out with my British friends, because they don't tip, or they tip 5, or 6 or 7 percent.

A: Well, that's interesting, 'cause in Britain, tipping's a part of the culture.

C: But it's flexible, and related to how mean you are.

B: Don't you have to tip taxis in London, though?

C: Yeah, well that's sort of another subculture, isn't it? And I hate that sort of thing, 'cause taxi drivers get really nasty when you don't tip them enough.

A: And also hairdressers and barbers. You have to tip them in Britain.

B: In Singapore, there are notices everywhere—you know, "Don't tip. We do not encourage tipping."

C: When we were in Vietnam last year, Charlie used to have fights all the time with this guy who was out there with us, because this guy would give huge tips. I mean this guy would just give

Modified Tapescript

A: It's just a different culture. I don't mind the American system. When I'm in Australia and get rotten service I can't show my dissatisfaction.

D: Well my attitude's changed a lot since living in the States for seven years. Now I'm pretty careful to give people their 15 percent unless I really dislike the service. And if I really like it, I'll give more than 15 percent. But I hate going out with my British friends, because they don't tip enough—maybe 6 or 7 percent.

A: Well, that's interesting, 'cause in Britain, tipping's a part of the culture.

D: But it's flexible, and related to how generous you are.

B: In Singapore, there are notices everywhere—you know, "Don't tip. We do not encourage tipping."

A: What about in Brazil, Adriana?

C: Oh, I guess it depends on the person. Most people work hard, and don't like to throw their money away.

Original Transcript	Modified Tapescript
any amount of money. He's a typical ignorant foreigner overseas, even though he's worked overseas a lot. You know, this local money is not real money, it's just toy money. You're supposed to give a small tip there, but he would give five or six times the right amount.	

TASK TYPES

There are many different ways of classifying task types. They can be classified according to the role of the learners: whether they are involved in reciprocal or nonreciprocal listening. They can be classified according to the types of strategies demanded of the listener: listening for gist, listening for specific information, making inferences based on what they hear, and so on. Alternatively, they can be classified according to whether the task focuses principally on linguistic skills (activating and extending the listeners' knowledge of phonology, grammar, and discourse), or whether the focus is on the experiential content of the material.

♦ RECIPROCAL VERSUS NONRECIPROCAL LISTENING

Reciprocal listening involves dialogues in which the role of an individual alternates between listener and speaker. Nonreciprocal listening involves listening to monologues. In listening courses, learners are involved in both reciprocal and nonreciprocal listening tasks. In the case of reciprocal listening, they can be cast in the role of participant, in which they alternate between listener or speaker, or they can be cast in the role of "eavesdropper" or "overhearer." In this second type of task, they listen in on conversations between two or more other speakers, but do not take part in the conversation themselves. Not surprisingly, this second type of listening is the more usual type in the listening class.

I try to simulate the interactive nature of listening, and also try to involve learners personally in the content of the language lesson through activities such as the following. In this task, the learners listen to one side of a conversation, and react to written responses. Obviously, this is not the same thing as taking part in an actual conversation, but I find that it does generate a level of involvement on the part of learners that goes beyond nonparticipatory listening. Because learners are providing personalized responses, there are variations between learners, and this creates the potential for follow-up speaking tasks, in which learners compare and

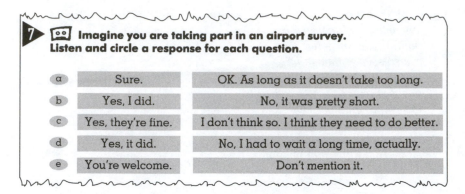

7 🔲 **Imagine you are taking part in an airport survey.
Listen and circle a response for each question.**

a	Sure.	OK. As long as it doesn't take too long.
b	Yes, I did.	No, it was pretty short.
c	Yes, they're fine.	I don't think so. I think they need to do better.
d	Yes, it did.	No, I had to wait a long time, actually.
e	You're welcome.	Don't mention it.

Figure 7-4 *Listen In* - Book 2, © International Thomson Publishing Asia.

share their responses with other learners. This particular task is taken from a unit of work set in an airport.

Text
Excuse me, we're doing a survey of what passengers think of facilities at the airport. Is it OK if I ask you a few questions? . . . Did you have a long flight? . . . Uh-huh. So what do you think of the airport? Is it clean? . . . What about the airport personnel? Are they efficient? . . . Right. Now, how about the baggage? Did it arrive quickly and in good condition? . . .
Well, that's all. Thank you very much.

Nonreciprocal listening tasks can draw on a rich variety of authentic data, not just lectures and one-sided anecdotes. In my own listening classes, I have used the following data:

answering machine messages
store announcements
announcements on public transportation

The increasing use of computerized messages on the telephone by companies and public utilities can also provide a rich source of data. The following text, used in a lesson on entertainment, was adapted from a system developed by a chain of movie theaters through which it is possible to call up, select, and pay for a movie over the telephone.

A: *(Jenny) Feel like seeing a movie?*
B: *(Bob) Sure. What's playing?*

A: Dunno. Let's try that new computerized booking service.

B: The what?

A: That new service I was telling you about. You know, I was telling you about that survey I did.

B: How does it work?

A: Well, you just call up this number . . . where is it? Here.

B: OK. (sound of telephone being dialed.)

C: Good afternoon, welcome to Ticketmaster. You can now book tickets to all current movies through Ticketmaster. To choose from a list of current movies, press 1 now. To choose from a list of theaters, press 2 now. To find out about Ticketmaster's new features, press 3 now. To repeat this list, press zero one.

B: Hit one.

A: OK. (beep)

C: The following is a list of movies. Enter your selection at any time. For The Nutty Professor press one now. For Danger in Space, press two, now. For Death at Midnight, press three now.

A: Let's do the Crazy Professor.

B: Oh no, I don't feel like a comedy.

A: OK. I hate sci fi, so let's go to Death at Midnight. I heard it's quite good.

B: OK. (beep)

C: Theaters showing Death at Midnight: For the Odeon Queensway, press one now. For the New York Cinema, press two now. For the ABC Theater Parkside, press 3 now. For . . .

B: OK. Queensway's the nearest.

A: Two?

B: Uh-huh.

C: You have selected the Odeon Queensway. Please select the day of show. For today, press one now. For tomorrow, please press two now. For the day after tomorrow, please press three now.
(beep) Please select a show time for today. For 12:30 p.m. press one now. For 2:30 p.m. press two now. For 5:30 p.m. press three now. For . . .

A: 5:30?

B: Uh-huh. (beep)

C: You have chosen 5:30. Please enter the number of tickets you wish to purchase. Up to nine. (beep). You have booked two tickets. If this is correct, press the pound sign to continue. To re-enter the number of seats, press zero two. (beep) You have confirmed two seats. Please select a credit card for payment. To pay by American Express, press one now. To pay by Mastercard, press two now. To pay by Visa, press three now.

A: Amex?

B: No. Let me pay. I'll put it on Visa. (beep)

C: You have selected Visa. Please punch in your number followed by the star key . . .

A: Wow! I'm glad we're not calling long distance!

Source: D. Nunan. 1997. Listen In. Book 2. International Thomson Publishing

◆ LISTENING STRATEGIES

A recurring motif in this book is the need to develop learners' awareness of the processes underlying their own learning so that, eventually, they will be able to take greater and greater responsibility for that learning. This can be done through the adoption of a learner-centered strategy at the level of classroom action, and partly through equipping students with a wide range of effective learning strategies. Through these, students will not only become better listeners, they will also become more effective language learners because they will be given opportunities to focus on, and reflect upon, the processes underlying their own learning. This is important, because if learners are aware of what they are doing, if they are conscious of the processes underlying the learning they are involved in, then learning will be more effective. Key strategies that can be taught in the listening classroom include selective listening, listening for different purposes, predicting, progressive structuring, inferencing, and personalizing. These strategies should not be separated from the content teaching but woven into the ongoing fabric of the lesson so that learners can see the applications of the strategies to the development of effective learning.

I particularly favor the development of inferential comprehension tasks because they force the learner to process the material more deeply. They also facilitate the development of vocabulary. In short, they require the learners to do more work than tasks that only require literal comprehension.

As indicated earlier, in addition to teaching direct strategies, such as selective listening and listening for gist, the teacher can also emphasize learning processes by stating goals at the beginning of each lesson. Such statements are important because learners are made aware of what the teacher is trying to achieve. The goal statement can be reinforced by self-check exercises at regular intervals during these courses. These will serve to remind learners of what they have learned, and give them an opportunity to monitor and evaluate their progress. See Table 7.2, at the end of this section, for a list of important listening strategies, along with examples.

◆ FOCUS ON LINGUISTIC SKILLS

Another basic distinction that can be made is between tasks that focus on aspects of the linguistic system, pronunciation, grammar, and discourse, and those that focus on the processing of content. With tasks focusing on pronunciation, a distinction is usually drawn between segmental tasks, focusing on discrete sounds, and those that focus on the suprasegmental features of stress, rhythm, and intonation. The tasks on pages 220 and 221 focus at the segmental level, requiring learners to distinguish between minimal pair contrasts.

Table 7.2 Summaries with examples of some of the most important listening strategies

Strategy	Examples
Listening for gist	◇ Is the speaker describing a vacation or a day in the office?
	◇ Is the radio report about news or weather?
Listening for purpose	◇ Are the speakers making a reservation or ordering food?
	◇ Is the speaker agreeing or disagreeing with the suggestion?
Listening for main idea	◇ Why is the speaker asking the man questions?
	◇ Did the speaker like or dislike the movie?
Listening for inference	◇ What are the speakers implying by what they said?
Listening for specific information	◇ How much did they say the tickets cost?
	◇ Did the speaker's husband say he picked up the kids?
	◇ Why did the speaker say he was studying Chinese?
	◇ Where did she say the meeting was being held?
Listening for phonemic distinctions	◇ Did the speaker say first or fourth?
	◇ Did the speakers say they can or can't come to the party?
Listening for tone/ pitch to identify speaker's attitude	◇ Did the speaker enjoy the wedding or not?
	◇ Is the speaker surprised or not?
Listening for stress	◇ What is more important, where he bought the watch or when?

Suprasegmental features focus the attention of the learner on the ways in which stress, rhythm, and intonation signal aspects of meaning, such as the speaker's attitude and the information focus within the text. In spoken language, these features are particularly important, because they help learners identify aspects of language that often go unnoticed. They are also an important preparation for speaking. While it is important for

Segmental versus suprasegmental features
Segmental features of language deal with isolated, individual sounds in the language, such as phonemes and phonemic distinctions, and how these signal semantic distinctions. Suprasegmental features focus on the way that stress, rhythm, and intonation function to signal differences of attitude, information focus, and so on.

PARTNER 1

1a. LISTENING DISCRIMINATION AND SPEAKING. Pair Practice Words for /θ/ and /s/.
PARTNER 1. Use this page. PARTNER 2. Turn to page 121.
DIRECTIONS: First you are the speaker. Say the words to your partner. You see the consonant sound before each word. For example, you say "Number 1 is *sing*." Repeat any words your partner does not understand.

1.	/s/	sing	6.	/θ/	tenth
2.	/θ/	thumb	7.	/s/	mouse
3.	/θ/	theme	8.	/s/	sank
4.	/s/	pass	9.	/s/	worse
5.	/θ/	thick	10.	/θ/	think

Now you are the listener. Your partner will say some words. Circle the words you hear. Ask your partner to repeat any words you do not understand. Number 11 is an example.

11.	(path)	pass	16.	thank	sank
12.	worth	worse	17.	thumb	some
13.	think	sink	18.	thick	sick
14.	mouth	mouse	19.	theme	seem
15.	thing	sing	20.	tenth	tense

Now compare answers with your partner.

PARTNER 2

1b. LISTENING DISCRIMINATION AND SPEAKING. Pair Practice Words for /θ/ and /s/.
PARTNER 2. Use this page. PARTNER 1. Turn to page 111.
DIRECTIONS: First you are the listener. Your partner will say some words. Circle the words you hear. Ask your partner to repeat any words you do not understand. Number 1 is an example.

1.	thing	(sing)	6.	tenth	tense
2.	thumb	some	7.	mouth	mouse
3.	theme	seem	8.	thank	sank
4.	path	pass	9.	worth	worse
5.	thick	sick	10.	think	sink

Now you are the speaker. Say the words to your partner. You see the consonant sound before each word. For example, you say "Number 11 is *path*." Repeat any words your partner does not understand.

11.	/θ/	path	16.	/θ/	thank
12.	/s/	worse	17.	/s/	some
13.	/s/	sink	18.	/s/	sick
14.	/θ/	mouth	19.	/s/	seem
15.	/θ/	thing	20.	/θ/	tenth

Now compare answers with your partner.

Figure 7-5 *Sounds Great* - Book 1, © Heinle & Heinle Publishers

learners to master both segmental and suprasegmental features of the language, suprasegmental features are inherently more interesting. Because they focus on aspects of language, such as speaker attitude, it is easier to develop communicative tasks to teach such features. The next

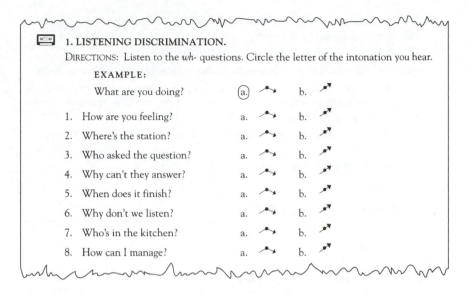

Figure 7-6 *Sounds Great* - Book 1, © Heinle & Heinle Publishers

task, Figure 7-6, illustrates this point. This task is designed to show learners how intonation in English can be used to differentiate between questions and statements.

◆ CONCLUSION

In this chapter, I have set out some of the theoretical, empirical, and practical aspects of listening comprehension. I have suggested that listening classrooms of today need to develop both bottom-up and top-down listening skills in learners. I have also stressed the importance of a strategies-based approach to the teaching of listening. Such an approach is particularly important in classrooms where students are exposed to substantial amounts of authentic data because they will not (and should not expect to) understand every word. Strategies described in the chapter include listening for key information, listening for gist, inferential reasoning, personalization, predicting, and intensive listening. In the final part of the chapter, I illustrated how these various principles can be applied to the practical task of designing listening materials and units of work.

In summary, we can say that an effective listening course will be characterized by the following features (see also the design features set out in Mendelsohn, 1994).

◊ Listening goals should be explicit: Learners should know what they are listening for and why;

◇ The materials should be based on a wide range of authentic texts, including both monologues and dialogues;

◇ Schema-building tasks should precede the listening;

◇ Strategies for effective listening should be incorporated into the materials;

◇ Learners should be given opportunities to progressively structure their listening by listening to a text several times, and by working through increasingly challenging listening tasks;

◇ The task should include opportunities for learners to play an active role in their own learning;

◇ Content should be personalized.

◆ CONCEPT MAP OF CHAPTER 7

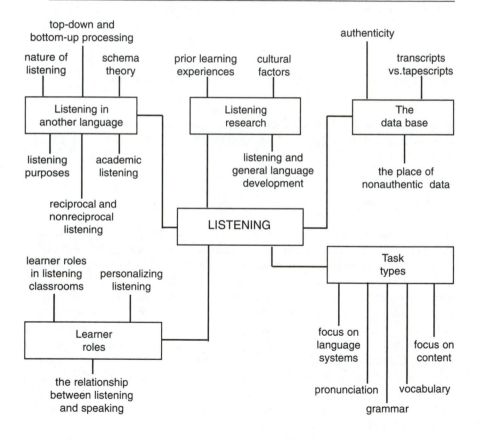

◆ QUESTIONS AND TASKS

1. What is the difference between top-down and bottom-up listening? Why are both important?

2. Find examples of top-down and bottom-up listening tasks in textbooks with which you are familiar.

3. What is schema theory, and why is it important for listening comprehension?

4. Analyze a listening textbook, and identify the key learning strategies underlying the text.

5. List the factors that determine the difficulty of a listening task.

6. What is comprehensible input, and why did it become an influential concept in language teaching?

7. Collect a sample of authentic listening data (or use a piece of data presented in the chapter), and design a series of listening tasks based on the data.

◆ REFERENCES

Anderson, A., and T. Lynch. 1988. *Listening*. Oxford: Oxford University Press.

Asher, J. 1982. *Learning Another Language through Actions*. Los Gatos Calif.: Sky Oaks.

Bartlett, F. C. 1932. *Remembering: A Study in Experimental and Social Psychology*. Cambridge: Cambridge University Press.

Beisbier, B. 1994. *Sounds Great: Beginning Pronunciation for Speakers of English*. Boston: Heinle & Heinle.

Brown, G. 1990. *Listening to Spoken English*. Second Edition. London: Longman.

Chaudron, C., and J. C. Richards. 1986. The effect of discourse markers on the comprehension of lectures. *Applied Linguistics*, 7, 2.

Brown, G., and G. Yule. 1983. *Teaching the Spoken Language*. Cambridge: Cambridge University Press.

Dunkel, P. 1993. Listening in the native and second/foreign language: Toward an integration of research and practice. In S. Silberstein (ed.), *State of the Art TESOL Essays*. Washington, D.C.: TESOL.

Foley, B. 1994. *Now Hear This!* Boston: Heinle & Heinle.

Foley, B. 1994. *Listen to Me! Beginning Listening, Speaking & Pronunciation*. Boston: Heinle & Heinle.

Krashen, S. 1982. *Principles and Practice in Second Language Acquisition*. Oxford: Pergamon.

Mendelsohn, D. 1994. *Learning to Listen*. San Diego, Calif.: Domine Press.

Nunan, D. 1987. Does instruction make a difference? Revisited. *TESOL Quarterly*, 21, 2.

———. 1997. Listening in Language Learning. Paper presented at the Korea TESOL Convention, Kyongju, Korea, October 1997.

Nunan, D., and L. Miller (eds.), 1995. *New Ways in Teaching Listening*. Washington, D.C.: TESOL.

Oller, J. 1979. *Language Tests in School*. London: Longman.

Ross, S. 1992. Program-defining evaluation in a decade of eclecticism. In Alderson, J. C. and A. Beretta (eds.), *Evaluating Language Education*. Cambridge: Cambridge University Press.

Rost, M. 1990. *Listening in Language Learning*. London: Longman.

Rost, M. 1991. *Listening in Action*. London: Prentice Hall.

Rost, M. 1994. *Introducing Listening*. London: Penguin.

Spada, N. 1990. In J. C. Richards and D. Nunan (eds.). *Second Language Teacher Education*. New York: Cambridge University Press.

Vai, M. 1998. *The Heart of the Matter. High-Intermediate Listening, Speaking, and Critical Thinking*. Boston: Heinle & Heinle.

Watson, K., and L. Smeltzer. 1984. Barriers to listening: Comparison between students and practitioners. *Communication Research Reports*, 1, 82–87.

CHAPTER **8**

Speaking

If listening is the Cinderella skill in second language learning, then speaking is the overbearing elder sister. The ability to function in another language is generally characterized in terms of being able to speak that language. When someone asks, "Do you know another language?" they generally mean "Can you speak the language?" In this chapter, we shall take a look at what it means to say that one can "speak another language." In the first part of the chapter, we look at the nature of speaking. Then, in a section that parallels the discussion on the difficulty of listening tasks in Chapter 7, we look at the issue of task difficulty in relation to speaking. The chapter covers the following issues and concepts:

The nature of speaking
◇ characteristics of communicative competence
◇ discourse versus dialogue
◇ transactional and interactional language
◇ purposes for speaking
◇ genre theory and speaking

The reluctant speaker
◇ prior learning experiences
◇ motivation
◇ dealing with the reluctant speaker

Task difficulty
◇ factors affecting task difficulty: task factors, learner factors, language factors
◇ listening to facilitate speaking

Course design issues
◇ goal setting
◇ influence of systemic–functional linguistics

Pedagogical tasks
◇ the restricted nature of most materials
◇ the "3P" instructional cycle
◇ key principles
◇ pedagogical versus real-world tasks

A sample speaking lesson

THE NATURE OF SPEAKING

◆ *CHARACTERISTICS OF COMMUNICATIVE COMPETENCE*

What is it that one needs to know and be able to do in order to speak in another language? Of course, one needs to know how to articulate sounds in a comprehensible manner, one needs an adequate vocabulary, and one needs to have mastery of syntax. These various elements add up to linguistic competence. However, while linguistic competence is necessary, it is not sufficient for someone who wants to communicate competently in another language. In (1974), the sociolinguist Dell Hymes proposed the notion of communicative competence as an alternative to Chomsky's linguistic competence. Communicative competence includes linguistic competence (although see Canale and Swain for an alternative perspective), but also includes a range of other sociolinguistic and conversational skills that enable the speaker to know how to say what to whom, when. In the early 1970s, Sandra Savignon conducted an important study into the development of communication skills built on a model of communicative competence containing several essential characteristics. She defined communicative competence as "the ability to function in a truly communicative setting—that is, in a dynamic exchange in which linguistic competence must adjust itself to the total informational input, both linguistic and paralinguistic, of one or more interlocutors" (p. 9). In addition to being dynamic, rather than static, and involving the negotiation of meaning, for Savignon, communicative competence is not restricted to spoken language, but involves writing as well. It is also context-specific, which means that a competent communicator knows how to make choices specific to the situation. Finally, it is distinct from performance. According to Savignon, competence is what one knows, while performance is what one does (See Savignon, 1972, 1983).

> **Characteristics of Communicative Competence**
> Communicative competence includes: (a) knowledge of the grammar and vocabulary of the language; (b) knowledge of rules of speaking (e.g., knowing how to begin and end conversations, knowing what topics can be talked about in different types of speech events, knowing which address forms should be used with different persons one speaks to and in different situations; (c) knowing how to use and respond to different types of speech acts such as requests, apologies, thanks, and invitations; (d) knowing how to use language appropriately.
> *Richards, Platt and Weber 1985: 49*

◆ *DISCOURSE VERSUS DIALOGUE*

Even the greatest of playwrights cannot capture the reality of genuine negotiation. Not even great modern playwrights such as Harold Pinter,

David Mamet, or Edward Albee are able to do so, although the latter had an acute ear for interpersonal discourse as the following extract shows.

Martha: *Our son does not have blue hair . . . or blue eyes for that matter. He has green eyes . . . like me.*

George: *He has blue eyes, Martha.*

Martha: *Green.*

George: *Blue, Martha.*

Martha: *GREEN! [To Honey and Nick] He has the loveliest green eyes . . . they aren't all flaked with brown and grey, you know . . . hazel . . . they're real green . . . deep, pure green eyes . . . like mine.*

Nick: *Your eyes are . . . brown, aren't they?*

Martha: *Green! Well, in some lights they look brown, but they're green. Not green like his . . . more hazel. George has watery blue eyes. Milky blue.*

George: *Make up your mind, Martha.*

Martha: *I was giving you the benefit of the doubt. Daddy has green eyes, too.*

George: *He does not! Your father has tiny red eyes . . . like a white mouse. In fact he is a white mouse.*

Albee, 1965: 50–51

Genuine interactions do not unfold like this. In the extract above, there is no ambiguity, there are no misunderstandings. In contrast, in authentic discourse, the interlocutors have a great deal of work to do to ensure that they are talking about the same thing. In most conversations there is the content of the discourse, but in addition, there is a meta-discourse, a conversation about the conversation, through which the interlocutors negotiate meaning and manage the conversation, ensuring that who says what about whom and when happens smoothly. In Chapter 2, we saw that this process of negotiation has been hypothesized as being beneficial for acquisition because it *pushes* the learners to the limits, and then extends, their competence.

Another aspect of speaking that is particularly relevant for second language speakers concerns whether or not the speaking is planned or spontaneous. We tend to assume that all conversations are spontaneous, and so they are to a degree. However, we all have routines, set phrases, and other expressions that we use to assist us when speaking spontaneously. In the case of second language learners, the provision of planning time can significantly increase levels of both fluency and accuracy. If you are teaching students who have to make oral presentations (either as students or in the workplace) in a second or foreign language, it is important to provide opportunities for them to give prepared, extended presentations in class.

◆ TRANSACTIONAL AND INTERACTIONAL LANGUAGE

You will recall from Chapter 4 that, in functional terms, most interactions can be classified as either transactional or interactional. Transactional talk is produced in order to get something, or to get something done. Interactional language is produced for social purposes. (I suggested in Chapter 4 that there were other functions, such as the aesthetic, but that transactional and interactional were by far the most common.) The other point to be remembered is that any given interaction will usually consist of both transactional and interactional language. These contrasting functions are illustrated in the two following conversational extracts. The first of these is basically transactional in nature, while the second is basically interactional. However, there is an interactional element in the first few turns of Extract 1. Similarly, the second interaction has a transactional element, when the father tells his daughter not to have the television on too loud.

Extract 1:
Store attendant: *Morning.*
Customer: *Morning.*
Store attendant: *Nice day.*
Customer: *Uh-huh. Can you give me two of those?*
Store attendant: *Sure.*
Customer: *Thanks.*

Extract 2:
Father: *Morning, Darling.*
Daughter: *Morning.*
Father: *Sleep well?*
Daughter: *Uh-uh. The thunder woke me up.*
Father: *Loud, wasn't it. And the lightning. . . . What are you doing?*
Daughter: *I'm going to finish watching that . . .*
Father: *Well, don't have it on too loud. Jenny's still asleep.*

◆ PURPOSES FOR SPEAKING

One of the most useful schemes for analyzing interactions from a functional perspective is that by Martin Bygate (1987). Bygate suggests that conversations can be analyzed in terms of routines. Routines are conventional (and therefore predictable) ways of presenting information. He discusses two types of routines: information routines (these would encompass what I have called transactional language), and interactional routines (corresponding to my interactional/social category). Information routines contain frequently recurring types of information structures. These can

Why do we speak?
What speaking tasks did you carry out today? This is what Burns and Joyce (1997) came up with:
◇   telling children to get ready for school
◇   chatting with a neighbor about the nice weather
◇   calling the garage to book a car in for a service
◇   discussing holiday plans with workmates
◇   calling your mother to ask her to pick up the dry cleaning
◇   gossiping with friends about a common acquaintance
◇   discussing your son's progress with his teacher
◇   answering a sales inquiry at work
◇   ordering a new passport
◇   discussing promotional prospects with a supervisor at work

be subdivided into routines that are basically expository in nature (for example, telling a story, describing something, giving a set of instructions, making a comparison), and those that are evaluative (giving an explanation, making a justification, predicting, coming to a decision). Interaction routines can be subdivided into service encounters (for example, a job interview) or social (a dinner party, a coffee break at work, etc.). Bygate adds a conversational management dimension to his scheme, suggesting that participants need constantly to negotiate meaning and to manage the interaction in terms of who says what, to whom, when, about what.

In my 1990 book on language teaching methodology, I proposed a rearrangement of this scheme. I suggested that, rather than being two different categories of event, the informational and interactional functions represented two different dimensions of interaction. In other words, the expository and evaluative subroutines were features of service and social interactions. I brought the two dimensions together in a grid. See Table 8.1. This facilitates the cross-referencing of functions with situations. The grid can be used in a variety of ways. In particular, it can be used for the functional analysis of transactional and interpersonal interactions. This information in turn can also be used in designing courses for speaking and oral interaction. I have also used versions of the grid with students to show them how particular functions are used across a range of communicative situations.

Bygate's routines facilitate communication for first language speakers because they make the interactions more predictable. If language were totally predictable, then communication would be unnecessary. If it were totally unpredictable, effective communication would probably be impossible. When people have conversations they work interactively to reduce unpredictability. This, as we saw earlier, is what people are doing when they negotiate meaning. For second language speakers, routines can be crucial in facilitating comprehension. In addition, by learning prefabri-

Table 8.1

	Information		
	Expository narrate describe instruct compare	*Evaluative* explain justify predict decide	*Negotiation of meaning* Management of interaction
Interaction			
S			
E Job interview			
R			
V Booking a			
I restaurant			
C			
E Buying stamps			
Enrolling in school, etc.			
S			
O Dinner party			
C			
I Coffee break			
A			
L			

cated, set conversational patterns, learners can "outperform" their competence. In fact, there is evidence that such prefabricated formulae are important precursors to acquisition.

◆ GENRE THEORY AND SPEAKING

This work on conversational routines is also closely related to the concept of *genre*. You will recall from Chapter 4, that genre theory proposed that different speech events result in different types of text, and that these texts are differentiated in terms of their overall structure and also by the kinds of grammatical items that are typically associated with them. A recount, probably the most common type of speech event in casual conversations typically begins with an introduction, followed by an orientation.

Genre
A genre is a staged, purposeful, socially-constructed communicative event (Martin, 1985). Such events generally result in spoken and written texts that can be differentiated according to their generic structure and grammatical features.

Then follows a series of events culminating in a comment and then a conclusion. Grammatically, the recount genre is characterized by the use of the simple past tense, and specific references to people and places.

The following extract from *Who's Afraid of Virginia Woolf?* illustrates the generic structure and grammatical elements associated with a recount.

When I was sixteen and going to prep school, during the Punic Wars,	*Introduction*
a bunch of us used to go into New York on the first day of vacations, before we fanned out to our homes, and in this evening, this bunch of us used to go to this gin mill owned by the gangster-father of one of us . . .—and we would go to this gin mill, and we would drink with the grown-ups and listen to the jazz. . . .	*Orientation*
And one time, in the bunch of us, there was this boy who was fifteen, and he had killed his mother with a shotgun some years before . . .	*Event*
and this one evening this boy went with us,	*Event*
and we ordered our drinks,	*Event*
and when it came time for his turn he said I'll have bergin . . . give me some bergin, please, bergin and water.	*Event*
Well, we all laughed . . . he was blond and had the face of a cherub, and we all laughed, and his cheeks went red	*Event*
and the assistant crook who had taken our order told the people at the next table what the boy had said	*Event*
and then they laughed,	*Event*
and then more people were told	*Event*
and the laughter grew . . .	*Event*
And soon everyone in the gin mill knew what the laughter was about, and everyone started ordering bergin, and laughing when they ordered it.	*Event*
We drank free that night, and we were bought champagne by the management, by the gangster-father of one of us.	*Event*
And of course we suffered the next day, each of us alone, on his train, away from New York, each of us with a grown-ups'	*Comment*
hangover	*Conclusion*
but it was the grandest day of my . . . youth.	
Albee, 1965: 62	

THE RELUCTANT SPEAKER

In a recent informal survey that I carried out with colleagues, reluctance to speak on the part of students was seen as their biggest challenge. Burns and Joyce (1997: 134) identify three sets of factors that may cause a reluctance on the part of students to take part in classroom tasks involving speaking. They suggest that this reluctance may be due to cultural factors, linguistic factors, and/or psychological/affective factors. Cultural factors derive from learners' prior learning experiences and the expectations created by these experiences. You will recall that in Chapter 1, I discussed the possible mismatches that can occur between teachers and learners from different cultural backgrounds. If learners come into your classroom believing that learning a language involves listening to the teacher or the tape, and doing written exercises, then they will be reluctant to become actively involved in speaking. It will be necessary to engage in a certain amount of learner training to encourage them to participate in speaking.

◆ PRIOR LEARNING EXPERIENCES

Many of the learners that I teach are reluctant speakers. This reluctance is partly due to their prior learning experiences. Many of them were educated in large classes in schools situated in noisy neighborhoods where opportunities to speak are severely limited. Others were taught in schools where speaking was simply not encouraged. However, I find that a period of learner training can go a long way towards overcoming this reluctance. Simple dynamics, and the management of classroom interactions, also helps. I never require students to speak out in front of the whole class at the beginning of a course. When students are working in pairs, I have them sitting facing each other rather than side by side. If I find myself with a particularly reluctant class, I change the dynamics by, for example, getting the students to stand up and move around while doing speaking tasks. I am never sure why this works, but it never fails. There seems to be something about the social nature of intermingling that creates an imperative to communicate. It also resonates with John Fanslow's notion of breaking rules. By allowing students to break the classroom rule that they should remain seated in class, I also allow them to break the rule that they should not speak in class.

According to Burns and Joyce, the linguistic facts that inhibit the use of the spoken language include difficulties in transferring from the learner's first language to the sounds, rhythms, and stress patterns of English, difficulties with the native speaker pronunciation of the teacher, a lack of understanding of common grammatical patterns in English (e.g., English tenses) and how these may be different from their own language, lack of familiarity with the cultural or social knowledge required to process meaning. Psychological and affective factors include culture shock, previous negative social or political experiences, lack of motivation, anxiety or shyness in class, especially if their previous learning experiences were negative.

◆ MOTIVATION

Motivation is a key consideration in determining the preparedness of learners to communicate. Motivation refers to the combination of effort plus desire to achieve the goal of learning the language plus favorable attitudes toward learning the language. That is, motivation to learn a second language is seen as referring to the extent to which the individual works or strives to learn the language because of a desire to do so and the satisfaction experienced in this activity. Effort alone does not signify motivation. The motivated individual expends effort toward the goal, but the individual expending effort is not necessarily motivated. Many attributes of the individual such as compulsiveness, desire to please a teacher or parent, or a high need to achieve might produce effort, as would social pressures, such as a demanding teacher, impending examinations, or the promise of a new bicycle (Gardner 1985: 10).

Why are learners unmotivated?

Lack of success over time/lack of perception of progress

Uninspired teaching

Boredom

Lack of perceived relevance of materials

Lack of knowledge about the goals of the instructional program

◆ Lack of appropriate feedback

What can be done?

Make instructional goals explicit to learners

Break learning down into sequences of achievable steps

Link learning to the needs and interests of the learners

◆ Allow learners to bring their own knowledge and perspectives into the learning process

Encourage creative language use

◆ Help learners to identify the strategies underlying the learning tasks they are engaged in

◆ Develop ways in which learners can record their own progress

In a detailed investigation of the reluctant second language speaker Amy Tsui (1996) came up with some fascinating insights into the reasons for reticence in the language classroom. She also has some practical solutions to the problem. Tsui and her informants collected their data in secondary school classrooms in Hong Kong. While English was supposed to be the medium of instruction in the schools, there was a great deal of mixed code speaking on the part of both teachers and students, and many schools, in fact, taught in Chinese. Tsui and the teachers she worked with identified five principal factors accounting for the reluctance of students to speak up in class:

1. *Students' perceived low proficiency in English:* videotaped data from secondary school classrooms showed that although students did have the competence to respond to teachers' questions in English, their lack of confidence, unwillingness to take risks, and a perception that their English was poor resulted in a marked reluctance to respond.

2. *Students' fear of mistakes and derision:* Students were also afraid of making fools of themselves in front of their peers. In addition, there is a cultural factor that functions in a number of Asian cultures inhibiting students from speaking up in front of their peers.

3. *Teachers' intolerance of silence:* Many of the teachers taking part in the study gave the students little or no wait time.

4. *Uneven allocation of turns:* From the data collected in the study it became clear that teachers favored the better students when soliciting responses. As Tsui points out, this is probably related to the intolerance of silence. By targeting the better students, teachers could be sure that there would not be periods of silence or confusion in their classrooms.

5. *Incomprehensible input:* The final factor identified by Tsui was the overly difficult teachers' language input. One teacher, for instance, having viewed herself teaching, reported that, "After viewing myself asking questions, I realized that what I thought were simple and clear questions were in fact quite difficult to understand. Not only this, but the questions were often confusing and not specific enough" (Tsui 1996: 154).

Interviewer:	*What stops you from speaking up?*
ESL student:	*'Cos my classmates also not speak up . . . they affect me very much . . . Sometimes I really frighten . . . I am afraid my classmate will laugh . . . I think my English level is not good, so I am shy to talk English . . . I hate English very much because I think English is quite difficult to learn . . . Educational system is stressful . . . because many people if fail in English . . . they affect (sic) their life.*
Interviewer:	*Are you worried about failing in English?*
ESL student:	*Very . . . very much.*

Tsui 1996: 145

◆ DEALING WITH THE RELUCTANT SPEAKER

Tsui and her teachers formulated six strategies for overcoming anxiety and reluctance to speak. The first strategy was to lengthen the amount of time between asking a question and nominating someone to respond. However, this strategy has limits, as one teacher found when she waited two minutes for a student to respond. The extended wait time, in fact, embarrassed the student who had been asked to respond and discouraged her from volunteering in the future. The second strategy was to improve questioning techniques. This strategy helped some teachers but not others. Another strategy tried by teachers was to accept a variety of answers. The fourth strategy was to give learners an opportunity to rehearse their responses in small groups or pairs before being asked to speak up in front of the whole class. Another strategy reported as effective was to focus on content rather than form. This lowered anxiety, particularly among lower proficiency students, presumably because they were not inhibited about making mistakes. The final factor identified by the teacher was to establish good relationships with the students. Tsui concluded from her study that the key to encouraging students to communicate was to create a low-anxiety classroom atmosphere. Strategies that contributed to a lowering of anxiety were the key ones in encouraging the reluctant student to speak.

Table 8.2 summarizes some of the practical steps that can be undertaken to enhance the motivation of learners to speak.

Table 8.2   Some preconditions for effective motivation

Factor	*Characteristics*
1. Supportive Environment	orderly classroom teacher is skilled in classroom management students nonanxious, and feel comfortable taking risks feedback is positive
2. Appropriate Level of Difficulty	tasks are neither too easy nor too difficult students know what they have to do criteria for success are clear
3. Meaningful Learning	students know what they are expected to learn and why activities are meaningful and worthwhile relationship between objective and activities is clear tasks are sequenced so that new tasks build on and extend ones that come before students are given a reason to be in class
4. Strategies	motivational strategy is matched to instructional need particular strategies are not overused teacher uses a range of strategies there is a learning-how-to-learn dimension to instruction
5. Content	students can relate content to own experience topics are interesting

TASK DIFFICULTY

◆ *FACTORS AFFECTING TASK DIFFICULTY: TASK FACTORS, LEARNER FACTORS, AND LANGUAGE FACTORS*

In Chapter 1, I pointed out the problems in determining difficulty when using *task* as a basic organizing principle. In terms of speaking, there are three sets of factors to be taken into consideration, and not all of the factors are under the control of the teacher or the instructional designer. In the first place there are factors to do with the data that learners are working with. (How dense/complex are the texts that learners are required to process? How abstract/concrete is the content in relation to the learners' experience? How much contextual support is provided?) The second set of factors has to do with the task itself. (How many steps are involved in the task? How relevant and meaningful is the task? How much time is available? What degree of grammatical accuracy is provided? How much assistance is provided? How clearly is the task set up for the learners? How much practice or rehearsal time is available?) Finally, there are factors that are internal to the speakers themselves. These factors, which are largely outside the teacher's control, include the level of confidence and motivation of the learners, prior knowledge of content, degree of linguistic knowledge and skill, extent of cultural knowledge, and the degree of familiarity with the task type itself.

Factors affecting task difficulty
◇ the degree to which the language event is embedded in a context that facilitates comprehension;
◇ the degree to which the language event makes cognitive demands on the learner;
◇ the degree to which background knowledge can be used;
◇ the amount of assistance provided to the learner;
◇ the complexity of the language that the learner is required to produce;
◇ the degree of emotional stress involved in completing the task;
◇ the interest and motivation of the learner.

With speaking tasks, there is also the interlocutor effect. Speakers behave differently when performing identical tasks depending on the person they are talking to (Martyn 1997). In her study, Martyn collected data from speakers as they performed similar tasks with different interlocutors. She found that different language was produced by the speakers according to the degree of comfort they felt with the learners they were working with. Another aspect of the interlocutor effect is the degree of competence of the other person or persons. As we have already seen, communication is a collaborative achievement in which the speakers negotiate meaning in order to achieve their goals. Therefore, a speaker's communicative success will be partly determined by the skills of the other person. This has implications, not only for research (and it has to be pointed out that most SLA research seems to have been conducted in an interpersonal vacuum), but also for the assessment of speaking performance.

The most extensive research into speaking task difficulty has been carried out in first language contexts. This work is reported in Brown and Yule (1983), who identify a number of factors that are significant in determining difficulty. In the first place, the degree of abstraction is a factor. Tasks requiring speakers to describe concrete, static objects are easier than tasks requiring the description of objects whose positions relative to one another are changing. Thus, describing a picture is easier than describing an accident. These concrete descriptions are easier than tasks involving abstract concepts such as expressing an opinion.

◆ LISTENING TO FACILITATE SPEAKING

Brown and her colleagues were not only interested in identifying those factors causing difficulty, but also in finding ways of helping speakers improve their performance. In some interesting work that dramatizes the symbiosis between speaking and listening, they found that prior experience as a listener helps speakers improve their performance as a speaker. (This insight would appear to validate the task-dependency principle of moving from reception to production that has already been discussed.) There are two possible reasons for this finding. In the first place, being a listener gives learners models to deploy when acting as a speaker. In addition, being a hearer first helps the learner appreciate the difficulties inherent in the task.

Giving speakers experience in the hearer's role is more helpful than simple practice in tasks in which a speaker is having real difficulties in appreciating what a particular task requires. In tasks in which speakers are largely successful in meeting a particular task demand, repeated practice may enable them to improve further their performance in this respect, and may indeed be a pleasant and motivating experience.

COURSE DESIGN ISSUES

◆ GOAL SETTING

In traditional approaches to curriculum development, having established the overall purposes for a course, the first step in the course design procedure is to specify what learners are to do. In other words, one has to set out the goals and objectives of the program. The broad communicative goal and attendant specific goals in Table 8.3 have been taken from a curriculum framework designed for teachers developing courses for general language proficiency.

While the value of goals and objectives are still recognized, in recent years, with the emergence of *task* and *text* as important curricular building blocks, curriculum developers have begun to explore alternatives to the "objectives first" approach. For a detailed exploration of task-based course design, see my 1989 book, *Designing Tasks for the Communicative Curriculum*.

◆ INFLUENCE OF SYSTEMIC–FUNCTIONAL LINGUISTICS

In Australia, where systemic–functional linguistics and the genre school of pedagogy have influenced course design, course designers have given much greater prominence to texts as the point of departure in course design. Table 8.4 illustrates the procedure developed by Burns and Joyce (1997) for developing a course based on such principles.

Having decided on the parameters for the course, the next (and, for many teachers, most interesting) step is to decide on the pedagogical tasks. In the section that follows, I discuss some of the issues that need to be considered in developing, modifying, or adapting classroom tasks

Table 8.3

Broad Goal	*Specific Goals*
Communication By participating in activities organized around use of the target language, learners will acquire communication skills in the target language, in order to widen their networks of interpersonal relations, have direct access to information in the target language, and use their language skills for study, vocational and leisure-based purposes	*To be able to use the target language to:* ◊ establish and maintain relationships and discuss topics of interest, e.g., through the exchange of information, ideas, opinions, attitudes, feelings, experiences, plans; ◊ participate in social interaction related to solving a problem, making arrangements, making decisions with others, and transacting to obtain goods, services, and public information; ◊ obtain information by searching for specific details in a spoken or written text and then process and use the information obtained; ◊ obtain information by listening to or reading a spoken or written text as a whole, and then process and use the information obtained; ◊ give information in spoken or written form, e.g., give a talk, write an essay, or a set of instructions; ◊ listen to, read or view, and respond personally to a stimulus, e.g., a story, play, film, song, poem, picture

Source: Adapted from the Australian Language Levels Framework

Table 8.4

Step	Discussion and Examples
1 Identify the overall context	The focus of a university course is preparing students to study at the university
2 Develop an aim	To develop the spoken and written language skills required to undertake university study
3 Note the language event sequence within the context	These could include: ◇ enrolling at university ◇ discussing course selection ◇ attending lectures ◇ attending tutorials ◇ using the library ◇ reading reference books ◇ writing essays ◇ writing reports ◇ undertaking examinations ◇ participating in casual conversation
4 List the texts arising from the sequence	These could include: ◇ enrollment forms ◇ service encounter/selecting courses ◇ lectures ◇ tutorial discussions ◇ service encounter/library encounter ◇ range of possible written texts, for example: discipline-specific essays discipline-specific reports ◇ range of possible reading texts, for example: discipline-specific journal articles discipline-specific books library catalogues lecture notes ◇ examination papers ◇ genres within casual conversation (e.g., the anecdote)
5 Outline the sociocultural knowledge students need	Students need knowledge about: ◇ academic institutions ◇ academic procedures and expectations ◇ the role of the student
6 Record or gather samples of texts	◇ Written texts: Gather examples of essays, catalogues, journals, etc. ◇ Spoken texts: You may need to; find available recordings prepare some semi-scripted dialogues yourself record authentic interactions

Table 8.4 Continued

Step	Discussion and Examples
7 Develop units of work	Classroom tasks should be sequenced within units of work to provide students with: ◇ explicit input ◇ guided practice ◇ an opportunity to perform independently

for your students. I shall then conclude the chapter by illustrating one way in which tasks can be sequenced into a unit of work.

PEDAGOGICAL TASKS

◆ *THE RESTRICTED NATURE OF MOST MATERIALS*

Most of the teaching materials in the pedagogical marketplace consist of what I would call reproductive language tasks. In completing such tasks, learners are required to do little more than reproduce, with degrees of variation, models provided by the teacher, the textbook, or the tape. Take, for example, the following list of tasks. These represent the sum total of task types in a popular textbook series, whose ostensible aim is to "help learners use the language essential to real-life situations." This is all the speaking practice that learners receive in the course.

1. Learner listens to and reads two-line dialogue and practices with a partner.
2. Listen and repeat.
3. Listen to a model dialogue and repeat, interpolating own name.
4. Read question cue and make-up question.
5. Read two-line skeleton dialogue and practice with partner.
6. Listen/read a model question and ask a partner.
7. Read a model dialogue and have a similar conversation using cues provided.
8. Study a substitution table and make up sentences.
9. Study questions and answers in a model dialogue and make up similar questions using cue words.
10. Look at a picture and study model sentences. Make up similar sentences about a similar picture.
11. Listen to numbers and dates. Read numbers and dates and say them.
12. Listen to tapescript and answer written comprehension questions.
13. Listen to an interview. Ask and answer similar questions with a partner.
14. Look at diagrams of clocks. With a partner ask and answer questions about the time.

15. Listen to a model, study a map, and describe the route from one specified point to another.

◆ THE "3P" INSTRUCTIONAL CYCLE

Despite the conceptual leaps made by the profession over the last twenty years, audiolingualism is still the dominant paradigm in many parts of the world. Underlying audiolingualism is a "3P" instructional cycle of presentation, practice, and production. At stage 1, the presentation stage, the teacher, textbook, or tape models a target structure for the student. At the practice stage, the student manipulates the structure through a series of drills. At the final stage, the production stage, the learner applies the structure in a series of application tasks.

While such tasks might well be necessary for establishing mastery over basic phonological elements and syntactic patterns, they do not go far enough. In addition to these reproductive exercises, learners need opportunities for creative language use. By creativity, I do not mean the opportunity to write poems or plays (although many learners could well benefit from such opportunities). By creativity, I mean the opportunity to recombine familiar language elements in new and unfamiliar ways.

◆ KEY PRINCIPLES

A considerable amount of research (see Chapter 2) as well as directions in pedagogical practice, suggest that in the speaking classroom, learners should be given the maximum number of opportunities possible to practice the target language in meaningful contexts and situation. While grammatical explanations and linguistic analysis facilitates acquisition, it seems to work better for some learners than others. However, opportunities to use the language appear to facilitate acquisition for all learners. When taking part in tasks that require the creative and relatively unpredictable use of language, learners are bound to make mistakes. These should be seen as a natural part of the learning process.

Table 8.5

	The 3P's Instructional Cycle		
	Stage 1 *Presentation*	*Stage 2* *Practice*	*Stage 3* *Production*
ROLE OF TEACHER	Model	Conductor	Monitor
ROLE OF STUDENTS	Listener	Performer	Interactor
ACTIVITY TYPE	Lecture	Substitution drill	Role play
CLASS ARRANGEMENT	Whole class	Pair	Small group

In my 1989 book on tasks, I suggested that we draw a distinction between pedagogical and target or real-world tasks. Tasks with a real-world rationale require learners to approximate, in class, the sorts of behaviors required of them in the world beyond the classroom. Tasks with a pedagogical rationale, on the other hand, require learners to do things that it is extremely unlikely they would be called on to do outside the classroom. As they cannot be justified on the grounds that they are enabling learners to rehearse real-world behaviors, they must have an alternative rationale. This usually takes a psycholinguistic form along the lines of: "Well, although the learners are engaged in tasks which they are unlikely to perform outside the classroom, the tasks are stimulating internal processes of acquisition" (1989; 40).

A SAMPLE SPEAKING LESSON

In this section, I shall describe a language lesson for a group of upper-intermediate learners. The material is based on The ATLAS Series, and I have selected it to illustrate some of the key principles described in the body of the chapter. The column on the left sets out the tasks carried out by the students the last time I taught a speaking lesson using these materials. On the right, I describe the rationale behind the tasks and their sequencing. The lesson was part of an intensive general English course run during summer school for students to brush up on their speaking skills.

Warm Up

1. In groups, brainstorm definitions of *culture, culture shock*, and *cultural identity*.

I began by describing the goals of the lesson, which were to express their opinions, and to give reasons for them.

2. Group work. Brainstorm. Make a list of the good things and the bad things about living in another country.

Good Things	*Bad Things*

The first two tasks were meant to be schema-building tasks, to remind students of what they already knew of the subject of the lesson. I reminded students of a lesson we had done the preceding week that had dealt with the issue of ''culture shock.''

Listening Tasks

1. Watch the video. Note where the people come from, and what they like most/least about living in another country and how they maintain their culture.

2. a. Listen. You will hear Dave, Anne, and Denise talking about what it's like to live in another country. None of them is living in the country where they were born. Make a note of the places you hear.

   b. Group work. Listen again. Use the information in the tape and the following fact sheet to complete the table showing where these three people were born and where they are living now.

Fact Sheet

◆ One of the people living in Australia was born in Britain.

◆ Denise was born in Australia.

◆ One of the people living in Australia is from Canada

Name	Where From	Where Now
Anne	_____	_____
Denise	_____	_____
Dave	_____	_____

   c. Group work. Discussion. What does each person say about "culture"?

Name	Topic	Comment
Anne	British culture	
Denise	Californian culture	
Dave	Popular culture	

   d. Listen to the tape again to confirm your answers.

The aims of the listening tasks were to give the student ideas for the speaking task to come, as well as to provide them with language models.

The first listening was based on a series of authentic videos of immigrants in the United States discussing the experience of living in another culture and maintaining their cultural identity.

The second listening was based on audiotaped interviews with three people who were living and working in countries other than the ones they were born in.

Finally, students had to listen again, and identify what each person has to say about ''culture.'' This is a challenging task, because they all define the term in somewhat different ways.

Speaking

1. a. Pair work. Make a list of the things that visitors would say about <u>your</u> culture.

   b. Make a list of the things that give Hong Kong a sense of identity, e.g., famous people, significant events in history.

2. Interview Tang and find out what she finds interesting, unusual, strange, good, and not so good about Hong Kong.

3. a. Pair work. You have just moved, or are about to move, to another country to take up a position as a computer programmer with a large firm. You know very little about this country. Brainstorm ideas for meeting people and finding out about the country.

The class was split into two. Half the class completed the A task and half completed the B task. They then formed A/B dyads to give feedback on the task they completed.

As luck would have it, on this particular day I had a visiting teacher from Beijing Foreign Studies University, so I was able to build her into the fabric of the lesson.

The final task in the lesson was designed to get students thinking about living and working in another country and thinking creatively about how they might get to meet other people.

Example:
A: I'd take classes in ceramics.
B: I had no idea you were interested in ceramics.
A: I'm not, but it's such a boring hobby, there must be lots of interesting conversations in the class.
B: That's a crazy idea. I'd find out about the place before I go. I'd read about the place in an encyclopedia, and I'd visit the local consulate. They always have lots of information.

   b. Work with another pair, and write down ten ideas. Rank the ideas from most to least interesting (1 = most interesting). Now rank them again from most to least practical (1 = most practical).

	Interesting	Practical
Ideas		
1. _____	_____	_____
2. _____	_____	_____

	Interesting	Practical
Ideas		
3. _____	_____	_____
4. _____	_____	_____
5. _____	_____	_____
6. _____	_____	_____
7. _____	_____	_____
8. _____	_____	_____
9. _____	_____	_____
10. _____	_____	_____

c. Compare lists. Which pair has the most interesting ideas overall?

Audio Tapescript

Anne: *Whenever I meet new people in this country I always have to explain where I'm from, whereas when I'm back in Britain, I'm surrounded by people who know about my background; friends, family and relatives are always around. When I first moved to Australia, I felt I had to explain my background to everyone I met because I came from a culture where everyone likes to know where you fit in. I got sick of it after a while.*

Denise: *I think that's your British background, Anne, 'cause I don't feel that way living in California. People are coming and going all the time, so they don't care that much about where you're from. They might say "Where're you from? Oh Australia," and then they'll talk about kangaroos or something and then that's it.*

Dave: *Well, a lot of times I feel really ignorant, especially about popular culture. You go somewhere and everybody knows someone's name—a famous actor or singer or whatever—who's only known in Australia. I found it time and time again when I first moved from Canada. Everybody knew someone or some event, but I didn't have a clue.*

Anne: *Right.*

Denise: *Well, that doesn't happen in California, 'cause Californian culture is the world's culture. Any person who's popular in California is going to be popular everywhere else 'cause they're going to be marketed everywhere else.*

♦ Conclusion

In the course of this book, I have traced the evolution of language education over the last thirty years. I have shown how changing views on the nature of language, language learning, and the role of the learner within the learning process have changed, and I have tried to spell out how these changing philosophies and view have affected, sometimes profoundly, what goes on in the classroom.

In this chapter, I have looked at the ways in which these changes have changed the ways in which we go about the task of helping our learners develop their speaking skills. Table 8.6 offers a summary of the ways in which these changing views have affected every aspect of the curriculum, from the days when audiolingualism dominated the speaking classroom through to the present time when communicative language teaching has come to dominate.

	Audiolingualism	*Communicative Language Teaching*
Theory of language interaction	Language is a system of rule-governed structures hierarchically arranged.	Language is a system for the expression of meaning: primary function—and communication.
Theory of learning	Habit formation; skills are learned more effectively if oral precedes written; analogy not analysis	Activities involving real communication, carrying out meaningful tasks, and using language that is meaningful to the learner promote learning.
Objectives	Control of the structures of sound, form, and order, mastery over symbols of the language; the goal is native speaker mastery.	Objectives will reflect the needs of the learner; they will include functional skills as well as linguistic objectives.
Syllabus	Graded syllabus of phonology, morphology, and syntax; contrastive analysis.	Will include some or all of the following: structures, functions, notions, themes, and tasks. Ordering will be guided by learner needs.
Activities	Dialogues and drills; repetition and memorization; pattern practice.	Engage learners in communication, involve processes such as information sharing, negotiation of meaning, and interaction.
Learner role	Organisms that can be directed by skilled training techniques to produce correct responses.	Learner as negotiator, interactor, giving as well as taking.
Teacher role	Central and active; teacher-dominated method; provides model, controls direction and pace.	Facilitator of the communication process; needs analyst, counselor, process manager.
Role of materials	Primarily teacher-oriented. Tapes and visuals; language lab often used.	Primary role of promoting communicative language use; task-based, authentic.

◆ QUESTIONS AND TASKS

1. What is communicative competence, and what are its individual components?
2. Why are conversational routines helpful for communication?

3. What is the negotiation of meaning, and why has it been hypothesized as being important for the development of speaking?

4. What is "genre"? How can an understanding of genre help us when it comes to the teaching of spoken language?

5. List the factors that determine the difficulty of a speaking task.

6. Study a textbook and identify the range of roles implicit in it for learners and teachers.

7. Summarize the key principles that you feel are important for developing speaking skills. Design a speaking lesson using the principles. Demonstrate how the principles are realized through the materials.

◆ CONCEPT MAP OF CHAPTER 8

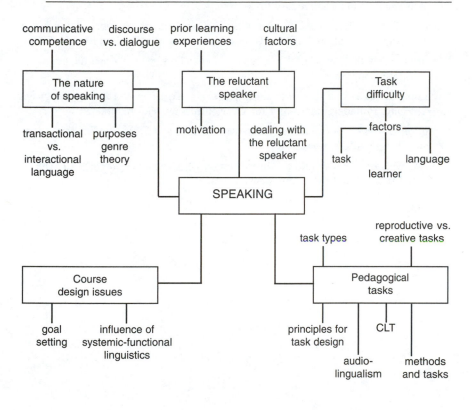

◆ REFERENCES

Albee, E. 1965. *Who's Afraid of Virginia Woolf?* London: Penguin.

Breen, M., and C. Candlin. 1980. The essentials of a communicative curriculum in language teaching. *Applied Linguistics*, 1, 2, 89–112.

Brown, G., and G. Yule. 1983. *Teaching the Spoken Language*. Cambridge: Cambridge University Press.

Burns, A., and H. Joyce. 1997. *Focus on Speaking*. Sydney: NCELTR.

Bygate, M. 1987. *Speaking*. Oxford: Oxford University Press.

Fanselow, J. 1987. *Breaking Rules*. New York: Longman.

Hymes, D. 1974. *Foundations in Sociolinguistics*. Philadelphia: University of Pennsylvania Press.

Gardner, R. 1985. *Social Psychology and Second Language Learning: The Role of Attitudes and Motivation*. London: Arnold.

McCarthy, M., and R. Carter. 1994. *Language as Discourse: Perspectives for Language Teaching*. London: Longman.

Martin, J. 1985. *Factual Writing: Exploring and Challenging Social Reality*. Geelong, Australia: Deakin University Press.

Martyn, E. 1997. Tasks and learner talk. Colloquium on task-based language teaching. International TESOL Convention, Orlando, Florida, March 1997.

Richards, J. C., J. Platt, and H. Weber. 1985. *Longman Dictionary of Applied Linguistics*. London: Longmaan.

Savignon, S. 1972. *Communicative Competence: An Experiment in Foreign Language Teaching*. Philadelphia: Center for Curriculum Development.

Savignon, S. 1983. *Communicative Competence: Theory and Classroom Practice*. Reading, Mass.: Addison-Wesley.

Tsui, A. 1996. In K. Bailey and D. Nunan (eds.), *Voices from the Language Classroom*. Cambridge: Cambridge University Press.

CHAPTER **9**

Reading

Reading, along with listening, is sometimes viewed as a *passive* skill. However, as we saw in Chapter 7, listening is anything but passive. In this chapter, we shall see that reading is anything but passive as well. There are, of course, similarities between reading and noninteractive listening (that is, listening to a monologue, news broadcast, lecture, etc.). Both involve processing ideas generated by others that are transmitted through language. Both involve highly complex cognitive processing operations. It is not surprising, then, that parallels are frequently drawn between both skills, nor that research outcomes developed in one area should be transferred to the other. Of course there are important differences. Listening is ephemeral: The words are gone as soon as they are uttered, whereas the written word is permanent, and can be revisited. In addition, reading involves the processing of written language, and, as we see in the next chapter, there are important differences between spoken and written language. The chapter covers the following issues and concepts:

Reading in another language
◇ reading purposes and strategies
◇ bottom-up and top-down approaches

Research into reading
◇ schema theory
◇ the transfer hypothesis
◇ cross-cultural aspects of reading comprehension

Task types
◇ the "good" reading task
◇ strategies-based approaches to reading tasks

Designing reading courses
◇ steps in the design process
◇ task-based course design

READING IN ANOTHER LANGUAGE

Unlike speaking, reading is not something that every individual learns to do. An enormous amount of time, money, and effort is spent teaching reading in elementary and secondary schools around the world. In fact, it is probably true to say that more time is spent teaching reading than any other skill. For hundreds of years, being literate has been the mark of the educated person. One of the greatest indictments of many education systems is that some children spend up to twelve years in school and do not become literate.

◆ READING PURPOSES AND STRATEGIES

Take a few minutes to reflect on all of the reading that you have done in the last twenty-four hours. Make a list. Now note the different purposes and strategies you employed for each of the different reading tasks that you carried out. The list is a nonexhaustive record of some of the things that I have read over the last twenty-four hours. I say nonexhaustive, because reading is so intimately a part of my daily existence, that an exhaustive list of every piece of written material than I processed would take up several pages, and would be extremely boring to read.

My 24-hour list of reading tasks

√ London, San Francisco and Sydney newspapers on the world Wide Web

√ Countless e-mail messages

√ The South China Morning Post newspaper

√ A memo from a staff member

√ Several poems from a newly published collection by a colleague

√ A Brazilian visa application form

√ Several academic texts

√ Page proofs of a forthcoming listening text

√ The University bulletin for senior staff

√ A past issue of TESOL Matters

√ The telephone directory

√ The label on a bottle of wine

√ The final chapter of a novel

When I carried out these reading tasks, I had different purposes in mind, and used different strategies. I read the novel for pleasure. Because I had enjoyed it so much, and because I was on the final chapter, I read it slowly, savoring every sentence. I read the colleague's poems for pleasure, and also out of curiosity. I skimmed the Senate minutes to ensure that the written record accorded with my own recollection of what had gone on. I scanned the issue of *TESOL Matters* because I was looking for a specific piece of information. I read the page proofs of the listening text slowly and painstakingly because I was looking for typographical errors.

(Something that I am not particularly skilled at.) I read the label on the wine bottle to check the grape varieties that had been used to make the wine. In summary, I read for pleasure, to obtain information, to verify information that I already know (or thought that I knew), and I read to check the accuracy of a text I had written. For each of these different tasks, I employed different strategies. I read slowly and carefully for both accuracy and pleasure, I skimmed to get a general idea of the information contained in some of the texts, and I scanned other texts for specific information.

Rivers and Temperly (1978: 187) suggest that there are seven main purposes for reading:

1. To obtain information for some purpose or because we are curious about some topic;
2. To obtain instructions on how to perform some task for our work or daily life (e.g., knowing how an appliance works);
3. To act in a play, play a game, do a puzzle;
4. To keep in touch with friends by correspondence or to understand business letters;
5. To know when or where something will take place or what is available;
6. To know what is happening or has happened (as reported in newspapers, magazines, reports);
7. For enjoyment or excitement.

Davies (1995) reviews studies by Lunzer and Gardner (1979) and Harri-Augstein and Thomas (1984) that set out the different types of reading that exist.

◇   The first of these is *receptive reading*, which is the rapid, automatic reading that we do when we read narratives;
◇   *reflective reading*, in which we pause often and reflect on what we have read;
◇   *skim reading*, in which we read rapidly to establish in a general way what a text is about;
◇   *scanning*, or searching for specific information.

Davies concludes, however, that in actual reading performance

> . . . it is difficult to draw clear boundaries between the types of reading termed *skimming* and *scanning*; in real life, scanning inevitably involves some skimming (and skipping) of large sections of text, and skimming, reciprocally, must embrace some scanning. Furthermore, skimming and scanning both involve fairly rapid superficial reading and both are aimed at searching, rather than deep processing of the text or reflection upon the content of the text.
>
> *Davies 1995: 137*

◆ BOTTOM-UP AND TOP-DOWN APPROACHES

In Chapter 7, we looked at bottom-up and top-down approaches to the development of listening. Similar approaches have been employed in relation to reading. The bottom-up approach views reading as a process of decoding written symbols into their aural equivalents in a linear fashion. Thus, one first discriminates each letter as it is encountered, sounds these out, matching the written symbols with their aural equivalents, blends these together to form words, and derives meaning. Arriving at the meaning of a word is therefore the final step in the process. On the face of it, this would seem to be a reasonable explanation of the reading process. Letters do represent sounds, and despite the fact that in English 26 letters have to represent over forty sounds, there is a high degree of correspondence between written symbols and their aural equivalents. In teaching beginning reading, it would seem reasonable to teach learners these sound–symbol correspondences, and, in fact, this is the procedure underlying the most popular approach to the teaching of reading, known as the phonics approach. The alternative, known as the whole-word approach, teaches words by their overall shape or configuration.

> **Phonics**
> An approach to the teaching of reading in which learners are taught to decode words by matching written symbols with their aural equivalents.

One of the assumptions underlying the phonics approach is that once a reader has blended the sounds together to form a word, then the word will be recognized. In other words, it is assumed that the reader will already know these words in their spoken form. This, in fact, is not an assumption that can be made with either second or first language learners. Most teachers who have taught initial reading using phonics are familiar with children who can "read" without understanding. In other words, they can sound out the words, but are unable to make sense of the text itself.

Phonics has come in for a great deal of criticism for the fact that it de-emphasizes meaning in the reading process. The complexity and relative unpredictability of sound–symbol correspondences in English have also been noted. In addition, research into human memory and speech processing has also shown that phonics is problematic. For example, it has been shown that it takes around a quarter of a second to match a letter of the alphabet with its aural equivalent. At this rate, given the average length of English words, good readers would only be able to process around 60 words per minute. However, we also know that the average reader can read between 250 and 350 words per minute. Reading, under the phonics approach, would appear to be a logical impossibility.

One of the most articulate critics of the phonics approach is Frank

Smith. In his (1978) book *Understanding Reading* , which purported to present a "psycholinguistic" approach to reading, he pointed out that, in speech processing terms, phonics simply does not work because in many words it is impossible to determine the sound represented by the word until one has read the entire word. If, for example, one encounters the sequence of letters *h - o. . .* , it is impossible to assign a phonemic value to the letter *o* until one knows whether the word is *house, horse, hot, hoot,* and so on as the letter *o* has a different sound in each word. Of course, when actually reading, context plays a crucial role in helping the reader to predict the meaning of a upcoming word. If the sentence in which the *h - o* sequence appears begins, "It was the dead of night, and the owl began to ho. . . " most readers would immediately predict that the upcoming word is *hoot*.

Evidence against the notion that reading is a matter of decoding letters to sounds in a linear fashion also came from work carried out in the 1970s by researchers using a technique called *miscue analysis.* The technique, pioneered by Goodman and Burke (see, for example, Goodman and Burke, 1972), involves the analysis of errors made by the reader when reading the text aloud. This technique shows that reading is more than mechanical decoding, that readers who are reading for meaning generate miscues that make sense semantically. For example, the person might read *It was a hot, sunny day,* when the original text was *It was a bright, sunny day.* (If someone read *It was a bright, sunny day,* we could reasonably conclude that he or she was decoding mechanically.)

Miscue analysis
A technique of identifying reading problems by having the reader read a text aloud, recording the reading, and then documenting and analyzing the deviations, or *miscues,* from the text.

Work by Smith, the miscue analysts, and others led to the development of an alternative to the bottom-up phonics approach. This alternative approach became known as the top-down or psycholinguistic approach to reading. According to this view, one begins with a set of hypotheses or predictions about the meaning of the text one is about to read, and then selectively samples the text to determine whether or not one's predictions are correct. Reading is a process of reconstructing meaning rather than decoding form, and the reader only resorts to decoding if other means fail.

However, there are also problems with this alternative hypothesis. Stanovich (1980), among others, has pointed out that if reading were a process of developing and testing hypotheses, as Smith suggests, then reading would actually take longer than the decoding approach.

One of the assumptions made by proponents of the top-down approach is that learning to read and reading fluently must necessarily involve the same process. Smith, for example, argues that fluent readers recognize words on sight. In other words, they function in the way suggested by proponents of the whole-word approach, and that, therefore, this is the way that children should learn to read. However, it does not necessarily follow that because fluent readers read by recognizing whole words on sight (assuming that this is how they read), that this is the way that they learned to read in the first place. It could well be that a phonics approach in the early stages of reading is the most effective and efficient way to teach reading. Or it could also be the case that different individuals learn to read in different ways, and that reading teachers need to adopt different strategies to meet these different needs.

Given these conflicting, and, in some ways, contradictory perspectives and approaches, how do readers make sense of text? What can we learn from the way the fluent readers make sense of texts that can guide us in developing effective pedagogical approaches for beginning readers?

I would argue that reading is an interactive process, in which the reader constantly shuttles between bottom-up and top-down processes. In order to explore this, I invite you to take part in a small experiment.

Study the text in the box below and answer these questions. As you do the task, make a mental note of the strategies you use to make sense of the text.

1. How many words can you make out?
2. What type of text do you think it is?
3. What do you think the text is about?
4. What do you think is the purpose of the text?
5. What language is the text written in?

TOK BILOG GAVMAN

Sipos yu painim sompela Japan i les long pait, yu gifim dispela pas. Sipos i savi wakabaut, i kan kam ontaim yupela nau painim soldia bilong yumi. Im i sik tumas, orait, yu brinim tok.

Tok im gut, mipela nokan kilim ol, kalabus dasol, nau salim ol iko long Astralia, na weitim pait i pinis.

WOK BILOG GAVMAN. I GAT PEI.

The text is written in a language that I am sure the vast majority of readers have never encountered: New Guinean Tok Pisin. The following extract is a conversation between two individuals who attempted to decode the

Tok Pisin text. In the extract they are discussing the strategies they used to make sense of the decontextualized text. As you read the transcription, you will see that they use both top-down and bottom-up processing strategies to construct a plausible interpretation of the text.

A: *I . . . I think one of the strategies is that is that . . . I feel I know a little bit of the language and I'm trying to draw on anything I've seen before or heard before that I can relate back to . . .*

B: *We're also using what we know about English and relating the words to English. But as well as that you start trying to decipher the actual grammar of the language, so things like (pronouns and)* sompela, yupela *and the other one which I've lost at the moment—*mipela*—presumably have something to do with umm (but also) the way in which the grammar is organized, like* som *and* yu *and* mi mifela, yufela, *and whatever.*

A: *But also, what we've done so far is try to decipher it more or less word by word, and we're only just beginning to get a sense of the context or the background knowledge or the kind of the discourse as a whole so um—it's interesting that we've started by trying to do it word-by-word . . .*

B: *Although we also get to bits that we can't do and leave it and then go on . . .*

A: *And then come back . . .*

B: *. . . when you've got a better sense of what comes after to try and actually . . . almost like a cloze test where you try to . . . to reconstruct what ought to go where on the basis of having read on.*

A: *I'm trying to think of what kind of connections there are between Australia and Japan and . . . in Papua New Guinea the kind of connections between Australia and Japan would be the war really, wouldn't they?*

B: *Either that or investment mining.*

A: *Yes, oh, that's true, could be investment, yeah.*

B: *So, it could be there's someone who's done this work and hasn't got paid.*

A: *Or it could be that they don't feel that investment with and contact with Australia have been very profitable and they're now turning to Japan for investment opportunities with other countries.*

Most people can decipher a few words, but have a great deal of difficulty in deciding the text type and purpose. However, given a context for the text, they can make much more sense of it. The next paragraph provides a context for the text.

The original text is printed on a piece of paper that I came across some years ago in a box of belongings owned by an uncle who had fought in the New Guinea highlands during the Second World War. The text is accompanied by two illustrations. The first of these shows a New Guinea highlander in a jungle setting peering around a tree at a wounded Japanese soldier who is holding up a piece of paper. The second illustration shows the highlander, the piece of paper in his hand, leading three Australian soldiers, one of whom carries a first aid kit, through the jungle. On the reverse of the paper is a message in Japanese.

The leaflet was designed by the Australian army and used in New Guinea during the Second World War. It was intended that the leaflet should be used by wounded Japanese soldiers to give to natives, who would lead Australian soldiers to the wounded Japanese soldier. Here is the translation of the message, written in Tok Pisin, and the Japanese text.

```
Tok Pisin literal translation

GOVERNMENT'S MESSAGE
If you find some Japanese who refuse to fight, you
give them this letter. If he is able to walk and
come on time, you (plural) must look for our sol-
dier. If he is very sick, OK, you bring the message.

Tell them clearly that we can not kill them, but (we
will) take them as prisoner only and send them to
Australia, and (they will) wait for the war to end.

GOVERNMENT'S WORK (JOB)
HAS A WAGE (REWARD)
```

[Translated by Philip Aratiso.]

RESEARCH INTO READING

◆ SCHEMA THEORY

Most of the research that is cited in scholarly books and articles on reading development and comprehension has been carried out in first language contexts with individuals who are learning to read their first language. According to Grabe (1993), the large amount of research into reading can be partly accounted for by the fact that cognitive psychologists, as much as educators, have been interested in the processes underlying literacy development. Studying children as they learn to read provides an important "window" into certain cognitive processes that can help psychologists understand the nature of the learning process, information processing, and other aspects of the human mind. As we have already seen, this research has shown that we do not process print in a serial, linear, step-by-step process. Nor do we process print as "visual tape-recorders." Rather, we interpret what we read in terms of what we already know, and we integrate what we already know with the content of what we are reading.

One interesting line of research in the second language area concerns the effect on reading performance of readers' own internalized models or beliefs about the reading process. Key questions here are: How do second language readers conceive of the reading process? and How do these internalized models affect their reading performance? Devine (1984) carried out a study with 20 low-intermediate ESL readers from a variety of backgrounds. The subjects were interviewed to determine their attitudes toward reading, and their ideas on what constitutes "good" reading. Based on their answers, Devine classified the subjects according to whether they were sound-, word-, or meaning-centered in their approach to reading. She then analyzed their oral reading, recall, and text comprehension. Miscue analyses (see above) of their oral readings revealed significant differences in the ways in which these three reader types went about the reading process, and what they took away with them from the reading process.

In a follow-up study Devine (1988) reported that:

> Evaluations of unaided retellings of the reading selections also sug-
> gested that the internalized models of reading held by the subjects af-
> fected recall and comprehension. Those readers who in their interviews
> indicated that they considered understanding what the author wanted
> to say as the measure of successful reading (that is, meaning-centered
> readers) not surprisingly demonstrated good to excellent recall and com-
> prehension of the text. On the other hand, and, again not surprisingly,
> readers who equated good reading with sound identification or good
> pronunciation usually failed to understand or recall what they had read.
>
> *(129)*

The practical implications of the work are intriguing. Devine suggests that meaning-centered readers are actually able to perform, when reading, at higher levels than predicted by their general levels of proficiency. In other words, their internalized assumptions and attitudes enable them to "outperform their competence." Perhaps one solution to the problems of second language readers is to work on their attitudes toward and assumptions about reading.

In Chapter 7, the concept of schema theory was introduced. You will recall that schema theory suggested that our knowledge and expectations about the world will strongly affect our ability to understand new informa-tion by providing a framework within which that new information might fit. Not surprisingly, a great deal of research with both first and second language readers has been carried out using schema theory. The basic principle behind schema theory is that texts themselves, whether spoken or written, do not carry meaning. Rather they provide signposts, or clues to be utilized by listeners or readers in reconstructing the original mean-ings of speakers or writers. Reading comprehension is thus an interactive process between the reader or the text, in that the reader is required to fit the clues provided in the text to his or her own background knowledge. (See, for example, Adams and Collins, 1979; Rumelhart, 1980). Schema theory is related to bottom-up and top-down processing, which we looked at in the preceding section, in the following way:

> According to schema theory, the process of interpretation is guided
> by the principle that every input is mapped against some existing schema
> and that all aspects of that schema must be compatible with the input
> information. This principle results in two basic modes of information
> processing, called bottom-up and top-down processing. Bottom-up pro-
> cessing is evoked by the incoming data; the features of the data enter
> the system through the best fitting, bottom-up schemata. Schemata are
> hierarchically organized, from most general at the top to most specific
> at the bottom. As these bottom-level schemata converge into higher
> level, more general schemata, these too become activated. Bottom-up
> processing is therefore called data-driven. Top-down processing, on the
> other hand, occurs as the system makes general predictions based on
> higher level, general schemata and then searches the input for informa-
> tion to fit into these partially satisfied, higher order schemata. Top-down
> processing is, therefore, called conceptually-driven.
>
> *Carrell and Eisterhold 1988: 84*

Schema theory has been used as a theoretical model in several important
areas of reading research. In the rest of this section I shall look at three
of these. The first is research into reasons why students who are good
readers in their first language have difficulty transferring their skills to
a second. Second, we look at work into cross-cultural aspects of reading
comprehension. Finally, we shall look at studies into the relationship
between background knowledge and linguistic knowledge in explaining
reading performance.

◆ THE TRANSFER HYPOTHESIS

A reasonable working hypothesis in the area of reading comprehension
is that good readers in a first language will be able to transfer their skills
to the second language. However, it has been found that L1 reading skill
does not predict second language reading proficiency. Limited linguistic
proficiency would appear to "short-circuit" the transfer of reading skills
from one language to another (Cziko 1978; Clarke, 1979). Cziko found
that the short circuit did not apply across proficiency levels, but appeared
to affect low and intermediate proficiency readers more than advanced
readers. Hudson (1988) suggests that schema theory might help to explain
the results obtained by Cziko and Clarke, in that readers, when functioning
in a second language, may be using the wrong schema to guide comprehension of the text.

> Basically, the issue here is whether the nonuse of semantic and
> discourse constraints by L2 readers is a symptom of low L2 proficiency,
> or whether it is a symptom of false schemata production and reconcilia-
> tion in conjunction with low language proficiency.
>
> *(p. 189)*

Hudson set out to determine whether schema theory was able to explain the L2 short-circuit of good reading strategies by proficient foreign language readers. Subjects for his study were 93 ESL students with different levels of proficiency in an intensive language institute in the United States, the majority of whom were planning to attend university in the United States. Test materials were nine graded reading passages matched to the proficiency levels of the subjects. Subjects were assigned to one of three conditions, termed Pre-Reading (PRE), Vocabulary (VOC), and Read-Test/ Read-Test (RT). The PRE condition was designed to help the reader apply the appropriate schema to the reading passage. The VOC method was designed to give readers essential vocabulary, while the RT method was designed for all readers to adjust their interpretation of the test passage.

The results indicated that the schema application treatment was more effective with readers at beginning levels of proficiency, while the vocabulary and read-test/read-test conditions were more effective for readers at intermediate and advanced levels. They show that readers at different levels of proficiency use different reading strategies, and benefit from different types of intervention. It seems clear from the study that for lower proficiency students at least, pre-reading tasks designed to help them apply what they already know about a subject can help significantly in reading comprehension.

◆ CROSS-CULTURAL ASPECTS OF READING COMPREHENSION

One line of research of particular interest to second language teachers is that into the effect of background knowledge, particularly cultural knowledge, on comprehension. One of the best known studies is that by Steffensen (1981) who compared the comprehension of readers from two different cultural backgrounds, one group from North America, and one group from India. She looked at the ability of her subjects to recover meaning from two texts, one describing a North American wedding, and one describing an Indian wedding. Steffensen found that her North American subjects had higher levels of comprehension on the passage describing the North American wedding, and the Indian subjects did better on the passage concerning an Indian wedding.

In the mid-1980s, I investigated the effect of background knowledge on the comprehension of secondary school students. I was particularly interested in the effect of background knowledge on readers' perceptions of cohesive relationships in two different texts. (For a discussion of cohesion, see Chapter 4.) Text A was on a familiar subject, while Text B was on an unfamiliar subject. A range of readability analyses indicated that Text B was linguistically simpler than Text A. (The analysis looked at such things as sentence length, the familiarity of the vocabulary, and grammatical complexity.) Ninety-six cohesive relationships were identified and matched across both texts, and a key marker of the relationships was deleted from each relationship. Examples of the cohesive relationships and the way they were used to construct test items are set out below:

Logical Relationship

Test item: Usually there would be no difficulty in deciding whether a living thing is a plant or an animal and it can be classified immediately. There are _____ some very tiny creatures which scientists know to be living, but cannot be sure whether they are plants or animals. (Deleted item 'however'. Cohesive type: adversative conjunction).

Referential Relationship

There is no difficulty in deciding that a bird is living and a stone is non-living, but not all things are as easy to distinguish as _____ . (Deleted item: 'these'. Cohesive type: referential demonstrative).

Lexical Relationship

Test item: Green plants grow towards the light. This is because plants need _____ for energy. (Deleted item 'light'. Cohesive type: lexical reiteration)

The study found that background knowledge was a more important factor than grammatical complexity in the ability of readers to comprehend the cohesive relationships in the texts. In other words, they had greater success in inserting acceptable words into the gaps in the familiar, yet grammatically more complex Text A, than the simpler, yet unfamiliar Text B. It was also found that certain types of relationships were more difficult than others for the subjects to comprehend. Logical relationships in particular were much more difficult than referential or lexical relationships.

More recently, Guyotte (1997) used a similar research procedure to investigate the reading comprehension of several groups of undergraduates in a Japanese university. Guyotte studied the comprehension of a three different groups on a passage taken from a medical text. One group consisted of students from a non-medical faculty, another consisted of students from a pre-medical course (these were students who were headed for medical school, but who had not yet started their medical studies proper), and a third group consisting of medical students. In general, Guyotte found that content knowledge had a significant effect on the ability of the subjects to identify logical relationships in the test passage.

There are several practical implications of this research. In the first place, it suggests that schema-building activities and tasks, carried out before the students read, will facilitate their comprehension. Training students to make links between the text and what they already know can also help. Finally, the research suggests that cohesive relationships should be taught explicitly. In particular, logical relationships should be taught in academic reading programs.

Compared with classroom-oriented research into speaking and listening classrooms, there has been comparatively little research into what goes on in second language reading classrooms. One interesting case study is that by Richards (1989), which presents research on a second language reading classroom. There were four different phases to the lesson. During the first phase, students worked on material from an SRA reading kit, focusing on inferencing skills. They then worked with the rate-builder portion of the kit, focusing on developing reading fluency. The third phase of the lesson involved readers in working on exercises from the vocabulary text, and they completed the lesson by taking part in an extensive reading activity.

Richards makes the point that, while it is relatively easy to describe what goes on in classrooms, moving beyond description to interpretation and evaluation is more difficult. However, as the purpose of the investigation was to identify what made the lesson an effective one, interpretation and evaluation were of central importance. From his analysis of the lesson and from interviews with the teacher, Richards concluded that the following principles capture the essence of effective instruction.

1. Instructional objectives are used to guide and organize the lessons. (The teacher formulated and conveyed to learners what the lesson was intended to accomplish.)

2. The teacher has a comprehensive theory of the nature of reading in a second language, and refers to this in planning his teaching. (The teacher used knowledge of L2 reading strategies, schema theory and the role of background knowledge rather than "common sense" to select learning experiences.)

3. Class-time is used for learning. (Students were "on task" for fifty of the sixty minutes.)

4. Instructional activities have a teaching rather than a testing focus. (He provided opportunities for learners to develop and improve skills and strategies rather than demonstrating mastery of such skills.)

5. Lessons have a clear structure. (The structure was outlined to students, and each activity was clearly framed.)

6. A variety of different reading activities are used during each lesson. (Variation and pacing contributed to the positive attitude of students.)

7. Classroom activities give students opportunities to get feedback on their reading performance. (The teacher provided information on the kinds of strategies they were using for different tasks, and on the effectiveness of these strategies.)

8. Instructional activities relate to real-world reading purposes. (Links were provided between the SRA activities and use of learners' textbooks for learning.)

9. Instruction is learner-focused. (Learners were encouraged to try and work things out for themselves.)

This is an interesting study because it actually takes us into a reading classroom and shows us what actually goes on there, through an extensive set of classroom transcriptions. It is interesting to note that the principles identified by Richards (explicit objectives, theory-driven, time on task, a teaching not testing orientation and so on) are characteristics of the "good" classroom in general, not just the reading classroom.

TASK TYPES

◆ THE "GOOD" READING TASK

The DART (Directed Activities Related to Text) model was developed by Davies and Green (1984), and Davies (1995) in reaction to traditional reading exercises, such as multiple choice, that, they argue, are extremely limited in their potential as learning activities. Davies argues for tasks that are characterized by the following features.

The good reading task:

◊ typically makes use of authentic and challenging texts;
◊ provides students with a rhetorical or topical framework for processing and analyzing the text;
◊ frequently involves an oral reading of the text by the teacher or a student followed by silent reading and rereading of the text;
◊ involves the students interacting with the text and with each other;
◊ involves students in direct analysis of the text instead of indirect question answering;
◊ frequently involves the transfer of information from text to a visual or dia-grammatic representation.

Through active reading tasks incorporating these features:

◊ students make their hypotheses explicit;
◊ hypotheses are evaluated by other students and checked against the text;
◊ there is discussion about alternative interpretations;
◊ students ask questions about what they do not know instead of answering questions to which they know the answers or which may be seen as irrelevant
◊ if necessary, the teacher can adopt a role of informant rather than inquisitor;
◊ students learn to be critical in their reading of a text.

Davies 1995: 144

These principles were used in the development of their DART (Directed Activities Related to Text) model (Davies and Green, 1984) as an alternative to the traditional approach to reading comprehension. Within this model, there are two different task types, reconstruction activities and analysis activities. Reconstruction activities require the reader to reconstruct a text. Analysis activities require the reader to transform the information in the text in some way. Table 9.1 exemplifies the types of tasks that can be developed within the model.

Table 9.1

Reconstruction Activities (using text modified by teacher)	*Analysis Activities* (using straight text)
PUPIL TASK: Pupils complete text or diagram, reconstructing meaning.	**PUPIL TASK:** Pupils locate and categorize text information by marking and labeling. Use marked text as basis for summary (diagrammatic or note form).

TEXT COMPLETION
◊ word completion (selected words deleted from text)
◊ phrase completion (selected phrases/clauses deleted from text)
◊ sentence completion (selected sentences deleted from text)

SEQUENCING
◊ selected segments of text arranged in logical/time sequence (text cut into segments representing steps, events, etc.)
◊ segments of text classified (texts cut into segments representing certain categories of information)

PREDICTION
◊ pupils predict next events/steps or stage after reading segments of text (text segments presented a section at a time)

TABLE COMPLETION
◊ pupils fill in cells of table using row and column headings and text as sources of information (teacher provides row and column headings)
◊ pupils devise row and column headings using texts and cells of matrix as sources of information (teacher fills in cells)

TEXT MARKING
◊ locating and underlining parts of text representing certain meaning of information targets

LABELING
◊ pupils label parts of text using labels provided by the teacher

SEGMENTING
◊ pupils break text into meaning or information units and label/annotate segments of text

TABLE CONSTRUCTION
◊ pupils produce column and row headings for tables and fill in cells using text(s) as source of information.

DIAGRAM CONSTRUCTION
◊ pupils construct and complete diagram appropriate for particular text, for example, FLOW DIAGRAM for text describing a process, BRANCHING TREE for a text describing a hierarchical classification, networks, etc.

PUPIL-GENERATED QUESTIONS
◊ pupils read text and generate questions they still need answers to

SUMMARY
◊ pupils produce headings and summarize information

Table 9.1 Continued

Reconstruction Activities (using text modified by teacher)	*Analysis Activities* (using straight text)

DIAGRAM COMPLETION
◇ label completion using text and diagram as sources of information (selected labels deleted from diagram)
◇ diagram completion using text and partly completed diagram as sources of information (teacher constructs original diagram: flow diagram, branching tree, network, etc.).

In this chapter, I have argued for a strategies-based approach to the development of reading skills. Strategies, you will recall from Chapter 2, are those mental processes and operations used by learners to learn and then communicate. A useful, if somewhat disorganized, typology of reading strategies is that developed by Grellet (1981: 12–13).

He identifies three main types of strategy:

◇ sensitizing
◇ improving reading speed
◇ going from skimming to scanning

Sensitizing is subcategorized into:
  ◇ making inferences
  ◇ understanding relations within the sentence
  ◇ linking sentences and ideas

Going from skimming to scanning includes:
  ◇ predicting
  ◇ previewing
  ◇ anticipation
  ◇ skimming
  ◇ scanning

Classroom techniques using these strategies include:
◇ ordering a sequence of pictures
◇ comparing texts and pictures
◇ matching, using illustrations
◇ completing a document
◇ mapping it out
◇ jigsaw reading
◇ reorganizing the information
◇ comparing several texts
◇ completing a document
◇ summarizing
◇ note taking

♦ STRATEGIES-BASED APPROACHES TO READING TASKS

One of the most comprehensive typologies of reading strategies is that developed by teachers in the ELTU at Chinese University. They note that by choosing the best strategies for different texts and purposes, it is possible for second language readers to significantly increase both their reading speed and their comprehension. Their typology is set out in Table 9.2.

Table 9.2   A typology of reading strategies

Strategy	Comment
1. Having a purpose	It is important for students to have a clear purpose and to keep in mind what they want to gain from the text.
2. Previewing	Conducting a quick survey of the text to identify the topic, the main idea, and the organization of the text.
3. Skimming	Looking quickly through the text to get a general idea of what it is about.
4. Scanning	Looking quickly through a text in order to locate specific information.
5. Clustering	Reading clusters of words as a unit.
6. Avoiding bad habits	Avoiding habits such as reading word-by-word.
7. Predicting	Anticipating what is to come.
8. Reading actively	Asking questions and then reading for answers.
9. Inferring	Identifying ideas that are not explicitly stated.
10. Identifying genres	Identifying the overall organizational pattern of a text.
11. Identifying paragraph structure	Identifying the organizational structure of a paragraph, for example, whether it follows an inductive or deductive pattern.
12. Identifying sentence structure	Identifying the subject and main verb in complex sentences.
13. Noticing cohesive devices	Assigning correct referents to proforms, and identifying the function of conjunctions.
14. Inferring unknown vocabulary	Using context as well as parts of words (e.g., prefixes, suffixes, and stems) to work out the meaning of unknown words.
15. Identifying figurative language	Understanding the use of figurative language and metaphors.
16. Using background knowledge	Using what one already knows to understand new ideas.

Table 9.2 Continued

Strategy	Comment
17. Identifying style and its purpose	Understanding the writer's purpose in using different stylistic devices, such as a series of short or long sentences.
18. Evaluating	Reading critically and assessing the truth value of textual information.
19. Integrating information	Tracking ideas that are developed across the text through techniques such as highlighting and notetaking.
20. Reviewing	Looking back over a text and summarizing it.
21. Reading to present	Understanding the text fully and then presenting it to others.

Adapted from ELTU, Chinese University of Hong Kong

DESIGNING READING COURSES

♦ STEPS IN THE DESIGN PROCESS

1. Decide Overall Purpose

In designing reading courses, the first step is to decide on the overall purpose of the course. Is it to develop the academic reading skills that your students will need for further study? Is it part of a workplace education program for workers who need to read manuals and sets of instructions, or is it part of a general EFL school curriculum? The purpose of your program, and the relationship of the reading component to the other skills that you might be wanting to teach will determine the overall goals and objectives of your course.

2. Identify Texts and Tasks

In the task-based approach advocated here, the next step, having identified the overall purpose, and the relationship of the reading component to other components of the course, is to identify texts and tasks. As we have already seen, tasks can be either target (relating to the kinds of things learners might want to do outside the classroom), or pedagogical. Target reading tasks might include following a set of instructions for assembling a piece of furniture, looking up currency exchange rates in the newspaper, reading a recipe, or reading the warranty for an electrical appliance to determine whether it is still valid. Pedagogical tasks might include reordering a set of scrambled sentences for a coherent paragraph, underlining the topic sentence in a text, comparing the ordering of information in a newspaper article about an incident with that in a radio report of the same incident.

3. Identify Linguistic Elements

Having selected appropriate texts and tasks, the next step is to identify the linguistic elements to incorporate into your program. These can be grammatical (for example, tenses, clause types), lexical and/or discoursal (reference items, conjunctions, linking expressions). Where do these items come from? When designing language courses, I keep sets of syllabus checklists to guide me in making decisions about which linguistic items to teach and when. I then make selections from these, based on the following factors:

◇   the proficiency level of the students (there is little point in teaching complex nominalizations to post-beginner students);

◇   the elements that students will need to know in order to reconstruct the meaning of the text (when introducing instructional texts, the imperative is important for law students, the functioning of modal verbs is important in tort law);

◇   the elements that help define the generic structure of the text (for example, narratives and recounts demand attention to past tense forms).

4. Sequence and Integrate Texts and Tasks

The next step in the design process is to sequence and integrate the texts and tasks into units of work. In sequencing and integrating tasks, a number of possibilities suggest themselves. In the planning framework set out by Hood, Solomon, and Burns (1996), several options are suggested. These include following the sequence in which texts would be dealt with in a real-world situation (for example, in a medical context the sequence might be looking up a telephone directory, following hospital signs, reading an appointment card, following signs to the pharmacy); ordering the texts in terms of their difficulty (for example, reading signs setting out opening hours would, all other things being equal, be easier than reading a letter to a magazine on health issues); beginning with texts most critical to students' needs, and then introducing less critical texts; grouping texts in terms of the type of language needed (telephone directories, appointment cards, opening hour signs could all be used to introduce numbers); sequencing texts in terms of strategies (here, it would be logical to move from skimming to scanning to reading for detail).

5. Link Reading to Other Language Skills

As it is comparatively rare to find courses dealing exclusively with reading, the final step in the design process is to link reading and other language skills. Here, Hood *et al.* suggest linking reading to other kinds of language interactions that mirror sequences in daily life. If we take the topic of health, for example, we might interact in the following ways when dealing with a matter of health (illness, injury, or a general checkup):

1. Find the relevant telephone numbers in a directory.
2. Telephone to make an appointment.
3. Make some written notes from the telephone conversation.
4. Read street directory signs to find the address.
5. Give information to a receptionist.
6. Consult with a doctor.
7. Read medicine labels.
8. Tell someone what happened.
9. Telephone work or school to notify them of your absence due to illness.

This sequence, which links all four skills, is similar to the action sequence approach to designing courses (Corbel, 1985).

◆ CONCLUSION

In this chapter, we have seen that reading in an interactive process involving the exploitation of linguistic knowledge (sound/symbol correspondences, grammatical knowledge), and real-world (content) knowledge. Skilled readers have a range of strategies at their disposal, and select those strategies that match the purposes for which they are reading.

In practical terms, the following implications for classroom action can be drawn:

◇ Use pre-reading, schema-building tasks, particularly with lower proficiency students to help them apply what they already know to the task of reading;
◇ Teach learners strategies such as predicting, skimming, scanning, and give them opportunities to match the strategies to the purposes;
◇ Provide a variety of reading purposes;
◇ With higher proficiency students, develop activities for helping them identify and track logical and referential relationships in texts;
◇ Use activities that require students to transform data from one modality to another and from textual to nontextual (e.g., diagrammatic) form;
◇ Give students opportunities to go beyond the texts, evaluating and critiquing what they read.

◆ QUESTIONS AND TASKS

1. Why is it important to take purpose into consideration in designing reading tasks?
2. What similarities and differences are there between listening and reading?
3. What arguments are offered against the phonics approach to reading in the chapter? Despite these criticisms, why might phonics be justified for beginning readers?

◆ **Concept map of Chapter 9**

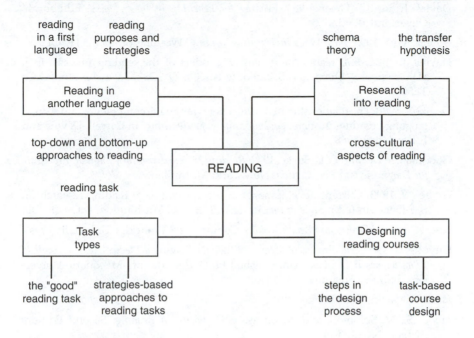

4. What is the "short-circuit" hypothesis and what are its implications for teaching reading?
5. Anayze a reading textbook and identify the range of strategies taught.
6. Find or devise tasks for some of the reading strategies set out in Table 9.2.
7. Summarize, in the form of a table, the research studies cited in the chapter. Indicate the researcher, the year, and, in a sentence or two, the main outcomes.

◆ **References**

Carrell, P., and J. Eisterhold. 1988. Schema theory and ESL reading pedagogy. In Carrell, Devine and. Eskey (eds.). *Interactive Approaches to Reading*. Cambridge: Cambridge University Press.

Carrell, P., J. Devine and D. Eskey (eds.). 1988. *Interactive Approaches to Reading*. Cambridge: Cambridge University Press.

Clarke, M. 1979. Reading in Spanish and English: Evidence from adult ESL students. *Language Learning*, 29, 121–150.

Corbel, C. 1985. The "action sequence" approach to course design, *Prospect*, 1, 1.

Cziko, G. G.A. 1978. Differences in first- and second-language reading: The use of syntactic, semantic, and discourse constraints. *Canadian Modern Language Review*, 34, 473—489.

Davies, F. 1995. *Introducing Reading*. London: Penguin.

Davies, F., and T. Green. 1984. *Reading for Learning in the Sciences*. Edinburgh: Oliver and Boyd.

Day, R. (ed.). 1993. *New Ways in Teaching Reading*. Washington, D.C.: TESOL.

Devine, J. 1984. ESL readers' internalized models of the reading process. In J. Hanscombe, R. Orem, and B. Taylor (eds.), *On TESOL '83*. Washington, D.C.: TESOL.

Devine, J. 1988. The relationship between general language competence and second language reading proficiency: *Implications for Teaching*. In Carrell, Devine and Eskep (eds.) 1988.

Goodman, Y. M., and C. L. Burke. 1972. *Reading Miscue Inventory Manual: Procedure for Diagnosis and Remediation*. New York: Macmillan.

Grabe, W. 1993. Current developments in second language reading research. In S. Silberstein (ed.), *State of the Art TESOL Essays*. Washington, D.C.: TESOL.

Grellet, F. 1981. *Developing Reading Skills*. Cambridge: Cambridge University Press.

Guyotte, C. 1997. *The Process of Japanese Students Reading a Medical Text in English: What Makes It Difficult?* Unpublished Ph.D. dissertation, Macquarie University, Sydney, Australia.

Harri-Augstein and Thomas 1984.

Hood, S., N. Solomon, and A. Burns. 1994. *Focus on Reading*. Second Edition. Sydney: NCELTR.

Hudson, T. 1988. The effect of induced schemata on the "short circuit" in L2 reading: Non-decoding factors in L2 reading performance. In Carrell, Devine and. Eskey (eds) 1988.

Lunzer, E., and Gardner 1979. *The Effective Use of Reading*. London: Heinemann.

Richards, J. C. 1989. *The Language Teaching Matrix*. Cambridge: Cambridge University Press.

Rivers, W., and M. Temperley. 1978. *A Practical Guide to the Teaching of English as a Second or Foreign Language*. New York: Oxford University Press.

Smith, F. 1978. *Understanding Reading: A Psycholinguistic Analysis of Reading and Learning to Read*. New York: Holt, Rinehart and Winston.

Stanovich, K. 1980. Towards an interactive–compensatory model of individual differences in the development of reading fluency. *Reading Research Quarterly*, 16: 32–71.

Steffensen, M. 1981. Register, Cohesion and Cross-cultural Reading Comprehension. Technical Report No. 220. Center for the Study of Reading, University of Illinois, Champaign, Illinois.

CHAPTER 10

Writing

In terms of skills, producing a coherent, fluent, extended piece of writing is probably the most difficult thing there is to do in language. It is something most native speakers never master. For second language learners the challenges are enormous, particularly for those who go on to a university and study in a language that is not their own.

In her review of 25 years of conceptual and empirical work on writing instruction, Raimes (1993) identifies four approaches to second language writing instruction. Until the mid-1970s, writing was a subservient skill, whose function was to support the development of oral language. Pedagogy was therefore dominated by form-focused techniques that were in line with the audiolingual ideology of drill and practice. In the mid-1970s, second language teachers discovered "process" approaches that were becoming popular in the first language classroom. As the term suggests, the process approach concentrates on the creation of the text, rather than on the end product. In the mid-1980s, two trends developed simultaneously. The first of these was a focus on academic content, looking at the demands made on readers by the nature of the academic subjects they were required to master. Along with content-based approaches came a focus on the requirements of the reader, and the implications of these requirements on the writer.

The chapter covers the following issues and concepts:

The nature of the writing process
◇   product versus process approaches,
◇   process writing
◇   spoken versus written language

Functional grammar and writing
◇   genre theory and writing
◇   the Disadvantaged Schools Project
◇   the SNAP Project
◇   problems with a functional model

A discourse-based approach to writing development
◇   discourse processes
◇   a discourse-based writing program

Contrastive rhetoric

THE NATURE OF THE WRITING PROCESS

◆ PRODUCT VERSUS PROCESS APPROACHES

One of the most controversial aspects of writing pedagogy has been the tension between process and product approaches to the teaching of writing. Product-oriented approaches focus on the final product, the coherent, error-free text. Process approaches, on the other hand, focus on the steps involved in drafting and redrafting a piece of work. Proponents of process writing recognize and accept the reality that there will never be the perfect text, but that one can get closer to perfection through producing, reflecting on, discussing, and reworking successive drafts of a text.

Product-oriented approaches to writing focus on tasks in which the learner imitates, copies, and transforms models provided by the teacher and/or the textbook. This is what, in an earlier chapter, I called "reproductive language work." The focus was also very much on the sentence level grammar, the belief being that sentences were the building blocks of discourse, and that discourse was created by fitting one building block on to the next. Such an approach was consistent with sentence-level structuralist linguistics and bottom-up processing. However, it was not consistent with emerging ideas in discourse analysis. Researchers working in this tradition were able to see that very often higher order choices determine lower order ones. In other words, decisions about how to package information within a sentence, and what grammatical forms to use (for example, whether to use the active or the passive voice, which tense to use, or whether to use a subordinate clause) can often only be made with reference to the discourse context within which the sentence is to be placed. In addition, an experiential philosophy, stressing learning by doing, argued more for a process approach. In such an approach, teachers focused less on a perfect final product than on the development of successive drafts of a text. Here the focus, in the first instance, is on quantity rather than quality, and writers are encouraged to get their ideas onto paper without worrying too much about formal correctness in the initial stages. They then share their work with others, getting feedback on their ideas and how they are expressed, before revising.

◆ PROCESS WRITING

Without doubt, a major impetus to writing pedagogy has come in recent years with the rapid growth of word processors, as well as the use of the Internet as a means of communication. In fact Stephen Marcus, a specialist in the use of technology in writing, maintains that process writing really became feasible with the development of word processing. Prior to that, the physical act of writing by hand was so laborious that it was unrealistic to expect writers to produce more than one or two drafts of their work.

Despite its attractions, process writing has been controversial. One criticism is that, left to themselves, young writers will produce recounts and narratives, but not the sorts of factual writing that they need to succeed in school. Martin (1985) argues that factual writing fosters the development of critical thinking skills, which in turn encourage the individual to explore and challenge social reality. Another critic of the approach is Rodrigues, who argues that the unfettered writing process approach has been just as artificial as the traditional high school research paper. Writing without structure accomplishes as little as writing a mock structure . . . [Students] need structure, they need models to practice, they need to improve even mechanical skills, and they still need time to think through their ideas, to revise them, and to write for real purposes and real audiences (1985: 26-7).

At several points in this book, I have dealt with the issue of authenticity. In Chapter 7, for example, I made a case for the use of authentic listening tasks in language learning. In relation to writing, the issue is not only what kinds of text learners are exposed to as models of writing, but also the types of text that learners are required to produce. In particular, the artificiality of much academic writing, particularly the writing of examination essays, has been criticized. Raimes deals with this issue by teaching two types of writing:

> . . . writing for learning (with prewriting, drafts, revisions, and editing) and writing for display (i.e., examination writing). Our students are aware of the different purposes and different strategies. They recognize that these are distinct. . . . In real questions, the speaker wants to know the answer; in exam questions, the speaker wants to know if the hearer knows. Similar distinctions can be made with writing. In a writing class, students need to be taught both how to use the process to their advantage as language learners and writers, and also how to produce an acceptable product on demand. A shortcoming of the debate around these issues is that process and product have been seen as *either/or* rather than *both/and* entities. However, while students certainly need to learn how to pass exams, they also need to perceive writing as a tool for learning, a tool that can be useful to them throughout their professional and personal lives.
>
> *(1993: 245)*

One of the clearest and most practical introductions to process writing is by White and Arndt (1991). They view writing as a complex, cognitive process that requires sustained intellectual effort over a considerable period of time. They suggest that producing a text involves six recursive procedures (recursive because they are nonlinear, as Figure 10.1 indicates).

These procedures can be realized in the classroom in a number of different ways. The following typical sequence of activities is suggested

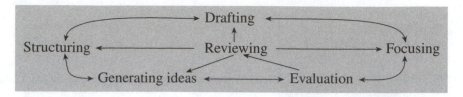

Figure 10.1   Procedures involved in producing a written text

by White and Arndt. It is worth noting that the learner completes six steps before actually producing a first draft. Note, also, the social, collaborative nature of the composing process.

1. Discussion (class, small group, pair)
2. Brainstorming/making notes/asking questions
3. Fastwriting/selecting ideas/establishing a viewpoint
4. Rough drafting
5. Preliminary self-evaluation
6. Arranging information/structuring the text
7. First draft
8. Group/peer evaluation and responding
9. Conference
10. Second draft
11. Self-evaluation/editing/proofreading
12. Finished draft
13. Final responding to draft

As White and Arndt point out, the process approach is aimed at helping the learner to develop a set of skills. As such, there is no reason why it need necessarily be inconsistent with approaches that focus more on the development of an acceptable final product. What we need in the writing classroom are both models and appropriate procedures. In other words, we need both process and product.

◆ SPOKEN VERSUS WRITTEN LANGUAGE

When developing courses for teaching writing (and for teaching speaking, for that matter), it is important to be aware of the differences between the spoken and written modes. Too often in the past, teachers attempted to teach spoken language by presenting learners with written language models, and vice versa, as though writing were "talk written down." This raises the question of just what the differences are between the two different modes. Again, while written language emerged from spoken language, it is more than "talk written down." According to Halliday (1985), writing emerged in societies as a result of cultural changes that created new communicative needs. These could not be readily met by the spoken language. In particular, with the emergence of cultures based on agriculture rather than hunting and gathering, people needed permanent records that could be referred to over and over again. This led to the emergence of a new form of language: writing.

Halliday (1985) suggests that written language is used for the following purposes:

◇ for action (for example, public signs, product labels, television and radio guides, bills, menus, telephone directories, ballot papers, computer manuals);
◇ for information (for example, newspapers, current affairs magazines, advertisements, political pamphlets);
◇ for entertainment (for example, comic strips, fiction books, poetry and drama, newspaper features, film subtitles).

These different purposes for language will be reflected in the characteristics of the texts themselves: Letters have different characteristics from newspaper editorials, which have different characteristics from poems, and so on. As we saw when we considered the concept of genre, these differences can be observed within the sentence at the level of grammar, and beyond the sentence at the level of text structure.

Written language does, in fact, serve a similar range of broad functions as does spoken language; that is, it is used to get things done, to provide information and to entertain. However, the contexts for using written language are very different from those in which spoken language is used. For example, in the case of information, written language is used to communicate with others who are removed in time and space, or for those occasions on which a permanent or semipermanent record is required. While most people in other cities or countries could be communicated with by telephone, there are certain types of message that would be more appropriate in written form, for example, postcard greetings to family and friends.

Can you tell the difference?

Study the following extracts from McCarthy and Carter (1994) and decide which has been taken from a spoken text and which from a written text. If you can't decide, circle "U" for "undecided."

A   . . . no, it'll shut. So, try it now. It's better . . .
B   . . . are erased away. Now, wouldn't you like to change your image . . .

C . . . and should be adjusted clockwise to reach the slowest
speed while still . . .
D . . . so, you know, up I get, bad temper . . .
E . . . well, eventually he came home and they had . . .
F . . . our answers to these questions may not be definitive or
complete, but even if . . .
G . . . your worries are over. Far from it. The little so-and-sos will
turn up again . . .
H . . . opportunities in space. Well, not strictly in space, but in
space research . . .
I . . . well, the place is gone now; not a stone remains . . .
J . . . into my eyes and said nothing. Well, it was a good
defense . . .

What was it about each extract that enabled you to decide whether it
was spoken or written?

Let us consider the discrimination exercise in the box above. These
extracts were taken from a study reported by Carter and McCarthy. Fifty-
five native and non-native speaking informants were asked to say whether
each fragment was predominately spoken or written.

Almost everyone agreed that extracts A and D suggested spoken
language; a sizable number also thought that extracts E, G, and H evoked
speech rather than writing. Extracts C and F were thought by significant
majorities to evoke writing, while extracts B, I, and J caused more of a
division of opinion and were felt to be neutral. (Carter and McCarthy
1994: 5)

As Carter and McCarthy observe, these responses are significant,
based as they are on such limited fragments, because they suggest that
people have a very clear idea of what it is that constitutes both spoken
and written language. Some of the linguistic exponents identified by
the informants as characteristic of spoken language included the use of
colloquialisms (*far from it, little so-and-sos*), discourse markers (*now, well,*
and *you know*), and contracted verb forms (*it'll, It's*).

For the record, the extracts came from the following sources:

A: Two people discussing a troublesome door closing mechanism
B: Written advertisement for consumer goods
C: Set of written instructions
D: Conversational extract
E: Conversational extract
F: Written academic text
G: Written advertisement for consumer goods

H: Advertisement for an academic post in a British university
I: Extract from novel
J: Extract from novel

From this exercise, you can see that the differences between spoken and written modes are not absolute, and that the characteristics that we tend to associate with written language can sometimes occur in spoken language and vice versa. This means that some spoken texts will be more like written texts than others, while some written texts will be more like spoken texts than others. Consider the following texts: Most native speakers would recognize 1 as being more like spoken language than 2, even though 1 is a written text and text 2 could conceivably be spoken.

Text 1
Annie,
Gone to the deli for milk. Back in a flash.
Go in and make yourself at home.
—Theo

Text 2
At times one's preoccupation with averages can cause one to lose sight of the fact that many of the most important workaday decisions are based on considerations of the extremes rather than on the middle of a distribution.

Despite the overlap between both modes, written language has certain features that are generally not shared by the spoken language, both in terms of its linguistic features and the contexts in which it will be interpreted. Linguistically, written language tends to consist of clauses that are complex internally, whereas with spoken language the complexity exists in the ways in which clauses are joined together. This is illustrated in the following extracts, Text 3 being the written text and Text 4 being the spoken one.

Text 3
Like Vincent d'Indy a disciple of Cesar Frank, Chausson shares with them a dreamy, even idle poetry, sumptuous but precise orchestration, and an energy that is intimate rather than powerful, ascetic rather than importunate.
Mordden 1980: 292

Text 4
This morning Associate Professor Joe Wolfe will talk about the science of music at half-past eleven, and we'll hear some fascinating things such as musicians playing music backwards, but most of it will be played forwards!
Author's data

We can see from the above texts that the written text seems to have more information packed into it. It contains only one main clause, in contrast with the spoken text in which there are several clauses chained together in an additive fashion. In a sense, spoken language is "unedited." If the speaker above had the opportunity to present the same content in written form, he might have produced something along the following lines:

> This morning at half-past eleven, Associate Professor Dean Wolf will present a program entitled "the Science of Music," in which the listener will experience a number of fascinating things, including music played backwards, although most will be played forwards!

Spoken and written language also differ in the ratio of content words to grammatical words (content words include nouns and verbs, while grammatical words include such things as prepositions, pronouns, and articles). The number of lexical or content words per clause is referred to as lexical density. The density of written language is also reinforced by the tendency to create nouns from verbs. Examples of this process are as follows:

Spoken
Good writers reflect on what they write.

Written
Reflection is a characteristic of good writers.

Lexical Density
The number of content words per clause expressed as a ratio of content words to function words.

Halliday calls this process of turning verbs into nouns *grammatical metaphor*. He suggests that the spoken forms are in a sense more basic than the written forms, and that, in writing, by turning verbs into nouns, we have altered the normal state of events. In other words, processes that in the grammatical system of English would normally be represented as verbs have been transformed into "things" and represented as nouns. It is this transformation that led Halliday to use the term *metaphor*.

These linguistic differences between spoken and written language are not absolutes. As I have already pointed out, there are some written texts that share many of the characteristics of spoken texts, and vice versa. Ultimately the linguistic shape of the text will be determined by a range of factors relating to the context and purpose for which it was produced in the first place.

Table 10.1 on page 279, from Burns and Joyce (1997: 13) summarizes the main differences between spoken and written language.

FUNCTIONAL GRAMMAR AND WRITING

In this book, I have adopted a functional view of language development and use. Functional models of linguistic analysis are developed to account

Table 10.1   Differences between spoken and written language

Spoken language	Written language
Context dependent	*Context independent*
generally used to communicate with people in the same time and place	used to communicate across time and distance
relies on shared knowledge between the interactants and often makes reference to the shared context	must recreate for readers the context it is describing
generally accompanies action	generally reflects action
Dialogic in nature	*Monologic in nature*
usually involves two or more speakers creating spoken texts together	usually written by one person removed from an audience
Unrehearsed and spontaneous but not unpredictable	*Edited and redrafted*
interactants build spoken, unrehearsed texts spontaneously within social and linguistic parameters	written language can be edited and redrafted any number of times
Records the world as happenings	*Records the world as things*
relies more on verbs to carry meanings	relies more on nouns and noun groups to carry meaning
Grammatically intricate	*Lexically dense*
tends to contain more grammatical words such as pronouns, conjunctions, etc.	tends to contain more lexical or content words as meaning is carried by nouns and noun groups
develops through intricate networks of clauses rather than complete sentences as it is jointly constructed and relies more heavily on verbs	relies on the process of nominalization whereby things that are not nouns can be turned into nouns

for relationships between the forms of the language, and the various uses to which the language is put. The systematic relationship between language structure and function is described by Halliday:

> Every text—that is, everything that is said or written—unfolds in some context of use; furthermore, it is the uses of language that, over tens of thousands of generations, have shaped the system. Language has evolved to satisfy human needs; and the way it is organised is functional with respect to those needs—it is not arbitrary. A functional grammar is essentially a 'natural' grammar, in the sense that everything in it can be explained, ultimately, by reference to how language is used.
>
> *Halliday 1985: xiii*

◆ GENRE THEORY AND WRITING

As we saw in Chapter 7, a key concept for many working within this functional perspective is *genre*. In written, as in spoken language, genres are typified by a particular structure and by grammatical forms that reflect the communicative purpose of the genre in question. It will be recalled that genre theorists argue that language exists to fulfill certain functions, and that these functions will determine not only the grammatical items that appear in a text, but also the overall shape or structure of the discourse that emerges as people communicate with one another. In other words, it will have certain predictable stages. The communicative purpose will also be reflected in the basic building blocks of the discourse, that is, the words and grammatical structures themselves. In other words, different types of communicative events result in different types of discourse, and these will have their own distinctive characteristics. Some events result in sermons, others in political speeches, and yet others in casual conversations. While each sermon, political speech, and casual conversation will be different, each discourse type will share certain characteristics that will set it apart from other discourse types.

At present, linguists are studying different text and discourse types in an effort to identify their underlying generic structure, and the linguistic elements that characterize them. In addition to identifying generic structure and linguistic features, genre analysts also look at other discourse features such as topicalization, the use of reference, and the operation of given/new structures in text. (In the next section, I shall look at some of this work.)

What are some of the practical applications of this model? In the rest of this section, I shall illustrate ways in which genre theory has been used in writing pedagogy and research. I shall do so by analyzing two research projects that I was involved in over the years. The first of these was the evaluation of an innovative curriculum program focusing on the development of written language in elementary and secondary schools that was known as the Disadvantaged Schools Project (DSP). The second was a needs assessment project known as SNAP.

◆ THE DISADVANTAGED SCHOOLS PROJECT

The Disadvantaged Schools Project was set up to improve the academic writing skills of children in inner-city schools in Sydney, Australia. The majority of children in these schools were from non-English-speaking backgrounds. The aim was to help them achieve the following goals:

◇ Perform effectively in written class assignments;
◇ Make effective notes;
◇ Do independent research;

◇   Complete written homework assignments;
◇   Participate fully in classroom discussions about writing.

The project worked towards these goals by implementing an innovative teacher education "package." This package, based on functional grammar, trained teachers in ways of sensitizing learners to the overall structure of different types of factual and imaginative texts, and to show them the grammatical resources that would help them produce successful texts.

After the package had been in place for some time, it was evaluated. I was involved in the evaluation along with three colleagues from Macquarie University in Sydney. The evaluation had three overall purposes. Firstly, it aimed to assess the impact of the program on children's writing. Secondly, it was to evaluate the impact of the program on teachers' capability to assess the effectiveness of students' writing as well as their classroom practice. Finally, it aimed to identify which elements of the package have been most beneficial and which require amendment.

In the course of the evaluation, we looked at around 1,500 pieces of children's writing. In assessing these pieces of writing, we used assessment criteria based on the functional model of grammar underlying innovation. A complete analysis was impossible, so we confined ourselves to three characteristic features:

◇   schematic structure
◇   topic development
◇   reference

In terms of the assessment criteria, we asked ourselves these questions:

1. **Schematic structure:**
    ◇   Is the schematic structure appropriate for the genre of the text? (In the model, it is argued that texts written for different purposes will exhibit different patterns of overall organization and text structure.)
2. **Topic development:**
    ◇   Does the writer explicitly identify the topic, and is the topic developed appropriately? (If the writer fails to develop the text topic or switches from one topic to another, then the text is confusing and difficult to follow.)
3. **Reference:**
    ◇   Does the writer use reference appropriately? (Appropriate use of reference is an indicator of text cohesion and that the writer has a sense of the "decontextualized" nature of writing in comparison to speaking.) (Nunan, 1992: 204).

Table 10.2 presents a text that was judged to be successful according to the assessment criteria. The text is broken down into individual clauses, and the schematic structure of the text is indicated in the left-hand column.

Table 10.2 Schematic structure of successful text

Structure Clauses		Text: The Skull and the Skeleton
	1	One day there was a poor orphan girl
ORIENTATION	2	She had to work with her stepmother
	3	Her hands were going to skin and bones
	4	So she decided to run away
	5	She saw a castle
	6	So she knocked on the door tap tap tap
	7	A skull with no body opened the door
	8	and he said "yes"
COMPLICATION	9	The girl told the skull [what had happened to her]
	10	She stepped into his castle
	11	She saw a body without a skull
	12	She knew that it belonged to the skull
	13	And the skull told the girl [what had happened]
	14	The they [sic] had dinner
	15	She stayed two night [sic]
RESOLUTION	16	and she kissed the skull
	17	They got married
	18	They lived happily after

It is followed by a discursive commentary on why the text was judged to be successful.

In terms of the criteria set out above, we judged this text to be successful for the following reasons:

> [This text] like many other narratives collected for this analysis contains no evaluation and reveals that this young writer, like many others, lacks full control of the narrative genre. However, for the purpose of this evaluation of young children's writing the essential stages of the narrative have been taken to be orientation, complication and resolution, and hence is assessed as satisfying criterion 1. The topic of [the text] is developed in the sense that the adventures of the 'poor orphan girl' are related to the meeting of the 'skull' and subsequent finding of its disengaged body. While the logical sequence of some events in the Narrative such as the skull telling 'what had happened' and 'having dinner' are not especially clear, there is enough information about the skull and skeleton for the reader to follow both the sequencing of events and the connection between complication and resolution. Hence the text is considered successful in terms of criterion 2. Reference is used appropriately in the text. The major participants are explicitly introduced: 'a poor orphan girl', 'a skull with no body' and thereafter referred to appropriately; 'she', 'the girl', 'he', 'the skull'. Thus it is clear at all times who or what is being referred to in the text.

Walshe et al. *1990: 20*

All in all, it was felt that the innovation had an overall positive response from participating teachers. There was also evidence that the innovation had a beneficial impact on students' writing. A comparative analysis of texts from schools taking part in the innovation and comparable schools not taking part in the innovation showed that, in terms of the evaluative criteria identified by the researchers, students in the innovation schools produced a greater range of factual texts, and produced them more successfully. (For a more detailed description and analysis of this innovation, see Nunan, 1992.)

◆ THE SNAP PROJECT

Another innovative program based on a functional approach is the SNAP (South Australian Needs Assessment Procedures) Project, which was initiated to develop a systematic procedure for diagnosing the strengths and weaknesses of students in their control over the spoken and written genres that they would need in order to succeed in school. Like the Disadvantaged School Project, this project was aimed at schools with high proportions of immigrant students. The project also took on the extremely ambitious task of attempting to develop a procedure for quantifying qualitative information. My role in this project, over a two-year period, was as consultant and adviser to the team and the principal researcher, Lexie Mincham.

Below, I have included examples of two different genres, an explanation and a recount, to illustrate the way in which the functional language model underlying the project has been used to provide a set of explicit criteria for evaluating students' writing. It is not difficult to see how the pro formas could also be used for instructional purposes. One of the key principles behind learner-centered instruction is that teachers have to be explicit about what learners are supposed to do and why, and so, in a

---

Example 1

Written Language Assessment Activity   **Years 8–10**

Explanation

An explanation is a factual text used to explain the processes involved in the evaluation of natural and social phenomena or how something works. Explanations are used to account for why things are as they are, focusing on causal relations. In the school curriculum, explanations are often found in Science and Social Studies.

Name of Student: _____ Year Level/Class: _____ Date: _____

Name of School: _____ Teacher: _____

Topic of explanation: _____

Criteria (Check appropriate box)	Very Competent	Competent	Limited Not Competent Yet	Comments
Ability to carry out the task	☐	☐	☐	☐
Did the student	☐	☐	☐	☐
–write an explanation with minimal support	☐	☐	☐	☐
Structure and organization:				
–introduce the issue/make a general statement	☐	☐	☐	☐
–use logical, sequenced explanation of how/why something occurs	☐	☐	☐	☐
–use paragraphs	☐	☐	☐	☐
Language features				
–use appropriate subject vocabulary	☐	☐	☐	☐
–use appropriate tenses	☐	☐	☐	☐
–use passive voice (optional)	☐	☐	☐	☐
–use relevant linking words, e.g., *if, when, because, consequently, since*	☐	☐	☐	☐
–express relationships between concepts, particularly time and cause/effect relationships	☐	☐	☐	☐
–use nominalized processes	☐	☐	☐	☐
–develop themes logically that are consistent with explanation	☐	☐	☐	☐
–use language to maintain appropriate tenor	☐	☐	☐	☐
–support text with diagram (optional)	☐	☐	☐	☐
Accuracy:				
–use grammar accurately, e.g., word order, verb endings, pronouns	☐	☐	☐	☐
–spell and use punctuation accurately	☐	☐	☐	☐

General comments _____

_____

_____

Global rating (circle)   Lowest 1__ 2__ 3__ 4__ 5 Highest

Example 2

Written Language Assessment Activity   Years 8–10

Recount

A recount relates a series of events. The focus of a recount is on events rather than on character development and plot, as in narrative. Recounts can be personal (retelling events in which the writer has been personally involved, e.g., an excursion); factual (recording details of an incident/event, e.g., news report or historical account); or imaginative (retelling events from an imaginary point of view, e.g., "A day in the life of a Roman slave" or "How radium was discovered."

Name of Student: _____ Year Level/Class: _____ Date: _____

Name of School: _____ Teacher: _____

Topic of explanation: _____

Criteria (Check appropriate box)	Very Competent	Competent	Limited Not Competent Yet	Comments
Ability to carry out the task	☐	☐	☐	☐
Did the student				
–write a recount with minimal support	☐	☐	☐	☐
Structure and organization:				
–provide an orientation, establishing *who* was involved, *where*, and *when* the events happened	☐	☐	☐	☐
–provide a sequence of events in chronological order	☐	☐	☐	☐
–use paragraphs	☐	☐	☐	☐
–provide a reorientation and/or personal comment (optional)	☐	☐	☐	☐
Language features				
–focus on individual participants, e.g., the San Francisco earthquake, Marie Curie	☐	☐	☐	☐
–focus on past tense, e.g., simple past	☐	☐	☐	☐
–use a range of action verbs, e.g., *erupted, discovered, worked*	☐	☐	☐	☐
–use a range of temporal and other connectives, e.g., *first, then, finally, because, however, although, as well*	☐	☐	☐	☐
–use pronoun reference, e.g., *it, she, this*	☐	☐	☐	☐
–use specific vocabulary appropriate to the information being recounted	☐	☐	☐	☐
Accuracy:				
–use grammar accurately, e.g., word order, verb endings, pronouns (*she, her, hers, they, their*, etc.)	☐	☐	☐	☐
–spell and use punctuation accurately	☐	☐	☐	☐

General comments _____

_____

_____

Global rating (circle)   Lowest 1___ 2___ 3___ 4___ 5 Highest learner-centered classroom, these pro formas could be extremely useful in helping the students understand what they need to do in order to produce acceptable texts of various kinds.

So far in this section, I have described some of the advantages of adopting a functional model of language for assessing students' writing. I have illustrated the approach with reference to a large-scale evaluation project, and also with reference to the development of checklists for assessing students' writing. However, I would not like to convey the impression that the approach is unproblematic, and in this section, I would like to deal with two particular problem areas as I see them.

◆ PROBLEMS WITH A FUNCTIONAL MODEL

The first of these relates to how one might compare assessment procedures based on a functional view of language with more conventional procedures. This is the problem that my colleagues and I encountered in our evaluation of the disadvantaged writing project. On one hand we wanted to adopt evaluative procedures that were fair to the innovation being evaluated. On the other hand, we did not want the evaluation process to lay itself open to charges of bias in favor of the functional approach to the teaching of writing. This dilemma relates to what Beretta (1986) calls "program fair evaluation." In selecting assessment procedures and instruments, the evaluators need to ensure that one of the assessment procedures or programs being investigated is not discriminated against.

In the case of the Disadvantaged Schools Project, we made the decision to adopt assessment criteria derived from functional grammar, even though this left us open to the charge of bias. We did so because one of our terms of reference was to determine the extent to which the innovation had an impact on students' writing. No doubt, had we embraced alternative criteria (such as evidence of creativity) the outcome may well have been different.

The second problem related to the so-called product-oriented bias of genre-based pedagogy. Certain proponents of "process" approaches to the development of writing have argued that genre-based pedagogy takes a normative approach to the production of texts, and focuses on the end product, the destination, as it were, rather than the route. (Some proponents of genre-based teaching, of course, have argued that process approaches focus on the route, and ignore the destination.)

> Genre theory grounds writing in particular social contexts, and stresses the convention-bound nature of much discourse. Writing, therefore, involves conformity to certain established patterns, and the teacher's role is to induce learners into particular discourse communities and their respective text types. By contrast, the process approach extols individual

creativity, individual growth, and self-realisation, and the teacher's role
is that of 'facilitator' rather than 'director.'

Bamforth, 1993: 94

Bamforth goes on to point out that the process versus product debate
represents a false dichotomy, and that certain individuals on either side
of the debate have taken up positions that are ideological rather than
empirical. He points out, quite rightly in my view, that ultimately "the
central issues of freedom and control are not alternatives between which
a choice has to be made. They are really interdependent, and effective
writing pedagogy will call upon both approaches" (p. 97).

The process/product debate has also suffered from confusion between
syllabus design and methodology. To my mind, the strength of the genre
approach rests on the principles it sets out for the selection of content. This
is essentially a syllabus design issue. The process approach, on the other
hand, is oriented toward classroom action, and its concerns are therefore
essentially methodological. Any comprehensive approach to pedagogy
must incorporate syllabus design, methodology, and assessment.

In the final part of this section, I have looked at two criticisms that
have been made of the functionally-based genre approach to pedagogy.
The first of these is in identifying methods of evaluating genre-based
curricular innovations against what, for want of a better term, we might
call "traditional" methods of teaching and assessing written language.
This first criticism is in the nature of a straw person argument, in that it
can be applied to any approach to pedagogy when the purpose of the
assessment is to evaluate whether or not the principles underlying the
innovation are actually reflected in the written (or oral) production of
the students. The second criticism relates to the product-oriented bias
of the adoption of a genre approach. Once again, I find the argument
fundamentally flawed for the following reasons. In the first place, the
argument that product-oriented approaches somehow stifle the creativity
of the writer overlooks the fact that creativity has to be measured against
something, and that something is generally taken to be a set of conventions
or "rules," if you will. In any field in which creativity plays a role, whether
it be painting, creative writing, or the production of academic discourse,
the creative artist must, in the first instance, master the conventions of
the discourse. In other words, one must master the rules in order to
transcend them.

A DISCOURSE-BASED APPROACH TO WRITING

In Chapter 4, I presented an organic approach to language, and argued
that discourse and grammar should not be seen separately. In this section,
I explore the implications of this view of grammar for the teaching of

writing. From this perspective, the creation of coherent and cohesive discourse is basically a matter of drawing on the grammatical and discourse features that exist in the language to turn multilinear and multirelated ideas into linear form. In this section, we shall explore ways in which this can be done.

◆ DISCOURSE PROCESSES

As we saw in Chapter 4, the concept of discourse coherence has fascinated discourse analysts and language educators, particularly those working with foreign language students in tertiary contexts. Discourse analysts inquire into what it is that constitutes coherent discourse. What is it, in other words, that distinguishes a text, which is perceived by the listener or reader as "hanging together," from a random collection of sentences? Language educators, on the other hand, are more concerned with the practical question of helping students produce coherent discourse. Ultimately, the two concerns should coincide, with language educators drawing on insights from discourse analysis to provide directions for pedagogy.

In the writing classroom. several specialists (Lautamatti, 1978; Witte, 1983; Connor and Farmer, 1990) have suggested that topical structure analysis is a promising technique for improving the coherence of written work. Lautamatti (1978) develops a technique for analyzing writing in terms of the relationship between the discourse topic and the sentence topics that make up a text. She argues that texts can be developed in three different ways, and that these ways are evident in the distribution of topics in succeeding sentences in a text. The first of these is through parallel progression, in which succeeding sentences in a text are semantically identical. The second is sequential progression. Here the topic of each succeeding sentence is different. In extended parallel progression, there is a return to a topic that has already been instantiated in an earlier sentence. Examples of each of these types of progression are set out below.

Several empirical investigations have been conducted into the use of topical structure analysis in teaching writing to second language speakers. Witte (1983) used the concept as a tool to investigate the revision process, and also as a device for studying perceptions of the quality of students' writing. More recently, Connor and Farmer (1990: 126–139) have reported on their experiences in using topical structure analysis as a revision tool for ESL students in intermediate and advanced-level college writing classes. Students are taken through the steps involved in identifying topics and producing topical structure diagrams. They then apply the techniques to their own writing, usually after the production of a first draft.

Connor and Farmer report success with the technique, although the data here are anecdotal. (Their paper is a report on a pedagogical innovation, not a presentation on the outcomes of a piece of empirical research.) They report that:

Table 10.3

Parallel Progression

The ability to carry electricity varies according to the extent to which substances contain electrons that are free to move. It is not something possessed by all substances.

1.   The ability to carry electricity
2.   It

Sequential Progression

The ability to carry electricity varies according to the extent to which substances contain electrons that are free to move. Some substances contain few such molecules, and are therefore poor conductors.

1.   The ability to carry electricity
2.   Some substances

Extended Parallel Progression

The ability to carry electricity varies according to the extent to which substances contain electrons that are free to move. Some substances contain few such molecules, and are therefore poor conductors. This ability has been closely studied by physicists in recent years.

1.   The ability to carry electricity
2.   Some substances
3.   This ability

> Student response has been positive; many have remarked that the procedure helps them to examine the meanings of their sentences and forces them to relate these meanings to the main topic and purpose of their writing. When we teach the analysis as a revision tool, we note improvement in student writing, specifically in regard to clearer focus (thanks to added extended parallel progression) and better development of subtopics (thanks to improved ratio of parallel and sequential progressions).
>
> *Connor and Farmer 1990: 134*

A number of years ago, I looked at the resources that second language writers used to create coherent discourse. I presented a group of second language writers in an English for Academic Purposes program with a set of propositional statements derived from a science report. The writers were asked to turn these statements into a coherent piece of discourse. Among other things, I found a great deal of diversity in the topical structure patterns that emerged from the students' writing.

While the technique of getting students to turn a set of propositions or simple sentences into coherent discourse is a relatively straightforward one, the processes that the writer must go through are extremely complex. To produce coherent discourse, writers must exploit what they already know about the subject at hand and integrate it with information from other sources; they must draw on knowledge of the way that grammar and discourse function together; they are required to use cohesion appropriately they must; sort out form/function; and they have to decide on the topic to form the point of departure of each succeeding sentence in the text. In the next section, we shall look at a sample unit of work designed to give students practice in these demanding tasks.

◆ A DISCOURSE-BASED WRITING PROGRAM

What will a discourse-based writing program look like? In this section I shall provide examples of tasks from a writing program developed from a functional perspective. Such a program will, naturally enough, begin with samples of discourse, rather than the production of isolated grammatical structures. It will show learners how to use their knowledge of grammar in the construction of coherent texts. Finally, it will focus them on looking at their writing from a functional perspective. The following sample tasks have all been taken from Nunan and Keobke (1997).

Sample Task 1:
Focusing on functions in introductory paragraphs

1. Here are ten ways writers create interest, give context, or outline direction. Check off the purpose of each one.
    1. Define important terms that appear in the title.
       ☐ interest ☐ context ☐ direction
    2. State what aspects of the topic will be discussed.
       ☐ interest ☐ context ☐ direction
    3. Give important background information about the topic.
       ☐ interest ☐ context ☐ direction
    4. Refer to other work that has been done in the field.
       ☐ interest ☐ context ☐ direction
    5. State the writer's own position or interest.
       ☐ interest ☐ context ☐ direction
    6. Give an (controversial) example that will be examined in detail.
       ☐ interest ☐ context ☐ direction
    7. State the strategy that the writer intends to use.
       ☐ interest ☐ context ☐ direction

8. Compare rival positions or options.
   ☐ interest   ☐ context   ☐ direction

9. State a problem or difficulty in dealing with the topic.
   ☐ interest   ☐ context   ☐ direction

10. Attract the readers' interest with a quotation, question, or anecdote.
    ☐ interest   ☐ context   ☐ direction

(Acknowledgment to Bill Littlewood for suggesting an earlier version of this task.)

2. Look at this introduction and complete the task.

"The issue of falling language standards in Hong Kong is long-standing and contentious." (South China Morning Post, September 16, 1997.) For many years, the older generation has decried falling standards of both English and Chinese. Over thirty years ago, one School Certificate examiner's report stated that, "In Chinese, clumsy sentence construction, wrong Chinese characters, irrelevancy and redundancy, and poor handwriting were found in the writings of many candidates." Today, the situation is, if anything, even worse. This week alone, there have been four articles and fifteen letters to the English language press on the declining standards of English. In fact, there is no evidence that standards have fallen, and considerable evidence that they have risen, and in this essay, I shall look at this evidence. Evidence in favour of rising standards comes from the changing demographics in high school and university, examination results provided by the Hong Kong Exams Authority, and a recent study carried out by the English Centre at the University of Hong Kong.

Task: Draw lines connecting the functions to examples in the text. Not all functions are represented.

◇ Define terms
◇ State key aspects
◇ Give background
◇ Refer to other work
◇ State writer's position
◇ Give an example
◇ State the strategy
◇ Compare positions
◇ State a problem
◇ Attract attention

Sample Task 2:
Focusing on paragraph development from a functional perspective

1. There are many different ways that a topic sentence can be developed. The writer can introduce a contrasting idea, give an example, elaborate on the idea, give a definition, qualify the claim made in the topic sentences, and so on.

Study the following possible ways of developing the topic sentence, and identify the functions being performed.

Topic Sentence:

All languages have the same purpose—to communicate thoughts—and yet they achieve this single aim in a multiplicity of ways.

a. All languages have the same purpose—to communicate thoughts—and yet they achieve this single aim in a multiplicity of ways.

Each language has its own unique set of grammatical and discourse features.

☐ Contrasting ☐ Exemplifying ☐ Elaborating ☐ Defining ☐ Qualifying

b. All languages have the same purpose—to communicate thoughts—and yet they achieve this single aim in a multiplicity of ways.

Animal communication, on the other hand, is constrained in many ways.

☐ Contrasting ☐ Exemplifying ☐ Elaborating ☐ Defining ☐ Qualifying

c. All languages have the same purpose—to communicate thoughts—and yet they achieve this single aim in a multiplicity of ways.

Time is expressed in different languages in many different ways.

☐ Contrasting ☐ Exemplifying ☐ Elaborating ☐ Defining ☐ Qualifying

d. All languages have the same purpose—to communicate thoughts—and yet they achieve this single aim in a multiplicity of ways.

Despite this, there are also universal features across languages.

☐ Contrasting ☐ Exemplifying ☐ Elaborating ☐ Defining ☐ Qualifying

e. All languages have the same purpose—to communicate thoughts—and yet they achieve this single aim in a multiplicity of ways.

By communication, of course, we mean the ability to press grammatical, lexical, and phonological resources into service in contexts of use.

☐ Contrasting ☐ Exemplifying ☐ Elaborating ☐ Defining ☐ Qualifying

2. Which of the above functions is the best way to develop a paragraph from the initial topic sentence? Can you say why?

Sample Task 3:
Focusing on cohesion

Read and think: A few questions about cohesion and topicalization

1. Rewrite the following text, replacing or deleting all unnecessary repetitions.

```
    John Smith arrived early at the hall. There was no
one else around at the hall. John Smith tried the
door of the hall. The door was unlocked. John Smith
opened the door. John Smith went through the door.
John Smith shut the door behind John Smith. Suddenly
```

there was a loud noise. The loud noise made John Smith jump.

2. Cohesion is the use of pronouns (*he, she, it*), demonstratives (*this, that*) and other referring expressions. Why do you think that cohesion is an important feature of written texts?

3. What do the boldface words refer to in the following text?

The words used by psychologists are a constant source of anxiety to them. **They** also cause rage to **their** readers (including other psychologists). If **they** coin a new term, in the belief that they have a new concept, and wish **it** to have its own term, they are often accused of creating an ugly and unnecessary neologism. If, on the other hand, **they** use an already existing word and try to extend it to fit the particular technical meaning **they** have in mind, they are often accused of debasing the language. **They** can also be accused of misleading the reader.

they = *the words use by psychologists*

their =

they =

it =

they =

they =

they =

4. There is a great deal of unnecessary repetition in the following paragraph. Rewrite the paragraph, using cohesion (that is, words such as *he, it, this, such*) to remove excessive repetition.

Languages are made by ordinary human beings, not by God or the pundits who stand in for him. Languages seem to be somewhat arbitrary collections of sounds, symbolized as written or printed signs, and the origins of language belong in the mists of prehistory. There was, when people became human, clearly a need for languages. We may think of a language as a system of communication used within a particular social group. Inevitably, the emotions aroused by group loyalty to the particular language we speak obstruct the making of objective judgments about language. When we think about making an objective judgment about language, we are often merely making a statement about our prejudices. It is instructive to examine our prejudices occasionally. I used to have powerful objections to the Americanization of British English. In having powerful objections to the Americanization of British English, of course, I was in complete agreement with many of the people in my country.

5. Compare the following (original) text with the one you produced, and make a note of similarities and differences.

> Languages are made by ordinary human beings, not by God or the pundits who stand in for him. They seem to be somewhat arbitrary collections of sounds, symbolized as written or printed signs, whose origins belong in the mists of prehistory. There was, when man became man, clearly a need for them. We may think of a language as a system of communication used within a particular social group. Inevitably, the emotions aroused by group loyalty obstruct the making of objective judgements about language. When we think about making such a judgement, we are often merely making a statement about our prejudices. It is instructive to examine these occasionally. I used to have powerful objections to the Americanisation of British English. In this, of course, I was in complete agreement with many of my fellow countrymen.
>
> *Adapted from Burgess, 1992*

6. Examine one of your own essays and identify/underline all the instances of cohesion. Ask another student if the referents for these are clear.

Sample Task 4:
Focusing on topicalization

1. What is the topic of the following sentences?

   Sentence 1. There are two aspects of English in Hong Kong that demand discussion.

   Sentence 2. Discussion is required of two aspects of English in Hong Kong.

   Would you follow sentence 1 with sentence 3 or 4 below? Why?

   Sentence 3. The first is the issue of "standards" and the second is the attitude of Hong Kong people toward English.

   Sentence 4. This is because there are currently many myths about the subject.

Topicalization
The process of giving prominence to particular entities, states of affairs, or processes within a sentence or utterance by shifting them to the beginning of the sentence.

2. Which of the following texts is more coherent (i.e., makes more sense to you)? Give reasons for your choice.

Text 1

Over the last few years, there has been a notice-able decline in the standard of English in Hong Kong. In universities and the workplace, this decline is evident. Casual visitors to Hong Kong also say it is apparent. Hong Kong needs to prosper next century, which won't happen if the decline is not reversed. Economic leadership will not be retained if the de-cline is not reversed.

Text 2

Over the last few years, there has been a notice-able decline in the standard of English in Hong Kong. This decline is evident in universities and in the workplace. It is also apparent to the casual visitor to Hong Kong. This decline must be reversed if Hong Kong is to prosper in the next century. If it is not reversed, Hong Kong cannot hope to retain its posi-tion of economic leadership.

3. Underline the topics in each of the sentences in both texts, and then fill in the topics in the following chart.

Sentence topics Paragraph 1   Sentence topics Paragraph 2

1. _____   1. _____

2. _____   2. _____

3. _____   3. _____

4. _____   4. _____

5. _____   5. _____

You can see that, even though both texts contain the same content, the informa-tion in Text 2 has been arranged so that there are fewer topics. The topic *the decline in English standards* has been topicalized in most sentences. As a consequence for most readers, the second text appears to be more coherent.

Sample 5
Using grammatical resources to create discourse

1. Consider the following pieces of information.
   Television is a medium of communication.
   Radio is a medium of communication.
   Video is a medium of communication.
   Books are media of communication.
   Magazines are media of communication.

Communication takes place between people.

People often use media to communicate.

This information can be packaged into a single sentence by using grammatical resources of various kinds. For example:

Sentence 1: "Communication between people often takes place through media such as television, radio, video, books, and magazines."

Sentence 2: "Media such as television, radio, video, books, and magazines can be used for communication between people."

The choice of whether to use Sentence 1 or Sentence 2, above, for beginning a paragraph about interpersonal communication, will be determined by whether we want the focus of the paragraph to be *media* or *communication between people.*

2.   Using Sentence 1 as the topic sentence in a paragraph, produce a coherent paragraph incorporating the following information (you can rearrange the order in which the information is presented):

◊   There is a form of communication called mass-mediated communication.

◊   Mass-mediated communication differs from interpersonal communication.

◊   Interpersonal communication typically involves face-to-face interactions between participants.

◊   Participants in an interaction affect, and are affected by, each other.

◊   Mass-mediated communication may affect people from different cultures.

◊   For example, some people from Russia might have learned about the United States from broadcasts.

◊   These broadcasts are on television and radio.

◊   These people will have a set of expectations.

◊   These people will have certain knowledge about the United States.

◊   Other people in Russia might have listened to the Voice of America.

◊   The Voice of America is a U. S.-sponsored radio station in Europe.

◊   These people might have a different set of expectations from other Russians.

◊   These people might have different knowledge from other Russians.

3.   Compare your text with the original (supplied separately). Make a note of similarities and differences. Can you explain the differences? Do different ways of combining information lead to differences of meaning?

CONTRASTIVE RHETORIC

In 1966, Robert Kaplan published an influential study into the relationships between cultural thought patterns and discourse. The study, based on an analysis of several hundred second language student essays, provided a foundation for the development of research in contrastive rhetoric. The basic argument of researchers in contrastive rhetoric is that certain culturally determined ways of thinking and communicating will transfer themselves to second language texts. For example, it has been noted that many Asian cultures are characterized by a high degree of indirectness. This indirectness manifests itself in a reluctance to state one's position explicitly. This, presumably, would create difficulties for L2 writers who are required to produce academic texts with an explicitly stated topic sentence followed by supporting evidence.

In a recent article, Chen (1997) draws on this tradition within contrastive rhetoric to compare approaches to academic writing in the United States and China.

> U. S. English writing is very direct and formulaic. Writers should first clearly identify the topic or goal of an article and then support their argument with specific examples. The paragraph and essay structure should clarify the relationship between details and the unifying ideas, and the conclusion should once again stress the unifying ideas. . . . The judgment of writing as good or weak is based on straightforward criteria: clarity, accuracy, detail and structure. The goal is clear communication. In contrast, Chinese writers prefer indirection and rely on metaphors to present their ideas. Writers do not assert their goal, or even their topic at the beginning of a paper; instead; they use metaphor to make subtle, implied connections between ideas. Examples must be subtly inserted, so that connections are neither obvious nor direct.
>
> *(p. 13)*

The idea that a second language writer's problem can be traced to the contrast between the culturally determined discourse patterns of first and second languages is by no means universally accepted. Mohan and Lo (1985), for example, are particularly critical of this notion. In an investigation of Chinese first language learners of English, they argue that the problems experienced by their subjects were due to the usual difficulties of inexperienced writers, not the contrasting rhetorical patterns of English and Chinese.

Leki (1991) is critical of much of the early work in contrastive rhetoric. She argues that a great deal of the work was intuitive rather than empirical, and tended to focus on disparate surface features of texts, such as anaphoric reference, that were incapable of explaining contrastive patterns in larger segments of discourse. According to Leki, it was not until the 1980s, with the work of linguists such as Robert de Beaugrande (1980) that more insightful analyses began to emerge. However, Leki goes on to question the extent to which insights from contrastive rhetoric are immediately applicable to pedagogy. While it can be enlightening for students to be made aware of differences in the ways in which their own language and English transform ideas into discourse, this enlightenment does not necessarily lead to improvements in students' writing. The real benefit of making learners consciously aware of distinctions between the discourse patterns of their own language and that of the target language is that it reassures learners that they do not suffer from individual inadequacies, but that their difficulties stem from the contrasts between both languages.

◆ CONCLUSION

In this chapter, I have explored some key issues in the development of second language writing. In the first part of the chapter I looked at the ongoing debate over product- and process-oriented approaches. Although proponents of these two approaches try to portray them as mutually incompatible, they are, in fact, complementary: There is no reason, in principle, why a writing program should not incorporate elements of both approaches.

The chapter also looks at the implications for writing pedagogy of adopting a functional, discourse-based perspective on writing, and in the penultimate section, I presented some sample tasks taken from a program based on such a perspective. The aim of these tasks is to show how functional grammar can provide practical insights for the writing teacher.

Finally, I attempted, in this chapter, to revise some of the key ideas and principles presented earlier in the book. In particular, I drew on concepts introduced in Section 1 and elaborated in Section 2. I hope that by thinking about these concepts and principles, and by testing them against their own reality, experienced teachers will be able to enrich their professional practice. For beginning teachers, I hope these ideas will provide a principled basis for creating their own professional practice in the teaching of second language writing.

◆ CONCEPT MAP OF CHAPTER 10

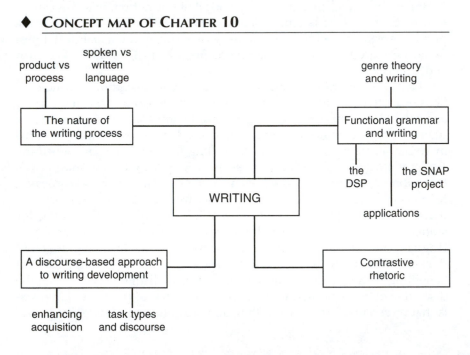

◆ QUESTIONS AND TASKS

1. Summarize the arguments for and against process approaches to the teaching of writing.
2. List some of the main differences between spoken and written language.
3. What is "lexical density"? What makes a text lexically dense?
4. How has genre theory been applied to writing?
5. What are the characteristics of a discourse-based approach to writing?
6. Develop some sample tasks similar to those contained in the chapter for teaching writing from a discourse perspective.
7. What is contrastive rhetoric, and why might it be important for teaching second language writing?

◆ REFERENCES

Bamforth, R. 1993. The genre debate. *Prospect*, 8, 4,

de Beaugrande, R. 1980. *Text, Discourse, and Process: Towards a Multidisciplinary Science of Texts*. Norwood, NJ: Ablex.

Beretta, A. 1986. Program-fair language teaching evaluation. *TESOL Quarterly*, 20, 1, 431–444.

Burns, A., and H. Joyce. 1997. *Focus on Speaking*. Sydney: NCELTR.

Chen, Kuang-Jung. 1997. English versus Chinese: World views and writing styles. *TESOL Matters*, 7, 1, 13.

Connor, U., and M. Farmer, 1990. The teaching of topical structure analysis as a revision strategy for ESL writers. In B. Kroll (ed.), *Second Language Writing*. Cambridge: Cambridge University Press.

Halliday, M. A. K. 1985. *An Introduction to Functional Grammar*. London: Arnold.

Kaplan, R. 1966. Cultural thought patterns in intercultural education. *Language Learning*, 16, 1, 1–20.

Kaplan, R. 1987. Cultural thought patterns revisited. In U. Connor and R. Kaplan (eds.), *Writing Across Languages: Analysis of L2 Text*. Reading, Mass.: Addison-Wesley.

Lautamatti, L. 1990. Coherence in spoken and written discourse. In U. Connor and A. Johns (eds.), *Coherence in Writing*. Washington, D.C.: TESOL.

Leki, I. 1991. Twenty-five years of contrastive rhetoric: Text analysis and writing pedagogies. *TESOL Quarterly*, 25, 1, 123–143.

McCarthy, M., and R. Carter, R. 1994. *Language as Discourse*. London: Longman.

Martin, J. 1985. *Factual Writing: Exploring and Challenging Social Reality*. Deakin, Victoria, Australia: Deakin University Press.

Mohan, B., and W. A–Y. Lo. 1985. Academic writing and Chinese students' transfer and developmental factors. *TESOL Quarterly*, 19, 3, 515–534.

Mordden, 1980. *A Guide to Orchestral Music*. New York: Oxford University Press.

Nunan, D. 1992. *Research Methods in Language Learning*. Cambridge: Cambridge University Press.

Nunan, D., and K. Keobke. 1997. *Writing Better Essays*. The English Centre: University of Hong Kong.

Rodrigues, R. J. 1985. Moving away from the writing-process workshop. *English Journal*, 74, 24–7.

Raimes, A. 1993. Out of the woods: Emerging traditions in the teaching of writing. In S. Silberstein (ed.), *State of the Art TESOL Essays*. Washington, D.C.: TESOL.

Walshe, J., G. Brindley, J. Hammond, and D. Nunan. 1990. *Evaluation of the Disadvantaged Schools Writing Project*. Sydney: NCELTR.

White, R., and V. Arndt. 1991. *Process Writing*. London: Longman.

Witte, S. P. 1983. Topical structure and writing quality: Some possible text-based explanations of readers' judgments of students' writing. *Visible Language*, 17, 177–205.

Glossary of Language Learning Terminology

achievement test An achievement test attempts to measure what students have learned from a particular course or set of materials. It contrasts with diagnostic tests, which attempt to identify what learners do and do not know, and proficiency tests, which are intended as tests of general ability and are not meant to be tied to any particular course.

acquisition The mental processes through which individuals develop the ability to understand and use languages as well as a description of the stages through which they pass in acquiring a language.

adjacency pair In discourse and conversational analysis, a pair of utterances produced by different speakers that are related in functional terms.

    For example: There's more coffee in the pot. (Offer)
                        I'm OK, thanks. (Decline)

analytic approach In course development, the use of topics, texts, and tasks that are not broken down into their separate constituents. (See *synthetic approach, linear learning, organic learning*). The approach is called "analytic" because the task for the learner is to analyze whole chunks of language and identify the individual, and usually heterogeneous, linguistic elements out of which they are constituted.

anaphora Within a text, the reference to a particular person, object, place, or event, in which the second and subsequent references are marked by some form of pronominalization. For example:

> *The handover of Hong Kong to China* was widely considered to be one of the most dramatic political events of the twentieth century. Not surprisingly, **it** was marked by considerable pomp and ceremony.

applied linguistics The application of linguistic theories, and methods of linguistic description and analysis, to practical issues and problems to do with human communication. These include language teaching and learning, second language acquisition, bilingualism, speech pathology, language disorders, communication in the workplace, deafness, lexicography and dictionary development, translation, and language planning.

approach General theories related to language teaching and learning.

aptitude A general ability to learn languages.

assessment Sets of procedures, techniques, and procedures for making judgments about what learners can and cannot do.

atomistic approach See *synthetic approach*.

audiolingualism Based on the notion that learning another language is a matter of acquiring new linguistic habits, this language teaching method has learners memorize and manipulate the target grammar through various manipulation and substitution drills.

authenticity Spoken and written texts used in language teaching are generally deemed to be authentic if they were produced in the first instance for purposes of communication, not for the purposes of language teaching.

back-channel In oral interaction, the provision of feedback from the listener or listeners to the speaker. The purpose of such feedback is to let the speaker know he or she is being attended to, and to encourage the speaker to continue. The feedback may be verbal or nonverbal (for example, head nodding).

> Example: A: I went to Big W yesterday . . .
> B: Uh-huh
> A: . . . and bought one of those Italian market umbrellas.

behavioral objective A precise description of the observable things that learners should be able to do after taking part in a course of study. Formal objectives have three elements: a task element specifying the performance, a conditions element, and a standards element, specifying how well they should perform.

> For example: In a classroom role play (condition), learners will exchange their names, addresses and occupations with other learners (task). Utterances will be grammatically well-formed and will be comprehensible to someone unused to dealing with second language speakers.

behaviorism A psychological theory that views all human behavior, including language acquisition, in terms of the development of sets of habits through processes of stimulus and response.

background knowledge The knowledge of the world that the reader or listener utilizes in interpreting a piece of spoken or written language.

bottom-up processing Decoding the smallest elements (phonemes and graphemes) first, and using these to decode and interpret words, clauses, sentences, and then whole texts. (See also **decoding**.)

cataphoric reference A form of cohesion in which the pro-form (the item used to stand in for the text referent) occurs first, and can only be interpreted with reference to the subsequent text.

> Example: I simply won't put up with this. All this fighting and bickering.

clarification request A strategy used by the listener for a more explicit formulation of the speaker's last utterance.

> A: Did y'see Theo last night? He was as pleased as a lizard with a gold tooth.
> B: Sorry? What do you mean by that exactly?

classroom discourse The distinctive type of discourse that occurs in classrooms. Special features of classroom discourse include unequal power relationships, which are marked by unequal opportunities for teachers and pupils to nominate topics, take turns at speaking, etc. It has been noted that the typical pattern of interaction in all sorts of classrooms is one in which the teacher asks a question to which he or she already knows the answer, one or more pupils respond, and the teacher evaluates the response.

> Example: [The teacher circulates around the room, asking questions about train travel. The students all have copies of a train timetable.]
> T: Now . . . back to the timetable. Where do you catch the train? Where do you catch the train?
> [She points to a student in the front row.]
> S: Keswick
> T: Yeah. . . . Now—what time . . . what time does the train leave?
> Ss: Nine. Nine o'clock. Nine pm. Nine pm. Nine am.

> T: [leans over a student and checks the timetable] OK. Depart nine am
> (Nunan 1991).

classroom management Techniques and procedures employed by the teacher in the classroom to control student behavior, including setting up different kinds of tasks, dealing with disruptive behavior, establishing and moving between different kinds of learning groups, and using audiovisual aids and other forms of realia and equipment efficiently.

closed task A task for which there is a single correct answer.

cloze procedure A procedure for developing teaching and testing materials by deleting words according to some predetermined ratio (for example, deletion of every fifth word). The task for the student is to replace the deleted words.

cognitive code teaching The learning of language rules through analysis and problem-solving. The approach developed in reaction to **audiolingualism.**

cognitive style The general approach adopted by a particular learner to the learning process. Some learners like to learn holistically. Others prefer to have tasks broken down for them.

coherence The extent to which discourse is perceived to "hang together" rather than being a set of unrelated sentences or utterances.

cohesion The formal links that mark various types of interclausal and intersentential relationships within discourse. Examples:
> Identity relationship: A: Do you know my brother *Pete*?
>   B: Yeah, I met *him* at the ball game last year.
> Logical relationship: I can't make it today. *However*, tomorrow's a possibility.

collocation A form of lexical cohesion in which two or more words are related by virtue of their belonging to a particular semantic field. In the following text, the underlined words belong to the semantic field of "gardening."
> Example: The <u>bulbs</u> should be <u>planted</u> in winter.
>   The <u>flowers</u> will appear in spring.

communication strategy A strategy used by a second language learner to get his or her meaning across with a limited amount of vocabulary and grammar.

communicative language teaching (CLT) The term *communicative language teaching* covers a variety of approaches that all focus on helping learners to communicate meaningfully in a target language. Early approaches downplayed the importance of grammar, some even advocating the abandonment of any focus on form. More recent approaches acknowledge the centrality of grammar [and try and teach learners the relationship between grammatical form and communicative meaning.]

communicative competence The ability to apply grammatical, discourse and cultural knowledge to communicate effectively in particular contexts for particular purposes.

Community Language Learning A language teaching method, developed by Charles Curran, based on techniques from counseling.

comprehensible input Messages addressed to the learner that, while they may contain structures and grammar that are beyond the learner's current competence, are made understandable by the context in which they are uttered. According to

Krashen's Comprehensible Input Hypothesis, acquisition occurs when learners understand messages that are just beyond their current stage of development.

comprehensible output A hypothesis developed by Swain in reaction to the Comprehensible Input Hypothesis. Swain argues that comprehensible input is necessary but not sufficient for language acquisition. Learners also need opportunities to produce comprehensible messages in the language.

comprehension Processes through which learners make sense of spoken and written texts.

comprehension approach An approach to second and foreign language teaching based on the belief that extensive listening comprehension should precede speaking.

comprehension check A strategy used by the speaker to ensure that the listener has understood correctly:
 A: The paper should go on the outside of the packet—know what I mean?
 B: Mmm.

concept mapping Showing the main ideas in a text, and the relationships between them in the form of a diagram or map.

confirmation request A strategy used by listeners to confirm that what they think they heard is correct.
 A: I saw a bank robbery a couple of weeks ago.
 B: A robbery?

conjunction Words and phrases, such as *however, on the other hand, in contrast,* that make explicit the functional relationships between different ideas in a text.

constructivism A philosophical approach to knowledge that argues that knowledge is socially constructed rather than having its own independent existence.

content-based instruction An approach to the teaching of language in which students are taught their regular school subjects, such as science, history, and math, through the target language. (Also known as **immersion.**)

content needs *What* learners need or want to learn, in contrast to process needs, which relate to *how* they need or want to learn.

content word A word that refers to a thing, quality, state, action, or event. (See also *function word*)

context The linguistic and experiential situation in which a piece of language occurs. The linguistic environment refers to the words, utterances, and sentences surrounding a piece of text. The experiential environment refers to the real-world context in which the text occurs.

contrastive analysis Procedures for comparing and identifying similarities and differences between the linguistic systems of different languages. The Contrastive Analysis Hypothesis suggests that, when languages share certain features, learning will be facilitiated, and that when features are not shared, learning will be impeded.

contrastive rhetoric This approach to text analysis is based on the view that certain culturally determined ways of thinking and communicating will transfer themselves to second language texts. For example, it has been noted that many Asian cultures are characterized by a high degree of indirectness. This indirectness manifests itself in a reluctance by writers from Asian first language backgrounds to state their position explicitly.

conversation An oral interaction between two or more people.

conversational analysis The study of how individuals negotiate and exchange meanings in interaction. The major focus of interest in recent years has been in the analysis and interpretation of casual conversation, that is, interactions that are carried out for social purposes rather than for obtaining goods and services.

cooperative principle This was formulated by the linguistic philosopher Grice (1975) as a way of accounting for how people interpret discourse. The principle is expressed in terms of four maxims: "Be true; be brief; be relevant; be clear." The maxims dictate that a speaker be truthful, brief, relevant, and clear, and that the interlocutor, in turn, should assume that the speaker is following the four maxims.

creative language Creative language practice occurs when learners are involved in tasks that require them to recombine familiar language patterns and elements in novel ways. It contrasts with reproductive language in which learners imitate or manipulate models provided by the teacher, textbook, or tape.

critical period hypothesis According to proponents of the critical period hypothsis, biological changes in the brain around puberty result in the two hemispheres of the brain functioning independently. After this neurological change takes place, acquiring native-like competence in a second language becomes difficult, if not impossible.

culture The (often implicit) norms and rules that govern the interactional and personal behavior between groups of individuals.

curriculum All elements and processes in the planning, implementation, and evaluation of learning programs. *Curriculum* includes **syllabus design** (selecting, sequencing, and justifying content), **methodology** (selecting and sequencing learning tasks and activities), and **evaluation** (which incorporates assessment and evaluation).

declarative knowledge Knowledge that can be stated or "declared," such as grammatical rules. It contrasts with "procedural knowledge," which has to do with the ability to use the knowledge to get things done, for example, being able to use grammatical rules and principles to communicate meaning.

decoding The process of determining the meaning of words and sentences by working out the meaning of individual letters and sounds. (See **phonics**.)

deductive learning The process of learning in which one begins with rules and principles and then applies the rules to particular examples and instances.

deixis Elements of discourse that serve to point the reader or listener to particular points in space or time. Example: "Put the boxes over there."

demonstrative The words *this, that, these, those*, which indicate the proximity of something to the speaker.

dependent variable In a formal experiment, the variable that is affected by the independent variable. In a study investigating the effect of two different teaching methods on listening comprehension, the methods would be the **indepen-**

dent variables, and the level of listening comprehension would be the dependent variable.

descriptive grammar A grammar that attempts to describe the way people use language, without prescribing what is correct or incorrect.

determiner Words that modify nouns to limit their meaning. Common determiners in English include articles (*a/an, the*), demonstratives (*this, that, these, those*), possessives (*his, their*), and quantifiers (*some, much, many*). Determiners are important elements of **cohesion**.

developmental error An error made by learners that shows that they are beginning to make generalizations about the target language.

dialogue A conversation intended to illustrate the function of some aspect of language (e.g., syntax, vocabulary, or functions) in context.

dialogue journal A learner's journal in which the teacher responds to each entry. The evolving entries form a sort of written "conversation."

dictogloss A procedure for teaching grammatical structures in context. The procedure involves the teacher in reading a short passage at normal speed. Learners note down all the words they hear, and then work in small groups, pooling their resources to reconstruct the original text.

direct method A method for teaching language that avoids the use of the native tongue, and that emphasizes listening/speaking over reading/writing.

discourse Recordings of naturally occurring samples of language within their communicative context.

discourse analysis The analysis of naturally occurring samples of written or spoken language with a focus on the communicative functions performed in the course of the comunication. Discourse analysis is sometimes contrasted with **text analysis**, which analyzes the formal, linguistic properties of a text. (See **cohesion**.)

drill A language teaching technique for helping learners develop fluency in a particular structural or functional item.

EAP (English for Academic Purposes) Courses and programs of study for helping learners develop the skills needed for speaking and writing for academic English, for example, writing essays and reports, taking part in tutorial discussions, giving academic presentations.

EFL (English as a foreign language) The teaching and learning of English in communities where it is not widely used for communication.

elicitation A procedure (usually employed by researchers and testers) for obtaining samples of language from second language learners. In the classroom, a procedure by which teachers stimulate students to produce samples of the structure, function, or vocabulary item being taught.

ellipsis The omission of clauses, phrases, or words that can be recovered from other parts of the discourse.

    Example: A: Are the guests here?
               B: Yes, they are.

In the above example, B omits *here*, which can be recovered from A's question.

ESL (English as a second language) The teaching and learning of English in communities where it is widely used for communication by the population at large. These days the distinction between ESL and EFL is widely regarded as an oversimplification.

ESP (English for Specific Purposes) Courses designed around the specific needs of particular groups of learners, for example "English for computer engineers," "English for accountants." ESP sometimes contrasts with EGP (English for General Purposes).

error A piece of speech or writing that is recognizably different in some way from native speaker usage. Errors can occur at the level of discourse, grammar, vocabulary, or pronunciation.

ethnomethodology A branch of sociology that is concerned with the analysis and interpretation of everyday speech.

ethnography A research tradition for studying interpersonal behavior in its cultural context.

evaluation Processes and procedures of gathering information about a program, or aspects of a program, for decision making purposes.

exchange A basic interactional pattern in classroom discourse. An exchange consists of three functional moves: an opening move, an answering move, and a follow-up move. These three moves are now more commonly known as initiation, response, and follow-up or feedback.

    Example: T: How many groups do we need? [Initiation]
                S: Three. [Response]
                T: Three. Very good. [Feedback]

experiential language learning In experiential learning, the learner's immediate personal experiences are taken as the point of departure for deciding how to organize the learning process.

face-saving An important principle, one which seems to underly a great deal of interpersonal interaction, is the need for interlocutors to "save face." This is most commonly achieved by the use of indirect speech act strategies. For example, if a speaker wishes to invite someone out, but is afraid of the possibility of a rebuff, he or she may avoid asking a direct question, such as "Would you like to come out with me?," asking instead, "Are you doing anything this evening?," or, even less directly, "There's a great movie playing at the Capri this evening."

feedback The provision of information to speakers about the message they have conveyed. Neutral feedback simply informs the speaker that the message has been received. It may be verbal ("Uhuh!," "Mmmm") or nonverbal (for example, a nod of the head). Evaluative feedback provides the speaker with information on whether the message has been positively or negatively received. Once again, it may be verbal ("Great!") or nonverbal (for example, a smile or a frown).

first language An individual's native tongue.

fluency The ability of an individual to speak or write without undue hesitation.

formative evaluation The collection and interpretation of information about a language program during the course of program delivery. It contrasts with summative evaluation, in which data about a program are analyzed when it ends.

function word A word that carries functional rather than experiential meaning. Function words include determiners, prepositions, modals, and conjunctions.

functions The things people do through language, for example, apologizing, complaining, instructing. (See also **speech acts**.)

functional syllabus A syllabus in which designers take lists of language functions or speech acts as their point of departure.

genre A purposeful, socially constructed oral or written communicative event, such as a narrative, a casual conversation, a poem, a recipe, or a description. Different genres are characterized by a particular structure or stages, and grammatical forms that reflect the communicative purpose of the genre in question.

given/new Any utterance or sentence can be said to contain given and new information. Given information is that which the speaker or writer assumes is known by the listener or reader. New information, on the other hand, is that which is assumed to be unknown. Given and new information will be reflected in the structure of sentences and utterances.

Examples: It is the cat that ate the rat.
(Given: Something ate the rat. New: The cat did the eating.)
What the cat ate is the rat.
(Given: The cat ate something. New: The rat was eaten.)

goals Broad general purposes for learning.

grammar The study of how syntax (form), semantics (meaning), and pragmatics (use) work together to enable individuals to communicate through language.

grammar-translation A language teaching method based on grammatical analysis and the translation of sentences and texts to and from the learners' first and target languages.

grapheme The smallest meaningful unit in the writing system of a language.

group work **Tasks** and exercises completed by learners working in small, cooperative groups. Group work is particularly important in **communicative language teaching.**

high structure task A task over which the teacher has all of the power and control.

humanism The philosophical approach known as humanism has found expression in education in approaches that place the experiences and feelings of the student at the center of the learning process. It thus provides the philosophical underpinning for learner-centered approaches to second language learning and teaching.

humanistic psychology An approach to psychology based on humanism.

ideational meaning That aspect of a text that relates to information about objects, entities, and states of affairs. In other words, the ideational meaning relates to what the utterance is about. It contrasts with the interpersonal meaning, which is related to the attitudes and feelings of the speaker or writer.

illocutionary force The **functions** performed by an utterance or piece of language. The illocutionary force of an utterance can only be understood if we know the context in which the utterance occurs.
Example: The statement "There's a dog out the back." could, depending on the context, be a description, a warning, an explanation, an invitation, and so on.

immersion An approach to the teaching of language in which students are taught their regular school subjects such as science, history, and math through the target language. (Also known as **content-based instruction.**)

imitation Repeating spoken or written models provided by the teacher, a textbook, or some other medium. Imitation and various forms of drills are the basic techniques underlying **reproductive language** practice. (See also **creative language** practice.)

inductive learning The process by which the learner arrives at rules and principles by studying examples and instances. (This contrasts with **deductive learning,** in which the process is reversed.)

information gap tasks Pair or group work tasks in which participants have access to different information. In order to complete the task, the information must be exchanged. Such tasks are hypothesized to promote acquisition by encouraging the **negotiation of meaning.**

information structure The ordering of elements within sentences and utterances according to (a) assumptions by the speaker or writer about the current state of knowledge of the listener or reader, and (b) according to the elements that the speaker or writer wishes to thematize.

innateness hypothesis The innateness hypothesis suggests that the ability to acquire language is a facility unique to the human species.

input The target language that is made available to learners.

interactional hypothesis According to this hypothesis, language is acquired as learners actively engage in attempting to communicate in the target language. The hypothesis is consistent with the experiential philosophy of "learning by doing." Acquisition will be maximized when learners engage in tasks that "push" them to the limits of their current competence.

interlocutor effect The effect that the other members of a conversation have on what the speaker says.

interpersonal task A communicative task in which the main purpose is to socialize rather than to obtain goods and services.

insertion sequence A sequence of utterances separating an **adjacency pair.** In the following example, the question/answer adjacency pair is separated by a subsidiary question/answer that constitutes an insertion sequence.

    A: Would you like mustard?
    B: Is it hot?
    A: Uh-huh.
    B: No, thanks.

interlanguage Language produced by learners in the course of acquiring the target language. Learners are hypothesized to pass through a series of interlanguages, each of which has a set of rules that, while deviating from the target language, have a degree of internal consistency.

interpersonal meaning That aspect of an utterance that reflects the speaker's attitude towards the topic of the utterance.

intonation Raising and lowering voice pitch to convey aspects of meaning. Intonation is one of the **suprasegmental** aspects of pronunciation.

language experience approach Applied principally to the development of first language literacy, this approach builds on the individual's experience of the world, and makes connections between the individual's experiential world and the literary world. (See **experiential language learning.**)

language transfer The effect of a learner's first language on the learning of another.

learner-centered instruction An approach to instruction that uses information about and from learners in selecting learning content and procedures. The phrase is also used to describe a classroom in which learners are required to learn actively, through doing, rather than through focusing on the teacher.

learning strategy The mental and communicative processes that learners deploy to learn a second language. For example, memorizing,
> **inductive learning, deductive learning.**

learning style A student's orientation toward learning.

lexicon All of the words in a language.

lexical To do with the words of a language.

lexical cohesion Lexical cohesion occurs when two words in a text are related in terms of their meaning. The two major categories of lexical cohesion are **reiteration** and **collocation**.

lexical density The ratio of content words to function words in a text.

lexical relationships The relationships that exist within a text between content words.
> Example: In the following text, the underlined words have the lexical relationship of synonymy:
> "I gave Sally a dictionary. The volume cost me a fortune."

linear approaches Approaches to syllabus design and methodology based on the belief that learners should master one item before moving on to the next.

linguistics The systematic study of language. Linguistics is divided into sub-branches, including **phonology**, **syntax**, **semantics**, and **pragmatics**.

literacy The ability to read and write a language.

locutionary force The propositional (as opposed to functional or illocutionary) meaning of an utterance or statement.

logical connectives Conjunctions, such as *therefore* and *however*, that mark textual relationships, such as causality, are also known as logical connectives.

low structure task A task in which the power and control over how the task is carried out rests with the students.

meaningful drill A language drill in which the student is required to understand the meaning of the utterance in order to produce a correct response. Meaningful drill contrasts with mechanical drill, in which understanding is not required in order to produce a correct response.

memory The ability to store and retain information in the brain.

metacognitive strategies Learning strategies that encourage learners to focus on the mental processes underlying their learning.

method A coherent and internally consistent set of principles for teaching language derived, at least in part, from a set of beliefs about the nature of language and learning.

methodology That subcomponent of the curriculum concerned with the selection and sequencing of classroom tasks and activities as well as the study of the theoretical and empirical bases of such procedures.

minimal pair Two words in a language whose meaning is signalled by differences in a single word or consonant, for example, /bit/ /pit/.

miscue analysis A procedure for analyzing the errors made by beginning readers as they read texts out loud. Originally developed for first language reading pedagogy, the technique has also been used by second language teachers.

modal verb Verbs for indicating speaker/writer attitude, (for example, possibility, permission) toward an event or a state of affairs. In English, the modal verbs are: *can, could, have to, may, might, must, shall, should, will, would.*

modality The dimension of an utterance that allows speakers or writers to reveal their attitude toward the propositional content or the illocutionary force of an utterance. Modality is most commonly achieved through modal verbs such as *may, might, should, ought.*

morpheme The smallest meaningful element into which a word can be analyzed. For example, the word *walking* consists of two morphemes, *walk*, which signifies an action, and *-ing*, which signifies progression.

motivation In language learning, the psychological factors determining the amount of effort a learner is prepared to put into language learning.

move A basic interactional unit in classroom discourse. Three-part exchanges consist of three moves: an opening move, an answering move, and a follow-up move. (For an example of these three types of move, see **exchange**, above.)

multilingualism The ability to communicate in more than two languages.

natural approach A set of principles for language teaching adapted from ways in which a first language is acquired.

natural order hypothesis A hypothesis that grammatical items will be acquired in a predetermined order that cannot be changed by formal instruction.

needs analysis Within curriculum development, sets of tools, techniques, and procedures for determining the language content and learning process for specified groups of learners.

negotiated curriculum A negotiated curriculum is one in which learners have a substantial degree of control over what is learned, how it is learned, and how it is assessed.

negotiation of meaning: The interactional work done by speakers and listeners to ensure that they have a common understanding of the ongoing meanings in a discourse. Commonly used conversational strategies include **comprehension checks, confirmation checks, clarification requests.**

nominalization The process of turning verbs into nouns. Nominalization has a number of purposes, including that of removing the doer of the action. It also allows for a process to be topicalized. For example:

"The politician deceived his electorate, and it shocked them."

"The deception shocked the electorate."

notions General concepts expressed through language such as temporality, duration, and quantity.

notional syllabus A syllabus organized around sets of general concepts.

objective A description of what is to be achieved in a course. (See also **performance objective**.)

open task A task in which there is no single correct answer. For example, "Discuss the pros and cons of euthanasia."

paralinguistics Nonverbal forms of communication, such as body movements and facial expressions.

pedagogical grammar A grammar intended for teaching purposes.

performance The actual use of language. Transformational-generative grammarians distinguish between competence (an individual's abstract knowledge of language) and performance (the actual use of language).

performance objective A precise statement of what learners are to be able to do at the end of a course of instruction. Formal performance objectives contain three parts: a task, the conditions under which the objective will be performed, and a standard. Example: In an employment interview role play (condition), the learner will answer questions for personal details (task). Five out of seven questions will be answered, and responses will be comprehensible to someone unused to dealing with non-native speakers (standards).

phoneme The smallest meaningful unit of sound in a language.

phonetics The description and analysis of the ways in which speech sounds are produced, transmitted, and received by speakers and hearers.

phonics An approach to the teaching of reading in which learners are taught to decode words by matching written symbols with their aural equivalents.

phonology The description and analysis of the distinctive sounds in a language, and the relationship between sound and meaning. (See also **segmental phonology** and **suprasegmental phonology**.)

pragmatics The study of the way language is used in particular contexts to achieve particular ends.

procedural knowledge The ability to use the knowledge to get things done, for example, being able to use grammatical rules and principles to communicate meaning. It contrasts with "declarative knowledge" which has to do with the ability to state or declare facts and principles, for example, the ability to regurgitate grammatical rules.

process needs How learners need or want to learn, in contrast to **content needs**, which relate to what they need or want to learn.

process writing An approach to writing pedagogy that focuses on the steps involved in drafting and redrafting a piece of work. Learners are taught to produce, reflect on, discuss, and rework successive drafts of a text.

productive language Used to refer to the skills of speaking and writing.

proficiency General language ability. The concept of language proficiency, its structure, and measurement continue to be controversial in language testing.

pronominalization The process of substituting a pronoun for an entire noun phrase. Example:

"I saw the <u>Yeungs</u> yesterday.
<u>They</u>'ve just come back from Hong Kong."

pronunciation The ways in which sounds are produced. Features of pronunciation are divided into **segmental phonology** (individual sounds) and **suprasegmental phonology** (stress, rhythm, and intonation).

propositional meaning The formal meaning of an utterance without reference to its function within a discourse. Propositional or locutionary meaning contrasts with pragmatic or illocutionary meaning.
Example: Propositionally, the utterance, "The window is open," is an existential statement about the state of an entity, i.e., a window. The illocutionary force of this utterance (which can only be recovered from the context in which it occurred) may be: a request ("It's awfully cold in here, would you mind shutting the window?"); a suggestion (A: I can't get out of the room, the door is stuck fast. B: The window is open, why don't you climb out?), and so on.

psycholinguistics The study of the mental processes underlying language acquisition and use.

realia Objects and teaching "props" from the world outside the classroom that are used for teaching and learning.

receptive skills Traditionally, listening and reading have been classed as "receptive" and speaking and writing classed as "productive" skills.

reciprocal listening Listening situations in which the listener also takes part as a speaker.

reference Those cohesive devices in a text that can only be interpreted with reference either (a) to some other part of the text, or (b) to some entity in the experiential world.

register The kind of language used by particular groups for particular communicative situations, for example, medical register. (See also, **genre**.)

reiteration A form of lexical cohesion in which the two cohesive items refer to the same entity or event. Reiteration includes repetition, synonym or near synonym, superordinate, and general word. In the following example, the underlined words refer to the same entity, and are therefore an example of reiteration.
   Example: I'm having terrible trouble with my <u>car</u>.
         The <u>thing</u> won't start in the morning.

repair The correction or clarification of a speaker's utterance, either by the speaker (self-correction) or by someone else (other correction). These repairs serve to prevent communication beakdowns in conversation.

reproductive language This is language produced by learners as they imitate or manipulate models provided by the teacher, textbook, or tape. Reproductive language tasks are usually designed to give learners basic language patterns that they can recombine in novel ways in **creative language** tasks.

rote learning Learning through repetition with minimal attention to meaning.

schema theory A theory of language processing based on the notion that past experiences lead to the creation of mental frameworks that help us make sense of new experiences.

second language acquisition The psychological and social processes underlying the development of proficiency in a second language.

segmental phonology The description and study of individual vowels and consonants in a target language. Of particular interest are **minimal pairs** (for example,
/bit/ /pit/), in which differences of meaning are created by contrasting sounds.

semantic network A network of words in which individual items are related in terms of their meaning.

semantics A study of the formal meanings expressed in language without reference to the context in which the language is used.

(The) Silent Way A somewhat idiosyncratic language teaching method based on the notion that the teacher should speak as little as possible, and that the learners should develop their own interior criteria for judging the acceptability of their language.

speech act An utterance seen in terms of its propositions (meanings) and functions. The propositional meaning is known as **locutionary force,** and the functional meaning is known as the **illocutionary force.**

structural syllabus A syllabus organized around lists of grammatical structures.

student-centered teaching and learning See **learner-centered instruction**.

substitution The use of proforms to represent entities or events mentioned earlier in a text. There are three types of substitution: nominal, verbal, and clausal.
Examples: *Nominal substitution:*
These cakes are great. These <u>ones</u> are pretty good, too.

Verbal substitution:
A: Tomoko always studies at night.
B: So <u>does</u> Keiko.

Clausal substitution:
A: Is Nigel <u>meeting us at the movies</u>?
B: I think <u>so</u>.

substitution table A table setting out a grammatical paradigm showing which items in a particular structure can be substituted for others.
Example:

This		my	brother
	is	your	mother
That		his	cousin
		her	
These		our	parents
		their	sisters
Those	are		aunts

suggestopedia An idiosyncratic method that claims that students can learn prodigious amounts of language in a short time under the correct relaxation techniques.

suprasegmental phonology The study of the role of rhythm, stress, and intonation in creating meaning. Segmental features of language serve many discourse functions, including the marking or highlighting of important information, the signaling of given and new information, the indication of speaker attitude, and so on.

systemic–functional linguistics A theory of language defines it as sets of interrelated systems, stresses its social nature, and attempts to account for grammatical features of language in terms of the communicative functions they perform.

syllabus That subcomponent of a **curriculum** concerned with the selection, sequencing, and justification of linguistic and experiential content. It contrasts with methodology, which is concerned with the selection, sequencing, and justification of tasks and activities. With the development of task-based and process approaches to a curriculum, the separation of syllabus and methodology has become increasingly difficult to sustain.

syntax The study of the rules that govern the formation of grammatical structures.

synthetic approach In course development, the prior analysis and breaking down of the language into its discrete grammatical, phonological, lexical, and functional elements. These are then sequenced and taught separately. The approach is called "synthetic" because the task confronting the learner is to synthesize, or integrate, these discrete elements.

task A pedagogic task is a piece of classroom work having a beginning, middle, and an end, and a focus principally (although not exclusively) on meaning. In contrast with pedagogic exercises, tasks have a nonlinguistic outcome.

> Example 1, below, is a task. Example 2 is an exercise.
>
> Example 1: "Listen to the weather forecast and decide whether you should wear a sweater when you go out."
>
> Example 2: "Turn the following active voice sentences into the passive voice using the examples provided."

task-based syllabus A syllabus in which the designer has taken a series of tasks (rather than a set of linguistic items, such as structures and/or functions) as the point of departure for the design process.

teachability/learnability hypothesis According to the teachability hypothesis, grammatical structures can be classified according to the demands, they make on the learner's working memory. The greater the demands, the more difficult the structure is to learn. An item will only be acquired, and therefore should only be taught, when the learner is developmentally ready to acquire it.

text The written record of a communicative event that conveys a complete message. Texts may vary from single words (for example, "Stop!," "EXIT") to books running to hundreds of pages.

text analysis The analysis of formal features of a text such as cohesion, text structure, and so on. The focus is on formal rather than functional analysis, and the analysis generally involves little reference to the extralinguistic context that gave rise to the text.

text-forming devices Within a text, formal linguistic devices, such as pronouns for making multiple references to entities, events, and states of affairs.

thematization The process of giving prominence to certain elements in a sentence or utterance by placing them at the beginning of the sentence or utterance. (See **theme** below.)

theme The initial element in a sentence or utterance that forms the point of departure for the sentence or utterance. The remainder of the sentence or utterance is known as the **rheme**. Examples:

Theme	Rheme
I	went to town yesterday.
DILLON, Mavis,	dearly beloved sister of Doris and aunt of Michael . . .
It	was the cat that ate the rat.

top-down processing The use of **background knowledge,** knowledge of text structures, and/or knowledge of the world to assist in the interpretation of discourse.

topic The experiential subject matter of a text.

topicalization The process of giving prominence to particular entities, states of affairs, or processes within a sentence or utterance by shifting them to the beginning of the sentence. Each of the following sentences is about the same participants and events, but each is topicalized differently.

I will finish this glossary tonight.
This glossary will be finished by me tonight.
Tonight, this glossary will be finished.

total physical response (TPR) A language teaching method in which learners listen to instructions in the target language, and carry out a sequence of physical actions.

transactional language Language that is used in obtaining goods and services. Transactional interactions are contrasted with interpersonal interactions, in which the purposes are primarily social.

transcription The written, verbatim record of spoken language.

transformational-generative grammar A theory of linguistics that attempts to specify the rules underlying a language that form or generate all grammatical utterances in a language, and that exclude all ungrammatical utterances.

turn One speaker's utterance, bounded by the utterances of one or more other speakers.

turn-taking The process by which opportunities to speak are distributed between two or more speakers. Rules for turn-taking differ in different cultural contexts.

whole-word approach Learning to read through memorizing words by their unique shape. This approach contrasts with phonics, in which words are recognized by working out the sounds each letter in the word represents.

Appendices

APPENDIX 2.1
The Effect of Strategy Training on Fifteen Key Learning Strategies

Identify Objectives

This item was glossed for students as "thinking about what you want to be able to do at the end of the course." It was included in the study because awareness of program goals and objectives has been identified in the literature as an important aspect of the learning process (see, for example, Green and Oxford 1995). Research carried out in other contexts has also demonstrated a significant correlation between the practice of making learning goals clear and student motivation (Jones and Jones 1990; Reilly 1994). When results on the post-instructional questionnaire were examined, it was found that 53 percent of the experimental group and 27 percent of the control group indicated that they were now more knowledgeable about this strategy. Fifty percent experimental and 40 percent control subjects indicated that they made greater use of the strategy. Thirty percent of experimental subjects, and 17 percent of control subjects indicated that the strategy helped them to develop their language skills.

◆ SELECTIVE LISTENING

In the questionnaire that students completed, selective listening was glossed as "listening for key information without trying to understand everything." In the pretreatment data collection exercise, this strategy was given a low rating by both control and experimental groups. By the end of the experiment, however, it was highly valued and deployed by the experimental subjects. In addition to opportunities to learn about and practice this strategy, this change probably reflects the changed listening demands made on students once they enter a university. Hong Kong schools are divided into Chinese Medium of Instruction (CMI) and English Medium of Instruction (EMI) Schools. In EMI schools (from which the great majority of University of Hong Kong students are drawn), instruction is supposed to be carried out in English. There is evidence, however, that the use of Cantonese in these schools is widespread (Littlewood and Liu 1997). In pretreatment interviews, students, who, it will be recalled, had just entered the university, did not perceive that listening would be problematic for them. However, once they began their studies, many of the students found themselves receiving instruction in English from lecturers from many different parts of the world. These instructors are both non-native and native speakers of English. They have a wide variety of accents, and many of the newly appointed native speaking teachers are unused to dealing with students whose first language is not English. Informal observations and analysis of lectures revealed many of these teachers using low frequency vocabulary, idiomatic expressions, and attempting to introduce humor into their lectures. In such situations, when students are struggling to come to terms with unfamiliar concepts and knowledge, they evidently come to value the opportunity to think about and practice strategies for identifying and recording the important information in a lecture. The fact that a dramatic difference was detected among experimental subjects, but not control subjects, probably indicated that for this strategy at least, students need opportunities for the strategy to be made salient through formal training, as well as opportunities to deploy the strategy in authentic communicative situations. (I am indebted to Andrew Cohen, personal communication, for pointing out to me the possible confounding effects on outcomes of training in the strategy and opportunities to use the strategy. I believe that this may be one of the side effects of conducting experimental studies in genuine classroom contexts.)

Predicting

Predicting, or thinking ahead and anticipating what is to come, was another strategy that students were introduced to and given practice in applying to academic learning. On this strategy, 33 percent of the experimental but only 4 percent of the control subjects reported an increase in knowledge about this strategy. In terms of utility and use, there was little difference between the control and experimental groups.

Confirming

The benefits of confirming, or checking one's answers with others, was discussed and systematically practiced throughout the semester. One third of the experimental group reported an increase in the value that they placed on this strategy. There was also an increase for the experimental group in terms of knowledge and deployment of this strategy. None of the control group subjects reported an increase in any of the areas investigated.

Reflecting

Reflecting, or thinking about ways one learns best, is, in a sense, a key strategy underlying all of the other strategies introduced in the course. It was therefore somewhat surprising to find that there was virtually no difference between the control and experimental groups on this particular probe. However, it is consistent with findings reported by Ho (1997), who found that Hong Kong students have difficulty with, and react negatively, in the short term, to reflecting on their learning. It may well be that this strategy is one that would only show improvement over the long term.

Self-evaluating

Self-evaluating, glossed as "thinking about how well you did on a task," was also a strategy that did not appear to have been affected by the intervention. This may have been because it was an "incidental strategy" (in much the same way as reflecting). In other words, it did not form the thematic focus of a lesson, as did most of the other strategies. Rather, students were given a series of informal opportunities to self-evaluate during the course of the study. In a follow-up study, it would be worth giving a more explicit focus to this particular strategy as it is central to a learning-centered approach to education. Another factor may be that self-evaluation is alien to the system in which the subjects received their secondary education.

Cooperating

Cooperating was glossed as "working with other students in small groups." This strategy was used extensively in the course, and the effect of its use is reflected in the data. Knowledge, use, and value of this strategy all increased, the most dramatic increase being in the areas of deployment, and the value placed on this strategy by the experimental groups. Hong Kong students have a cultural predilection for cooperative rather than competitive learning (Tsui 1996), and this may partly account for the relatively high initial scores for both control and experimental groups on the knowledge dimension of the study. However, opportunities to reflect on this strategy also seems to have had an effect on experimental subjects' use of this strategy in their learning (43 percent reported an increase in their use of the strategy as opposed to 23 percent of the control group), and also on the importance they placed on it as a strategy in university level learning (40 percent reported placing greater value on the strategy at the conclusion of the experiment, while none of the control subjects gave it greater value). Inspection of lesson plans and teaching notes confirmed that the control groups had relatively fewer opportunities to take part in small group, cooperative activities.

Summarizing

Summarizing, or creating a short version of a text recording key information, is an important academic strategy that all students use extensively in university study. In follow-up interviews, control and experimental subjects revealed that they made extensive use of the strategy in their academic subjects. This extensive use may explain the results obtained on this particular item, with control subjects outperforming experimental subjects on both utilization and use. (None of the experimental subjects reported an increase in use, compared with 23 percent of control subjects. 7 percent of the experimental subjects gave greater value to the strategy compared with 17 percent of control subjects.) Observation revealed that the control groups, while not being explicitly taught this strategy, had relatively greater opportunity to use the strategy in class.

Memorizing

Memorizing is also a strategy that is widely used in Hong Kong secondary schools. All subjects were therefore familiar with the strategy. While experimental subjects outperformed control subjects, the results were not significant, and the experiment seemed to have little effect on subjects' knowledge, utilization, or appreciation of this strategy. In rank-order terms, however, there was a large difference between pre- and post-intervention. Before the experiment, this was the most popular strategy overall. At the end of the experiment, a number of other strategies, including inductive learning and selective listening, had overtaken it.

Inductive and Deductive Learning

Two contrasting cognitive strategies were inductive and deductive learning. Inductive learning was glossed as, "working out rules from examples," while deductive learning was characterized as, "learning rules and then applying them in using language." At the beginning of the experiment, these strategies (along with selective listening) were among the least popular items in the survey. At the end of the study their rankings had changed dramatically. This was particularly true for inductive learning in the case of the experimental group. However, some caution needs to be exercised in interpreting these results. Inspection of lesson plans and protocols revealed that both strategies were used extensively in lessons and tutorials in both control and experimental classrooms (although it was only in with the experimental groups that the strategies were made explicit). Deployment of these key cognitive strategies is hardly surprising in a university environment, and it is quite likely that these strategies were also significant features of students' content classes. (Students were majoring in a wide range of subjects from psychology and geography to comparative literature and Japanese.) This observation underlines the difficulty of carrying out, in naturalistic contexts, research designed to isolate and examine relationships between dependent and independent variables. By conducting the research in context, the external validity of the study was strengthened at the expense of internal validity.

Developing Independent Learning Skills

Developing independent learning skills, that is, encouraging learners to learn and use language without the aid of the teacher, was another of those general strategies for which considerable growth was evident from the beginning to the end of the study. This was the case for both experimental and control groups, although the control groups did considerably better when it came to knowledge of this strategy. Once again, the qualitative data were of considerable help in attempting to interpret these data. It showed that the control subjects, as well as the experimental subjects, had an independent study component to their course, although the rationale for this component was not made explicit in the control groups as it was for the experimental groups.

Applying

The idea of activating English outside of class was a strategy that appeared to benefit significantly from being made explicit, particularly in terms of knowledge and use. Twenty-five percent of the experimental group reported an increase in their use of English outside of class, while none of the control group reported an increase. It may seem strange that this strategy needed an explicit focus with the context of Hong Kong, where English is generally considered to be a second rather than a foreign language, and where it is assumed that the use of English in the community is widespread. However, recent research indicates that such views may be inaccurate, and that the use of English in nonacademic contexts is far more circumscribed than had previously been thought. In a study involving almost 6,000 undergraduates, Bacon–Shone, Bolton, and Nunan (1997) found that only a tiny percentage of students ever used English outside the classroom. (See Chapter references).

Classifying and Personalizing

Evidence that strategy training makes a difference can also be found in the results obtained on the probes for classifying (glossed for the students as "putting similar things together in groups") and personalizing ("sharing your own opinions and ideas"). In the case of classifying, there were no differences between the control and experimental groups in terms of knowledge, there was a slight difference in favor of the experimental groups in terms of use, and a similar difference in favor of the control groups in terms of value. In the case of personalizing there was a slight difference in favor of the control groups in terms of knowledge and values, and a similar slight difference in favor of the experimental groups in terms of use.

APPENDIX 5.1:
Needs Analysis Questionnaire

Part 1: General Learner Needs Survey

Name ____   Current proficiency level ____

Age ____   Educational background ____

Language learning history ____   Other languages ____

Intended occupation ____   Aptitude ____

Purposes for English ____   Where language will be used ____

People with whom learner will   Degree of mastery required ____
interact ____

Target variety or dialect ____   Language genres required ____

Part 2: Language Contact Survey

We would like you to tell us which of the following uses of language are important for you. Please put an X in the box beside each if you think it is Very Useful, Useful, Not Useful.

	Very Useful	Useful	Not Useful
Do you want to improve your language so that you can:			
1. Tell people about yourself	☐	☐	☐
2. Tell people about your family	☐	☐	☐
3. Tell people about your job	☐	☐	☐
4. Tell people about your education	☐	☐	☐
5. Tell people about your interests	☐	☐	☐
6. Use buses, trains, ferries	☐	☐	☐
7. Find new places in the city	☐	☐	☐
8. Speak to tradespeople	☐	☐	☐
9. Speak to landlord/real estate agent	☐	☐	☐
10. Buy furniture/appliances for your home	☐	☐	☐
11. Deal with door-to-door salesmen	☐	☐	☐
12. Communicate with your friends	☐	☐	☐
13. Receive phone calls	☐	☐	☐
14. Make telephone calls	☐	☐	☐
15. Do further study	☐	☐	☐

	Very Useful	Useful	Not Useful
16. Get information about courses/schools, etc.	☐	☐	☐
17. Enroll in courses	☐	☐	☐
18. Get information about the education system	☐	☐	☐
19. Help children with schoolwork	☐	☐	☐
20. Apply for a job	☐	☐	☐
21. Get information about a job	☐	☐	☐
22. Go to an employment service	☐	☐	☐
23. Attend interviews	☐	☐	☐
24. Join sporting or social clubs	☐	☐	☐
25. Join hobby or interest groups	☐	☐	☐
26. Watch TV	☐	☐	☐
27. Listen to the radio	☐	☐	☐
28. Read newspapers, books, magazines	☐	☐	☐
29. Give, accept, refuse invitations	☐	☐	☐
30. Make travel arrangements	☐	☐	☐
31. Talk to your boss	☐	☐	☐
32. Talk to doctors/hospital staff	☐	☐	☐
33. Talk to neighbors	☐	☐	☐
34. Talk to children's teachers	☐	☐	☐
35. Talk to government officials	☐	☐	☐
36. Talk to English-speaking friends	☐	☐	☐
37. Get information about goods and services	☐	☐	☐
38. Complain about or return goods	☐	☐	☐
39. Arrange credit/hire-purchase/layaway	☐	☐	☐

From this list, choose five you want to learn first.

1. _____

2. _____

3. _____

4. _____

5. _____

Part 3: Methodological Preferences

How do you like learning? Put a circle around your answer.

(a) In class do you like learning

    (1) individually?   YES/NO

    (2) in pairs?   YES/NO

    (3) in small groups?   YES/NO

    (4) in one large group?   YES/NO

(b) Do you want to do homework?   YES/NO

If so, how much time do you have for homework outside class hours?

_____ hours a day   _____ hours a week

How would you like to spend the time?

    (1) Preparing for the next class?   YES/NO

    (2) Reviewing the day's work?   YES/NO

    (3) Doing some kind of activity based on your personal experience, work experience, or interests?   YES/NO

(c) Do you want to

    (1) spend all your learning time in the classroom?   YES/NO

    or

    (2) spend some time in the classroom and some time practicing with people outside?   YES/NO

    or

    (3) spend some time in the classroom and some time in an individualized language center?   YES/NO

(d) Do you like learning

    (1) by memory?   YES/NO

    (2) by problem-solving?   YES/NO

    (3) by getting information for yourself?   YES/NO

    (4) by listening?   YES/NO

    (5) by reading?   YES/NO

    (6) by copying from the board?   YES/NO

    (7) by listening and taking notes?   YES/NO

    (8) by reading and making notes?   YES/NO

    (9) by repeating what you hear?   YES/NO

Put a cross next to the three things that you find most useful.

(e) When you speak, do you want to be corrected

    (1) immediately, in front of everyone?   YES/NO

or . . . .

(2) later, at the end of the activity, in front of everyone?   YES/NO

(3) later, in private?   YES/NO

(f) Do you mind if other students sometimes correct your written work?   YES/NO

Do you mind if the teacher sometimes asks you to correct your own work?   YES/NO

(g) Do you like learning from

(1) television/video/movies?   YES/NO

(2) radio?   YES/NO

(3) tapes/cassettes?   YES/NO

(4) written material?   YES/NO

(5) the blackboard?   YES/NO

(6) pictures/posters?   YES/NO

(h) Do you find these activities useful?

(1) Role play   YES/NO

(2) Language games   YES/NO

(3) Songs   YES/NO

(4) Talking with and listening to other students   YES/NO

(5) Memorizing conversations/dialogues   YES/NO

(6) Getting information from guest speakers   YES/NO

(7) Getting information from planned visits   YES/NO

(i) How do you like to find out how much your English is improving? By . . . .

(1) written tasks set by the teacher?   YES/NO

(2) oral language samples taken and assessed by the teacher?   YES/NO

(3) checking your own progress by making tapes, listening to them critically and comparing?   YES/NO

(4) devising your own written tasks for completion by yourself and other students?   YES/NO

(5) seeing if you can use the language you have learnt in real-life situations?   YES/NO

(j) Do you get a sense of satisfaction from:

(1) having your work graded?   YES/NO

(2) being told that you have made progress?   YES/NO

(3) feeling more confident in situations that you found difficult before?   YES/NO

INDEX